Dickinson Unbound

Dickinson Unbound

Paper, Process, Poetics

Alexandra Socarides

OXFORD
UNIVERSITY PRESS

OXFORD
UNIVERSITY PRESS

Oxford University Press is a department of the University of Oxford.
It furthers the University's objective of excellence in research, scholarship,
and education by publishing worldwide.

Oxford   New York
Auckland   Cape Town   Dar es Salaam   Hong Kong   Karachi
Kuala Lumpur   Madrid   Melbourne   Mexico City   Nairobi
New Delhi   Shanghai   Taipei   Toronto

With offices in
Argentina   Austria   Brazil   Chile   Czech Republic   France   Greece
Guatemala   Hungary   Italy   Japan   Poland   Portugal   Singapore
South Korea   Switzerland   Thailand   Turkey   Ukraine   Vietnam

Oxford is a registered trade mark of Oxford University Press
in the UK and certain other countries.

Published in the United States of America by
Oxford University Press
198 Madison Avenue, New York, NY 10016

© Oxford University Press 2012

First issued as an Oxford University Press paperback, 2014.

Material from *The Poems of Emily Dickinson* reprinted by permission of the publishers and the Trustees of
Amherst College. *The Poems of Emily Dickinson*, edited by Ralph Franklin, Cambridge, Mass.: The Belknap
Press of Harvard University Press, Copyright © 1998, 1999 by the President and Fellows of Harvard College.
Copyright © 1951, 1955, 1979, 1983 by the President and Fellows of Harvard College.
Material from *The Letters of Emily Dickinson* reprinted by permission of the publishers.
The Letters of Emily Dickinson, Thomas H. Johnson, ed., Cambridge, Mass.: The Belknap Press of
Harvard University Press, Copyright © 1958, 1986 by The President and Fellows of
Harvard College; 1914, 1924, 1932, 1942 by Martha Dickinson Bianchi;
1952 by Alfred Leete Hampson; 1960 by Mary L. Hampson.

"Rethinking the Fascicles: Dickinson's Writing, Copying, and Binding Practices"
was first published in *Emily Dickinson Journal* 15, no. 2 (2006): 69–94.
Reprinted with permission by The Johns Hopkins University Press.

"The Poetics of Interruption: Dickinson, Death, and the Fascicles" was first published in
A Companion to Emily Dickinson, ed. Martha Nell Smith and Mary Loeffelholz. Malden,
MA: Blackwell (2008): 309–333. Reprinted with permission by Blackwell Publishing.

Library of Congress Cataloging-in-Publication Data
Socarides, Alexandra.
Dickinson unbound : paper, process, poetics / Alexandra Socarides.
p. cm.
Includes bibliographical references and index.
ISBN 978-0-19-985808-8 (cloth : acid-free paper); 978-0-19-938023-7 (paperback : acid-free paper)
1. Dickinson, Emily, 1830-1886—Criticism and interpretation. I. Title.
PS1541.Z5S675   2012
811'.4—dc23   2011043282

CONTENTS

Acknowledgments   *vii*
Abbreviations   *xi*

Introduction   3
1. Dickinson's Sheets   *20*
2. Epistolary Practices and the Problem of Genre   *49*
3. Sewing the Fascicles: Elegy, Consolation, and the Poetics
   of Interruption   *78*
4. Dickinson's "Sets" and the Rejection of Sequence   *105*
5. Methods of Unmaking: Dickinson's Late Drafts,
   Scraps, and Fragments   *130*
Afterword   *168*

Notes   *173*
Bibliography   *193*
Poems Referenced   *199*
Index   *203*

ACKNOWLEDGMENTS

I am grateful to the many archives and special collections that provided me with access to their holdings, with time amongst their materials, and in some cases, with financial support, without which this book would not have been possible. To Mike Kelly, Margaret Dakin, Peter Nelson, Mariah Sakrejda-Leavitt, and Daria D'Arienzo at the Amherst College Archives and Special Collections; to Leslie Morris at the Houghton Library; to Sean Casey and Eric Fraser at the Boston Public Library Rare Books and Manuscripts Department; and to Caroline Sloat, Jaclyn Penny, Thomas Knoles, and the family of Stephen Botein at the American Antiquarian Society. Thanks, also, to each of these archives for providing me with the fantastic images that appear in this book, and to Dinah Fried for making the perfect illustration of how Dickinson made her fascicles. This project has been funded by many sources over the years, and I am indebted to the people at institutions (both large and small) who read my many proposals and thought that such a book was worth their support. Thanks to Rutgers University for the Kalstone Grant, a Mellon Travel Grant, and a Mellon Summer Seminar Grant; to the Emily Dickinson International Society for a Graduate Research Fellowship and the Scholar in Amherst Award; to the National Humanities Seminar for a spot in Sharon Cameron's 2008 Summer Literary Institute on Dickinson; and to the University of Missouri's Research Council, Research Board, and Center for Arts and Humanities. An earlier version of part of Chapter 1 appeared in the *Emily Dickinson Journal* and an earlier version of part of Chapter 3 appeared in *A Companion to Emily Dickinson*. I am grateful to Johns Hopkins University Press and Blackwell Publishing for giving me permission to reprint them here; thanks also to the editors—Cristanne Miller, Martha Nell Smith, and Mary Loeffelholz—for including my work in these publications. Lastly, I am enormously lucky to have had this book fall into the hands of Brendan O'Neill at Oxford University Press; he took care of it (and me) at every stage and secured three fantastic anonymous readers, each of whom saw what I was trying to do and helped me to do it better.

If the institutions and funding sources made the research possible, it was the people who surrounded me that made the writing of this book possible. For early inspiration in the ways of reading poetry, I would like to thank Robert Farnsworth, Marie Howe, and Suzanne Hoover. They each made it so that by the time I arrived at graduate school, I already knew how to eat, sleep, and breath the poems I loved.

At Rutgers University, I had the privilege of learning from a wonderful assortment of scholars, including and in particular, Carolyn Williams, Michael McKeon, Michael Warner, Myra Jehlen, Colin Jager, and Richard Miller. Alison Shonkwiler, Kristie Allen, and Sunny Stalter-Pace read the earliest drafts, offered incisive feedback, and generally made writing a dissertation a whole lot less painful. Since arriving at the University of Missouri, I have had the pleasure of working in an enormously supportive and stimulating environment. Thanks, in particular, to Pat Okker, John Evelev, Tom Quirk, Noah Heringman, and Andy Hoberek, who have offered invaluable guidance along the way. I couldn't ask for a better writing group than that which is composed of Anne Myers and Frances Dickey. I am indebted to the graduate students who took my Dickinson seminar for talking Dickinson with me during the final stages of my writing, and to Mike Horton for crucial research assistance. In recent years I have come to know a fantastic assortment of nineteenth-century Americanists, many of whom have offered feedback, discussion, and criticism on this project, as well as their friendship. I am grateful to the members of the Midwest Nineteenth Century Americanist Group—especially Melissa Homestead, Susan Harris, Laura Mielke, and Stephanie Fitzgerald—for commenting on the first chapter; to Faith Barrett, Theresa Strouth Gaul, Desirée Henderson, Jennifer Putzi, and Elizabeth Stockton for taking me under their wings and being the best interlocutors imaginable; to Chris Lukasik for being the most demanding of readers; and to Vivian Pollak for her curiosity and conversation at a crucial stage of my writing.

Throughout, I have been lucky enough to be guided by three amazing mentors, each of whose scholarship and spirit are visible on every page. To Martha Nell Smith, for modeling how to be, in equal parts, excited about what I think and humble to the work that surrounds me. To Virginia Jackson, for forcing me to rethink everything I knew and start all over again. And to Meredith McGill, for over a decade of guidance, mentorship, and friendship. When I tell my students that the most important decision they make in graduate school is choosing an excellent advisor, I speak from experience. Thanks to each of you for taking me on before I had anything to show for myself and for continuing to be there long after I should have figured it all out for myself. I hope these pages make each of you proud.

And now to my friends and loved ones: Thanks for tolerating my constant need to go home to write my book and for asking about how it was going even when you weren't totally sure what I was writing about. Nothing would be possible without the love and friendship of Bibi Prival, Liz Mayer, Debbie Neft, Jessica Morowitz, Katie Cushmore, Zanny Wood, Kathy Lubey, Joanna Luloff, Amanda Hinnant, and Sheri Harrison. Thanks to Lynn Duryee for reading this book in its entirety, to Jeremy Faro for helping me come up with a title, and to Meredith Martin for helping it find a home.

Lastly, I want to acknowledge my family. To my mother, Barbara Bonner, for instilling in me early an interest in art, in how artists work, and in all kinds of beauty;

to my brothers—Charlie Socarides, Richard Socarides, and Bob Stolorow—each of whose passion for and dedication to what they do inspires me; and to my extended family—Claudia Rosen, Lisa Rudikoff, Don Fried, and Vera Rosen—for having no obligation to love me and for doing so anyway. In memory of my sister, Dede Socarides Stolorow, who I have come to learn is present in all I do. To Gabe Fried, who gave me Dickinson's *Manuscript Books* for my twenty-fourth birthday, long before I knew I would ever write a book about them, and who, years later, read all 1,789 poems out loud with me, just to make sure I really loved them. And lastly, to Archer and Nate (my heart and my soul), who were both born during the writing of this book: boundless gratitude.

ABBREVIATIONS

F Dickinson, Emily. *The Poems of Emily Dickinson: Variorum Edition.* Ed. R. W. Franklin. 3 vols. Cambridge, MA: Belknap Press of Harvard University Press, 1998.

L Dickinson, Emily. *The Letters of Emily Dickinson.* Ed. Thomas H. Johnson and Theodora Ward. Cambridge, MA: Belknap Press of Harvard University Press, 1958.

Dickinson Unbound

Introduction

This book takes up the question of how Emily Dickinson made her poems, the significance of the materials she used when doing this, and the interpretive possibilities and problems that attention to the details of poetic practice raises for a study of this remarkable writer's work. While Dickinson's poems have garnered attention from hundreds of critics since her introduction to a reading public wider than family and friends in 1890, we have yet to understand how she made the very texts that have enraptured, puzzled, frustrated, and elated her readers. Indeed, part of the allure of reading Dickinson is that her poems give the impression that they have *not* been made—not labored over, not drafted and redrafted, not abandoned and revised. They have, instead, as Thomas Wentworth Higginson put it, been "torn up by the roots, with rain and dew and earth still clinging to them."[1] Or not. As any poet knows, poems may present themselves as pieces of nature, unshaped by human hands—but this is always a fiction. Instead, poems are made objects, and that making takes place in specific times and specific places, with certain materials on hand that make such a making possible. In this book I will return us to these scenes of making, so that we might better understand the work of America's seemingly most inaccessible poetic genius.

This book concerns itself with Dickinson's sites of composition—with the practices she employed in these spaces and with the surfaces on which she executed these practices—in order to investigate the relationship between the way she made her poems and the poems themselves. How I navigate that move from paper to poetics is the topic of this introduction. By "paper" I mean, literally, the materials on which Dickinson copied her poems: sheets of stationery (loose and sewn), leaves of paper (whole, torn, and mangled), letters, envelopes, and scraps of household paper. By "poetics" I mean something in an entirely different register: the way a poem works; the impulse, desire, or motivation that seems to drive it; the meaning that can be extracted from it; and the conventions that are both embedded in and highlighted by its form. Because we have yet to see the materials that lay across Dickinson's desk and we have yet to know her writing through them, this book highlights a different poetics at work in Dickinson's poems than the ones regularly narrated by literary history. I discuss here a poetics that is guided by paper.

This is, on the one hand, to say that Dickinson was thinking about her compositional practices inside her poems. Whether she was copying poems onto folded sheets of stationery that she might sew to each other, pinning together jagged scraps of household paper on which she had written lines that might have been related, or embedding pieces of what had once been poems into the letters she would send far and wide or deliver over the hedge by hand, Dickinson was developing both poems and a theory of poetry to which the methods of composition and the materials taken up in the act of composition are integral. To know Dickinson's writing through what may, at first, look like idiosyncratic practices and arbitrary materials is to understand her writing as a reflection upon the very problems of making that her reception has largely effaced. On the other hand, the relationship between paper and poetics is not simply causal, for Dickinson's preoccupation with her own practices doesn't simply produce what we might call a fully-articulated poetics of composition. While there are stunning examples of how the paper itself shapes the poems, it is also important to acknowledge that the opposite is also sometimes true: that the poem being written can demand that Dickinson use certain paper. In some cases, this requires that Dickinson construct a methodologically complicated system of engaging with and utilizing paper.

As should be clear by now, when I refer to Dickinson's act of making, I am talking about her actual, literal, and physical methods and processes of writing, not our later accounts of what may have been the workings of her imagination or sources of her inspiration.[2] In doing so, I draw attention to the text in a historically-specific scene of writing. In *The Textual Condition*, Jerome McGann explains how imagining this scene runs counter to dominant critical practices: "Today, texts are largely imagined as scenes of reading rather than scenes of writing. This 'readerly' view of text has been most completely elaborated through the modern hermeneutical tradition in which text is not something we *make* but something we *interpret*."[3] McGann advocates turning our attention to "much more than the formal and linguistic features of poems or other imaginative fictions. We must attend to textual materials which are not regularly studied by those interested in 'poetry': to typefaces, bindings, book prices, page format, and all those textual phenomena usually regarded as (at best) peripheral to 'poetry' or 'the text as such.'"[4] Although McGann's "today" was twenty years ago, we have yet to pay this kind of attention to Dickinson's textual materials. The reason for this is obvious: Since the protocols of reading that twentieth-century readers of Dickinson had been taught depend on poems in print isolated from each other and from the paper on which they were written, this paper simply didn't—or couldn't—matter.

By the time Ralph Franklin put the manuscripts in readers' hands (sort of) with his 1981 publication of *The Manuscript Books of Emily Dickinson*, it was practically impossible to revise our reading habits.[5] Additionally, there has been active resistance to attention to textual materials by critics who have expressed the worry that turning to the scene of writing might turn the critic's attention ever inward, making the study of Dickinson even more insular and isolated than it already is. Margaret Dickie, for instance, worries that attention to Dickinson's manuscript books (the objects of analysis in this book's first and third chapters) seals her off by "recreat[ing] the poet in her workshop," thereby posing a problem for feminist critics who have been "working to bring her out into the world, to place her in the context of other women poets or of her male contemporaries, to examine her craft, her experiments with language, her finish."[6] It is this book's position that, instead of concealing or sequestering Dickinson, placing emphasis on the poet's material practices radically expands our understanding of this poet, as it reveals her to have been a writer whose poetics were engaged with contemporary forms and concerns. It shows us a writer who was absorbed in and influenced by nineteenth-century material culture, women's copying and bookmaking practices, familiar epistolary networks, and contemporaneous poetic discourse.

This is not to say that critics have not paid close attention to Dickinson's manuscripts. They have, and a great debate in this subfield rages on about how to read these objects. While very different in their methodologies and conclusions, many of these studies highlight Dickinson's manuscripts as a rich field for inquiry. Of particular interest to me have been Sharon Cameron's *Choosing Not Choosing: Dickinson's Fascicles*, Martha Nell Smith's *Rowing in Eden: Rereading Emily Dickinson*, Marta L. Werner's *Emily Dickinson's Open Folios: Scenes of Reading, Surfaces of Writing*, Domhnall Mitchell's *Measures of Possibility: Emily Dickinson's Manuscripts*, and Virginia Jackson's *Dickinson's Misery: A Theory of Lyric Reading*.[7] The last of these, Jackson's *Dickinson's Misery*, has made available the particular questions that drive this book, and for that reason I am most directly engaged with its arguments. Jackson interrogates the ways in which twentieth-century criticism has insisted upon reading Dickinson as a lyric poet and showcases the radical warping of Dickinson's texts that has been produced by that narrative. By asking readers to look at what Dickinson actually wrote, Jackson exposes our assumptions about the identity of Dickinson's texts and brings to light a story about the diversity of now-collapsed genres that circulated and thrived in nineteenth-century literary culture. Jackson's assertion that Dickinson was concerned with "the material circumstances of writing" and not with "what that writing will be taken to (figuratively) represent" invites this book's investigation of process, material culture, and the relation between the two.[8] In this way, the problem at the center of this book was made visible by Jackson's insights about "lyric reading"—the act by which we read a wide variety of texts as lyrics—but is, in essence, an entirely different problem. In short, once we accept that Dickinson's poems have been misread lyrically, then the question that follows is what those poems were before that misreading.

My focus on paper, then, is related to the work being done on Dickinson's manuscripts, but because I am interested in textual materials and writing protocols, I have found the interdisciplinary space of media studies particularly relevant to the questions I ask. While it might seem strange to use the word "media" in relation to Dickinson, it is important to acknowledge that Dickinson's paper is exactly that. As we will see in the chapters ahead, Dickinson used various paper-based media—sewn fascicles, letters and envelopes, loose sheets, household scraps—in ways that were both conventional and strange. While she appropriated certain cultural conventions for the composing and copying of poetry, she departed from these by treating paper not simply as the material that holds her lines, drafts, and fair copies, but as a constitutive and meaningful part of the making and dissemination of the poems themselves. Once we begin to think about paper as media, we can ask new kinds of questions about the poems written on that paper. For instance, does it matter how poems reach their readers? What difference does it make (both to the poem itself and its reader) if it was written on a formal sheet of stationery or on, say, the back of a candy wrapper? When there is not an explicit reader, towards what horizon of interpretation (if any) do they—the paper and the poem—propel themselves? In the words of Lisa Gitelman and Geoffrey B. Pingree, a focus on media shows us that "looking for content apart from context just won't work."[9]

If the questions above about paper and media have gone unasked largely because of ingrained reading habits and active resistance, then the result has been a history of editing (and criticism based on that editing) that redoubles the problem. When a reader encounters a Dickinson poem either in an anthology or in most collections of her work, that reader is given no indication that this is just one of what often were multiple incarnations of a poem, all of which were written at different moments and on (or with, or around) different kinds of materials. Under those circumstances, there is no way to think about the relationship between the making of the poem, the materials Dickinson used when making it, and the poem itself. Take, for example, the poem that begins "It sifts from Leaden Sieves—" (F 291). Most accounts of this poem point out that it was probably influenced by Dickinson's reading of Emerson's poem "The Snow-Storm" and that there are resonances with other Dickinson poems, such as the one that begins "The Snow that never drifts—" (F 1155), within it.[10] Critics like to speculate, in particular, on what the "it" in the opening line may be a symbol for: for Magdelena Zapedowska the poem is about a peaceful "annihilation" of the world, while for Domhnall Mitchell it is about, on one account, the relationship between democracy and immigrants and, on another, about how "print buries the unique characteristics of handwriting under a blank uniformity."[11] What these accounts don't take into account is the fact that Dickinson produced at least five drafts of this poem over a twenty-one year period, copying each one on a different kind of paper, often with radical revisions and reworkings of the one that had come before it. We might ask, then, which version are critics looking at when they read Emerson's influence or speculate on Dickinson's relationship to democracy?

Let us back up so that I can tell the story of this poem: The first manuscript that we have was sent to Susan Huntington Dickinson. Sue, as Dickinson and others called her, was Dickinson's sister-in-law, closest friend, next-door neighbor, and the recipient of more poems and letters than any of Dickinson's other correspondents. In 1862, on three sides of a folded sheet of off-white paper (fig. I.1), Dickinson wrote:

It sifts from Leaden
Sieves—
It powders all the Wood.
It fills with Alabaster
Wool
The Wrinkles of the Road—

It makes an Even
Face
Of Mountain, and of
Plain—
Unbroken Forehead
from the East
Unto the East again—

It reaches to the Fence—
It wraps it Rail by Rail
Till it is lost in Fleeces—
It deals Celestial Vail

To Stump, and Stack—
and Stem—
A Summer's empty Room—
Acres of Joints, where
Harvests were,
Recordless, but for them—

It Ruffles Wrists
of Posts
As Ankles of a
Queen—
Then stills it's Artisans—
like Ghosts—
Denying they have been—
                              Emily

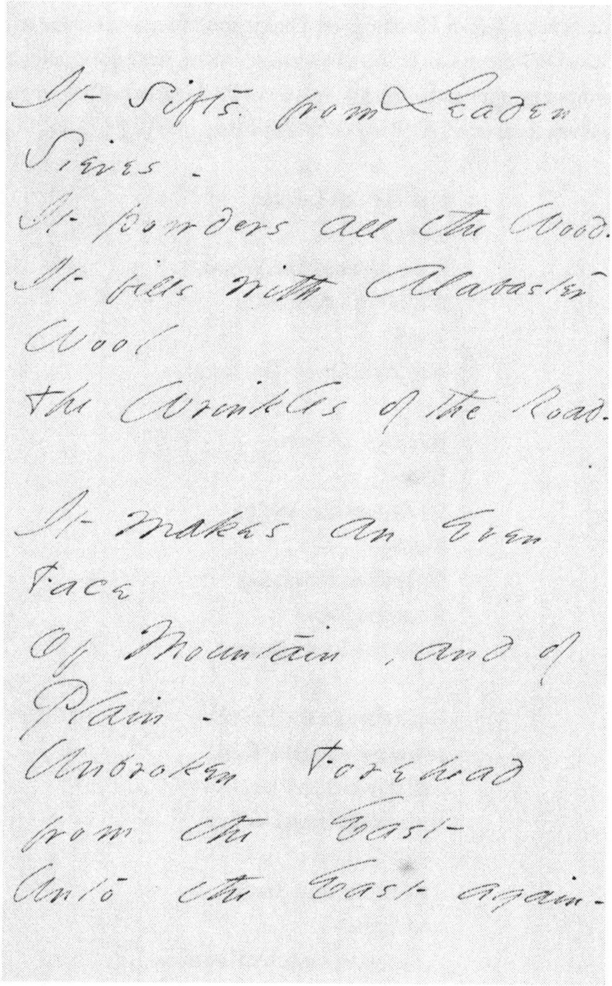

Figure I.1
"It sifts from Leaden Sieves—" (F 291). Sent to Susan Huntington Dickinson in 1862. By permission of The Houghton Library, Harvard University, MS Am 1118.3 (278) © The President and Fellows of Harvard College.

These lines describe the falling of snow onto the earth by comparing snow to flour and wool and by comparing the earth to a face, with wrinkles and a forehead, with wrists and ankles. In this rich description of the snow, its generating force is both everywhere (wrapping the fences, filling the rooms where summer harvests had been) and nowhere (when it "stills," at the end of the poem, there is

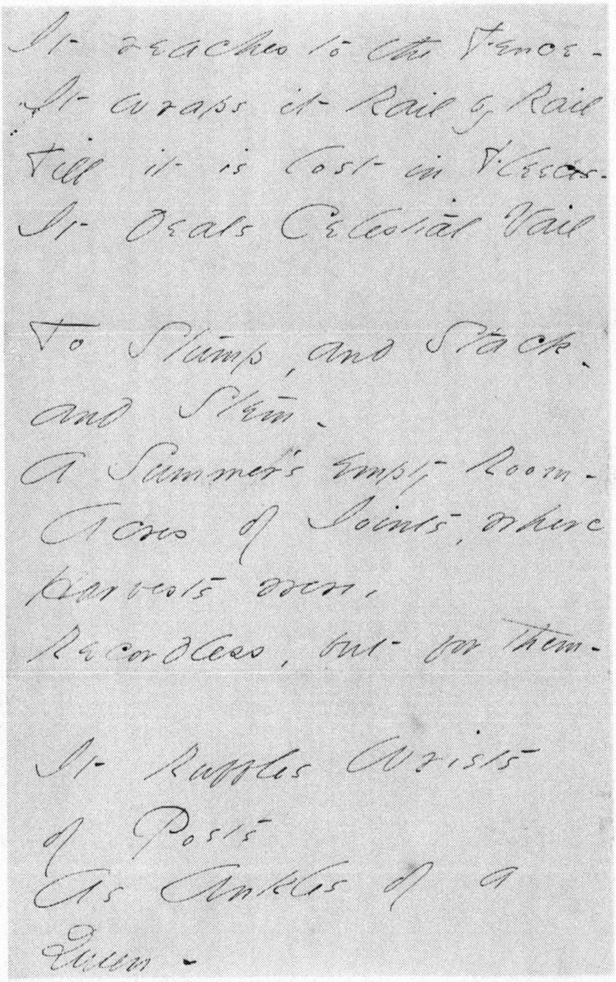
It reaches to the Fence -
It wraps it Rail by Rail
Till it is lost in Fleeces -
It deals Celestial Vail

To Stump, and Stack -
and Stem -
A Summer's empty Room -
Acres of Joints, where
Harvests were,
Recordless, but for them -

It Ruffles Wrists
of Posts
As Ankles of a
Queen -

Figure I.1 *(continued)*

the possibility of denying that these "Artisans" or "Ghosts" had ever been present on this landscape). When Dickinson copied these lines onto a folded sheet of stationery the following year—a sheet that she would eventually sew into the group we now call Fascicle 24—she retained the basic structure of the poem she had sent to Sue, but revised certain words: the snow now falls on "the Field" instead of "all the Wood"; it "flings a Crystal Vail" instead of "deals a Celestial Vail"; and the "Artisans" that had been compared to "Ghosts" in the earlier draft are now

Then stills its Artisans -
Like Ghosts -
Denying they have been -

Emily -

Figure I.1 (*continued*)

compared to "Swans." In this draft Dickinson also included several variants whose placements she indicated with + markings both within the poem and below it: "Myrmidons" for "Artisans"; "Seams" for "Joints"; and all the words (except for "all the Wood") that had been used in the previous version. In the draft that Dickinson included on formal stationery, then, she expanded the poem's options but she also situated the scene in a more visible landscape and tempered the mysterious element of the snow.

Already we might think about what difference it makes to send a poem to Sue and to copy a poem onto a sheet of stationery that, by 1863, Dickinson probably knew she would sew to other sheets. We might, in other words, ask what effect the shift in paper and practice had on the changes Dickinson made to the poem. But Dickinson did not stop there. Two years after making the fascicle copy, Dickinson revised the poem quite drastically, reducing it by almost half its size (fig. I.2). She copied this new version in pencil on a small piece of paper and folded the paper in thirds, as if she were going to mail it:

> It sifts from Leaden
> Sieves
> It powders all the Wood
> It fills with Alabaster
> Wool
> The wrinkles of the
> Road—
> It scatters like
> the Birds
> Condenses like a Flock
> Like Juggler's Flowers
> situates
> Opon a Baseless Arc—
> It traverses—yet halts—
> Disperses, while it stays
> Then curls itself in
> Capricorn
> Denying that it was—

In shortening the poem Dickinson did away with much of the description of what the snow does to the landscape and replaced it with lines that describe the movement of the snow itself: it now "scatters," "Condenses," "situates," "traverses," "Disperses," "stays," and "curls." It is the contradictory images of the snow that then allow it to be, as it was in the final lines of the earlier drafts, "Denying that it was." In this draft the poem moves more quickly to the heart of the matter: there is, we might say, something about the erratic and unpredictable movement of snow that allows for its ability to deny itself. In 1871, six years after revising the poem down to these twelve lines and retaining them, Dickinson copied and sent them to Higginson (in this version the snow is "Disputing" instead of "Denying"), and twelve years after that, in 1883, she copied and sent them to the editor of Roberts Brothers, Thomas Niles.

Figure I.2
"It sifts from Leaden Sieves—" (F 291). Copied in 1865 and retained. Courtesy, Archives & Special Collections, Amherst College.

To summarize: What we have here are five drafts of this poem, written over a period of twenty-one years. Three drafts were sent to correspondents, one was sewn into a fascicle, and one was retained on loose paper. Two drafts are long, and three are short. Each version was copied on a different kind of paper that was sewn, folded, or placed in an envelope. Each version has, at the very least, a word or two that is different from the others. The compositional history of this poem generates certain questions—questions that occur by approaching it as a made object instead of as a printed text. For instance, how might we read the fact that the domestic images for the snow are dominant in the draft that went to Sue and the draft that was sewn into a fascicle (objects themselves that stayed close to home), but were omitted in the versions that Dickinson sent to the professional men—Higginson and Niles—with whom she corresponded later in life? Did moving to a small piece of loose paper in 1865 have an effect on the way Dickinson chose to render this snow as an element of nature whose essence is rooted in erratic, opposing movements as opposed to more leisurely, formal ones? What difference does it make that the version sent to Niles was copied with the lines that begin "Further in Summer than the Birds" (F 895) and that both poems were, according to Dickinson's letter, sent in return for the "delightful Book" that he had previously sent her (L 813)? While Dickinson did not draft every poem as many times as she did this one, enough of them were composed and revised in such a way as to warrant our attention. For instance, at least forty-five of the poems that she copied onto sheets of folded stationery and sewed into her fascicles have three or more extant material contexts, and at least eleven of these have more than four.[12] Once Dickinson had stopped making fascicles, she placed at least eighty-three poems in three or more material contexts, and at least thirty-one of them in more than four.[13] Tracking a poem through its multiple contexts is often the best way to understand the relationship between Dickinson's paper, process, and poetics.

Reading Dickinson's materials allows us to see her poems as something other than lyrics without histories. Instead, we become aware of the fact that she was, among other things, interrogating assumptions about the literary genres with which she was engaged. While it is important to keep in mind Jonathan Culler's warning that all writing "is made possible by the existence of the genre . . . as surely as the failure to keep a promise is made possible by the institution of promising," in the pages ahead I treat Dickinson's genres as a topic that is still very much open for investigation.[14] By not assuming that we already know what genre Dickinson was writing in—or towards, or around—this book reveals how Dickinson was actively appropriating and questioning the conventions of a wide array of poetic genres that were available to her—sequences, elegies, narratives, lyrics, and fragments, in particular—as well as pressing on the boundary between poetry and prose. By including the lyric as one of Dickinson's available genres, I am putting into practice Jackson's idea that "to say that lyrics are part of the Dickinson archive is not necessarily to say that the discursive system of the lyric inevitably governs everything that can be said about Dickinson's work."[15] Additionally, I treat none of these aforementioned genres as stable. Indeed, it is precisely their instability—the murkiness of their boundaries, their resistance to proscriptive definitions—that allows Dickinson to engage them with such fervor.

This combination of an interest in Dickinson's materials and her navigation of the generic issues that would have been present to a nineteenth-century American poet structure this book's analysis. Each of the five chapters immerses itself in the details of a specific compositional practice and the materials taken up in that practice: copying poems onto folded sheets of stationery; inserting and embedding poems into correspondence; sewing sheets together to make fascicles; scattering loose sheets; and copying lines on often torn and discarded pieces of household paper. Understanding these five roughly chronological stages of Dickinson's practices produces new ways of approaching her poems and paints a picture of Dickinson as a nineteenth-century American writer who was navigating the problems of genre. While each chapter provides descriptions and overviews of Dickinson's methods as they apply to each kind of practice, they primarily concern themselves with the details of specific poems. This is partly because this is the most interesting way of telling this particular story, but also because I hope that the analyses that emerge over the course of this study are ultimately teachable both as a group and in their individual instances.

Instead of proceeding from the assumption that Dickinson's fascicles are meant to be read as books of poetry, Chapter 1 begins by situating Dickinson's method of copying poems onto folded sheets within conventions of nine-teenth-century verse-copying and homemade book-making practices. By turning our attention to the material differences between Dickinson's fascicles (otherwise known as her manuscript books) and other objects (commonplace books, autograph albums, scrapbooks, diaries, and sermons), I highlight the individual folded fascicle sheet as Dickinson's primary unit of construction. Instead of imposing on the fascicles a coherence that we have long assumed Dickinson was aiming for, this chapter argues that attention to the sheet ren-ders the poems as much more loosely tied together (into pairs and clusters) than current readings of them as narratives or sequences permit. Approaching Dickinson's fascicles along these lines allows us to see more clearly the reasons for and results of her resistance to print.

Before, during, and after the years in which she was constructing the fascicles, Dickinson copied poems onto sheets that she enclosed in her letters, inserted poems into the body of her letters proper, and embedded poems into the prose itself. Chapter 2 explores Dickinson's method of sending what had once been or would later become poems and pieces of poems in her correspondence. Instead of treating either the letters or the fascicles as Dickinson's privileged site of compo-sition, this chapter argues that analyzing where the two practices meet highlights how Dickinson relied on the existence of both to rethink the formal structures and the rhetorical strategies of her poems. By looking closely at "As if I asked a common alms—" (F 14), a poem that was first copied on a sheet of stationery and sewn into a fascicle and then later recopied in letters and sent to different corre-spondents, this chapter investigates the relationship between verse and episto-lary prose in nineteenth-century literary culture, in Dickinson's understanding, and in current editorial and critical practice.

Chapter 3 addresses Dickinson's act of sewing her folded sheets together, adding to and complicating my analysis of fascicle sheets in Chapter 1. By taking up Dickinson's poems about death as they appear in the fascicle context (across sheets, now that they are sewn together), this chapter exposes Dickinson's in-terest in revising the conventions of consolation and closure on which the ele-giac genre has always depended. This chapter argues that by sewing her sheets together, Dickinson created a material and formal framework in which her poems could refuse the finality typically associated with the elegy, allowing them the latitude to return over and over to the scene and subject of mourning. Reading several of Dickinson's poems about death in the context of the fascicles highlights her intervention into the genre so popular with women poets of the time and, in turn, allows us to read their work as contributing to the develop-ment of the genre.

While the first three chapters isolate specific material practices that Dickin-son engaged as she made her poems, Chapter 4 asks what, at first, looks like a biographical question about her process: why, temporarily in 1863 and then decisively between 1864 and 1875, did Dickinson stop sewing sheets together and instead allow loose sheets to scatter? By looking closely at the poem that begins "I felt a Cleaving in my Mind—" (F 867) and a variety of manuscripts to which it is related, Chapter 4 analyses Dickinson's strategies for drafting poems during these years and places those strategies in relation to her decision to stop sewing sheets. In doing so, it reveals that a certain dependence on the temporal and spatial elements of sequence had been, albeit in deeply conflicted ways, necessarily built into the fascicle project from the very beginning. As opposed to most critics who highlight the fascicle years as Dickinson's most successful, I argue that it is when Dickinson recognizes the limitations of this project—a realization that becomes manifest in the materials of this period—that she is able to produce some of her greatest poems.

In an effort to wrestle with one of the central questions of this book—do the materials produce the poetics or do the poetics demand the materials?—Chapter 5 looks closely at the drafts, scraps, and fragments that Dickinson, in her final years, wrote on equally scrap-like materials from her home. Unlike the fascicles of Dickinson's early career, which offer the critic formal containers to ground and contextualize the sometimes elusive poetry, these under-studied late lines exist in now un-apprehendable space, as part of the poet's every day. Yet attention to the lines that Dickinson wrote on the inside flaps of discarded envelopes and the back sides of shopping lists, advertisements, bills, and recipes show that in the midst of what has previously seemed like a disintegration of her systematic compositional practices, Dickinson was actually returning to the fascicles to rewrite, revise, redact, and what I call "unmake" this poetry in a new material context. By looking closely at this largely untreated stage in Dickinson's compositional process, I argue that Dickinson's paper continues to make all the difference to the poems themselves, as the scrap-like paper prompts Dickinson to write poems which, as the draft manuscripts show so vividly, have a very hard time coming to their ends.

Far from offering a narrative in which I move from a position of ignorance and awe to one of understanding and mastery, I found that the more time I spent with Dickinson's materials, the more they challenged my understanding of what Dickinson was doing and the identity of what she was writing. Rather than arguing that manuscripts provide the definitive source for an interpretation of poetry, then, this book aims to navigate the complicated implications of archival work and material history for the study of Dickinson. In short, while I use manuscripts to uncover aspects of Dickinson's practices that we have not yet seen, I also articulate where the limits of such a methodology lie. In the Afterword I make this explicit by thinking through some of the questions that this method makes available to scholars of poetry. Because I argue that material textual analysis of Dickinson's writing is most fruitful when it raises (rather than settles) questions about genre and the boundaries of the literary, this Afterword aims to open up new territory for investigation. In this end, this book describes a process that readers can do on their own, and (potentially) in relation to a number of different writers: it looks closely at paper, pinholes, slips, string, and folds, not merely as the often-overlooked details of manuscripts, but as elements of a practice that, because it can be contextualized historically, can lead to a fuller understanding of a writer's process and poems.

My attention to manuscripts raises several issues that need to be addressed upfront. The first is the issue of Dickinson's speaker. All readers and critics of Dickinson's poems make certain decisions about who the "I" of her poems is. As I see it, there are three ways that this speaker is interpreted: first, critics read along purely biographical lines and assume that Dickinson (the actual person writing the poem) is the "I," giving voice to her innermost thoughts and communicating her knowledge and experience to those who are both historically situated and purely imagined; second, they assume that when Dickinson writes "I," that "I" can be appropriated (and voiced) by anyone reading the poem, such that Dickinson is actually writing about you; and third, they understand the "I" to be someone other than the writer or the reader—an imagined figure whose history, desires, and motivations drive the poem.[16] This last way of reading the speaker turns Dickinson's poems into something akin to dramatic monologues, something that she herself urged Higginson to do when she wrote him, "When I state myself, as the Representative of the Verse—it does not mean—me—but a supposed person" (L 268). Yet to infer the presence of a speaker at all implies at some level that these poems are being spoken, that there is some voice that owns the words by speaking them. Sharon Cameron's now famous formulation that "the lyric voice is solitary and generally speaks out of a single moment in time," for instance, was articulated in a book about how Dickinson pushed the lyric genre to its limits.[17] This approach assumes that Dickinson believed in, manufactured, and was invested in some position of subjectivity through which a poem passed, an assumption that Jackson urges us to challenge, since, in her words, Dickinson "so strenuously resists substituting the alienated lyric image of the human—the very image the modern reading of the lyric has created—for the exchange between historical persons between whom the barriers of space and time had not fallen."[18] Instead, Jackson proposes that we think about who these historical persons were, because "to say that where or who 'you' are makes a difference in, among other things, historical questions of genre."[19]

To impose a twenty-first century understanding of who "speaks" in a Dickinson poem on those, admittedly, now twenty-first century readers, is to undo the work that recontextalizing the poet in her nineteenth-century moments of composition achieves. Because this book is about how a real woman living in Amherst, Massachusetts in the middle of the nineteenth century put words on a page (or a slip, or a shopping list, or a flyer), I will look at that paper instead of hearing voices. In doing so, I situate the readers of this study in that historical space and I urge them to think about the poems themselves as texts that were

made by Dickinson and that do work. This is work that we can come to understand by thinking about how poems move, about how they reveal and hide things,
about how they develop, and about how, sometimes against their better efforts,
they get blocked.

The second issue that my approach raises is the question of intention. Because
looking at manuscripts makes the writer present (or creates the fiction that the
writer is present), it self-evidently problematizes how and where and why to attribute intention. In Walter Benn Michaels's introduction to *The Shape of the Signifier: 1967 to the End of History*, "The Blank Page," he raises a crucial question
about the relationship between materiality, intentionality, and the position of the
reader.[20] He argues that Susan Howe's attention to the materiality of Dickinson's
writings (to the spaces between words and the way that certain letters are written)
implicitly rejects an interest in the writer's intentions and instead foregrounds
the subject position of the reader. This becomes the formula of Michaels's po-
lemic: an interest in materiality necessitates a critical disavowal of intentionality
and demands that the subject position of the reader is the only thing that matters.
The implication, for Michaels, is that materiality and identity (through an emphasis on the reader) are inextricably linked. Your relationship, then, to the question
of whether or not materiality matters dictates the other positions you take as a
critic. Because Howe approaches Dickinson's manuscripts in order to understand them as drawings, Michaels's assessment that Dickinson's intentions don't
matter to Howe seems precisely right, for all that matters is what Howe's experience with these details is and what kind of interpretation she might construct
from this position. But Michaels himself is working with an impoverished distinction between intention and matter that disappears when we see Dickinson's
materials not as inert objects but as steps in a process. When we turn our attention to the details of the material objects that point to how Dickinson made these
poems—creases, pin holes, blank spaces, types of paper, and other texts that appear on that paper—we find that the material object and the intention of the
writer are intimately connected.

In *Thinking Through Material Culture*, Carl Knappett reminds scholars from all
disciplines of the archeological paradigm that has governed the study of material
objects, delineating the interpretive path that archeologists take from finding an
object to discerning the behavior of the people who used or created that object to
deducing the thoughts that governed those people.[21] This archeological paradigm
comes closer to the work I do in this book: Because I am looking at (albeit not
unearthing) objects and because I am discerning what Dickinson did with those
objects, I am necessarily concerned with her thoughts, or, we might say, her intentions. When we follow a writer's hand along her page, track when and where she
revised and recopied a given poem, and register the interruptions of the page or
the potentials of the string she used to sew those pages together, we seek to understand how that writer worked and what those methods of working both made
possible and limited. While I never attempt to say what Dickinson may have been

privately thinking or planning when she made her poems—this is a version of intention that we might guess at but can never know—I allow the objects to lead us to better understand Dickinson's writing practices, the cultural and literary landscape within which those practices took form, the writer who developed in the process, and, ultimately, the poems themselves.

Finally, writing about manuscripts presents the problem of how to represent those manuscripts, as the writing I do (and you read) about them appears in print, while the manuscripts themselves do not. In the pages ahead I have provided images of manuscripts whenever it is both necessary and possible. That being said, the words written on those manuscripts are sometimes difficult to read—a problem for Dickinson criticism that I address at length in Chapter 5—and many of them, simply for the purpose of following the interpretations that I then provide, need to be translated into print. While I am not directly entering into the long-standing debate on how best to represent *all* of Dickinson's poems, I have had to take a position on how the readers of this study will encounter Dickinson's poems in print. This is a loaded position because, as Cristanne Miller states, "in quoting a Dickinson poem, scholars now implicitly manifest their theoretical position as to what constitutes a Dickinson poem."[22] This is particularly problematic, according to Miller, because a translation that stresses the poem as an aural object (in metrically-lineated lines and stanzas, without the variants Dickinson often included on the manuscript page) treats it as a nineteenth-century object, whereas a translation that stresses the poem as a visual object (words as they appear on the page, with variants) "implicitly support[s] postmodern readings of plurality, visual intentionality, and the poet's deliberate construction of fluid texts of one form or another."[23] In the pages to come I disrupt this equation by representing Dickinson's scriptural lineation and variants, yet I do this in conjunction with a set of interpretive practices that place Dickinson very firmly in the nineteenth century. In other words, as one can see in my transcriptions of two of the drafts of "It sifts from Leaden Sieves—," I attempt to reproduce—always with the knowledge that such reproduction is impossible—in print what it is I see on the manuscript (words and marks as they appear on the page), yet this is not a move to present Dickinson as a proto-modernist experimenter with form. In complicating the equation on which debates about how to print (and read) Dickinson's poems seem to implicitly stand, I aim to broaden how we think about the relationship between manuscripts, print, and interpretive practices.

While the "unbound" in *Dickinson Unbound* most directly refers to the materials that themselves reside at the center of this study—the sheets before Dickinson sewed them and the sheets she never sewed; the letters and poems as they emerged from envelopes to be read; the scraps that are no longer held together by pins—I also use this term to refer to a method of analysis that itself unbinds Dickinson's readers from what may have previously fettered their interpretations of her poems. By placing emphasis on the processes that Dickinson employed and on the paper she used to make her poems, we have the opportunity to re-enter poems we may have thought we already knew and the chance to understand in new and more concrete ways the poet who has heretofore eluded, and perhaps always will elude, our grasp.

CHAPTER 1

⌒⋎⌒

Dickinson's Sheets

Between 1858 and 1864 Emily Dickinson copied over eight hundred of her poems onto folded sheets of stationery and sewed them into the forty groupings that we have come to call the "fascicles." After Dickinson's death in 1886, her first editor, Mabel Loomis Todd, cut the string that held these sheets together in order to publish the poems as individual lyrics. Disturbed by the fact that Dickinson's later readers had never been given the chance to study the fascicles as they were assembled by her and curious as to what a reconstruction of them could make possible, in the late twentieth century Ralph Franklin undertook the major textual project of dating handwriting, comparing pressure marks, and matching pin holes. Ninety-five years after the delicate red string had been cut, the fascicles were returned, as closely as possible, to their original form.

In the aftermath of Franklin's reconstruction, several new studies of Dickinson's poems were published, many of which asked important questions about how knowledge of the fascicle context can widen, shift, and even radically alter our understanding of Dickinson's individual poems. Each treatment of the fascicles considered them from a different angle: while some argued that each fascicle tells a specific narrative, others considered that, taken together, all forty fascicles construct a single story. Scholars who preformed non-narrative readings of the fascicles instead located dominant tropes, themes, and ordering mechanisms; placed the fascicles within various poetic traditions; and isolated their particularly meaningful features. One of the great byproducts of Franklin's reconstruction has been the disparate critical and methodological approaches that scholars have taken in relation to these objects—approaches that were not available to critics in the years between the dismantling and reconstruction of the fascicles.[1]

Attention to this story's sometimes scandalous-seeming details of string cutting and lyric extraction, as well as to the subsequent heroic efforts of reconstruction has, ironically, long obscured what it was Dickinson was doing when she made the fascicles. Even in Franklin's introduction to *The Manuscript Books of Emily Dickinson*, in which he reproduces images of the fascicles, he comments on the great critical interest in them "as artistic gatherings—as gatherings intrarelated by theme, imagery, emotional movement" and declares himself more interested by investigations that might explain "why she assembled the fascicles—by what principles and for what purposes."[2] Franklin knew, as he matched ink stains and lined up pin holes, that Dickinson's project was rooted in a specific time and place, that it had been driven by a set of unique compositional practices and cultural influences, yet his facsimile edition provoked the kinds of literary readings that suspended the very knowledge it should have made visible.

This chapter makes that other story visible—the one about a woman who took up specific materials and engaged in particular practices in order to write over eighteen hundred of the most riveting, peculiar, and enduring poems in the English language. It does so by extending the move that, over two decades ago now, Barton Levi St. Armand urged scholars to make when he placed Dickinson's fascicle poems in a wider cultural context by asking them to further investigate her material writing practices. "This art," St. Armand writes, "was not exclusively literary in nature but originated in Dickinson's situation as a nineteenth-century woman who was part of a community where many nonliterary or nonacademic arts were practiced."[3] St. Armand suggests that Dickinson's poetry was "in the popular tradition of the portfolio or sketchbook," a tradition that he traces to Washington Irving and Fanny Fern, but that had been applied to Dickinson in different terms as early as 1890, when Thomas Wentworth Higginson suggested that her poems were the sort of manuscript expressions defined by Ralph Waldo Emerson's 1840 essay, "New Poetry."[4] There, Emerson had written: "Only one man in the thousand may print a book, but one in ten or one in five may inscribe his thoughts, or at least with short commentary his favorite readings in a private journal."[5] Into this journal, according to Emerson, the writer would copy "confessions," "faults," "the imperfect parts, the fragmentary verses, the halting rhymes."[6] While tracking the cultural influences on Dickinson back through Emerson provides some of the context that allows us to see her working within the literary and nonliterary arenas of her time, it is through returning to the specifics of Dickinson's materials and practices that we are able to take our cues for how to read her poems from the poet herself.

This first chapter is concerned with the paper Dickinson ordered from the local stationer and onto which she copied many of her most well-known poems. What might seem like a minor detail in the larger story of her fascicle project is the material that sits at the very center of this endeavor. This chapter will look closely at these folded sheets of paper—at all that their presence conveys, at all that Dickinson's use of them reveals—in order to argue that understanding Dickinson's act of copying poems onto folded sheets of stationery is the very thing that reveals the fascicles to *not* be the narratives, book-length-sequences, or thematically-grouped poems that many critics have described them as ever since

Franklin's reconstruction. By acknowledging the sheet as Dickinson's primary unit of composition, we can begin to see how her poems were composed according to a complex understanding of the relationship of the individual poem to the cluster, to realize her preference for minor accumulations over dominating and oppressive wholes, and to recognize the formal play that pairings, in particular, made possible for her. Copying poems onto sheets that always contained more than one but never more than eight poems forced Dickinson to ask what may sound like simple questions, but they are precisely the ones that Dickinson scholarship, with its attachment both to the individual poem and to a desire to read these poems in the context of entire fascicles, has obscured: What is the relationship of one poem to another poem? What are the different forms of possible relation and how do poems find their ways into these relations? What do these relations make possible and what do they repress?

This chapter will begin with a detailed description of how Dickinson made the fascicles and analyze some of the ways that she drafted poems in the years leading up to the fascicle project, as this history makes visible her later decision to commit poems to sheets of stationery. In the second section I ask where Dickinson learned how to make such objects, why she did not, say, copy her poems into bound blank books, and what kinds of materials she must have come in contact with that somehow resemble what it is she strove to make. In order to do this, I look closely at a variety of nineteenth-century conventions for verse copying and book making that Dickinson was engaging as she made the fascicles, as they reveal what kinds of cultural and literary practices she had experienced. In the third section I turn to the words, lines, and poems that Dickinson copied on the sheets from which she would eventually make her fascicles. Reading the sheets in the context of the compositional processes and details of material culture provided in the previous sections allows me to explore how this specific material artifact is connected to the poetics that Dickinson was developing during these years. In the final section I explain how attention to Dickinson's sheets allows critics new access to the question that continues to preoccupy them: why Dickinson chose not to have her poems printed.

MAKING THE FASCICLES

Making the fascicles was a detailed and time-consuming project. Dickinson made clean copies of her already-drafted poems onto folded sheets of stationery, stacked these sheets, made two holes through them along the left-hand margin, and sewed them together with string (fig. 1.1). Each one measures approximately five inches across by eight inches long and is composed of paper that is mostly cream, either wove or laid, with light ruling. Each of the forty fascicles contains between four and seven sheets of folded stationery, although in several of them Dickinson included single leaves and slips of smaller paper, usually to accommodate the end

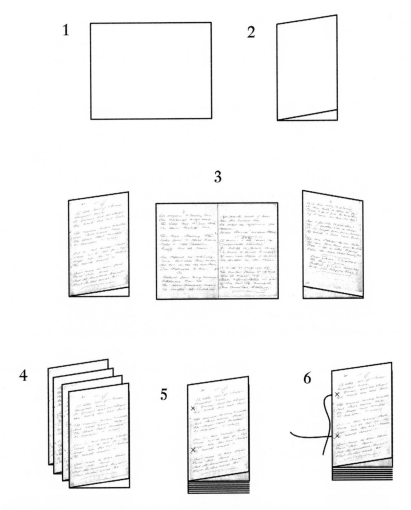

Figure 1.1
Making a Fascicle. Illustration by Dinah Fried.

of a poem or its variant words. She did not number, title, or otherwise mark the fascicles or the poems that she copied onto the sheets. In almost all cases, when she was finished copying, she destroyed her earlier drafts.

Although some critics have argued that the fascicles were simply a way of keeping order or tidying up what, by 1858, had become a large number of poems in Dickinson's possession, certain clues indicate that other forces motivated her.[7] For instance, Dickinson did not copy onto these sheets everything that she wrote during these years, nor did she copy poems as they were written or sew sheets as they were completed. Consequently, poems written in different years sometimes appear on sheets sewn into the same fascicle, and in several instances the same poem appears in more than one fascicle.[8] Additionally, Dickinson maintained certain rules about how poems were to be copied: She most often marked the end of each entry and the beginning of the next with a portion of blank space, a single line drawn horizontally across the page, or simply the beginning of a new side. Her entries often consume more than one side of the same folded sheet, but only once did she allow a poem to continue onto the next sheet.[9] In other words, Dickinson had a particular method for copying that kept poems distinct from each other and preserved the unit of the folded sheet. Poems were not copied here randomly, nor were the fascicles used as storage containers for all of her poems.

One of the reasons critics simultaneously pay so much attention to the fascicles and do not think more about how they were made is because we know of only a few poems that Dickinson wrote before she began copying poems onto fascicle sheets. We have access to only four poems written before 1858, one of which was later copied onto a sheet that was sewn into a fascicle, and critics have been largely left to speculate about what else Dickinson may have written before this time. In other words, because we have almost no access to Dickinson's pre-fascicle process, the fascicles present themselves as both more originary and stable than they actually are. In light of this dearth of materials, it is important to remember that while it looks as if Dickinson's poems sprang spontaneously and fluently from her pen in 1858, her letters point to the fact that she was drafting poems far earlier than this, and, I would argue, developing a sense of how she wanted to organize her poems. As early as 1853, after learning that her brother Austin was writing poems, she wrote to him, in that jovial yet competitive tone that she often took with him: "Now Brother Pegasus, I'll tell you what it is—I've been in the habit *myself* of writing some few things, and it rather appears to me that you're getting away my patent, so you'd better be somewhat careful, or I'll call the police!" (L 110). That same year she sent Sue the lines that begin "On this wondrous sea" (F 3) with a command at the top of the page to "Write! Comrade, write!" (L 105).

Not only did Dickinson consider herself to be a poet who, by virtue of this designation, must have been writing poems, but, according to Franklin, she may have even been making something resembling fascicles as early as 1853. Franklin theorizes that the "little manuscript" (L 121) and "little volumes" (L 150) that she sent to Henry Vaughan Emmons that year may have been individual folded sheets, something akin to what Dickinson would have learned to make at Amherst Academy where "student writing was put out in a manuscript called 'Forest Leaves,' a form of juvenile journalism often hand-copied on single sheets of folded paper to form a volume."[10] While my analysis of the fascicles in this chapter will show that Dickinson probably would not have thought of the fascicles as "volumes" and therefore was most likely not referring to them in her correspondence with Emmons, it is clear that Dickinson was engaged in an early practice of drafting, copying, saving, and sending material that is now largely lost to us. Although we cannot know what form this practice took or what kinds of objects Emmons received from Dickinson, looking closely at her early compositional practices reveals the kind of labor that Dickinson put into both making her poems and constructing a system that, while continuously revised during the fascicle years, must have already been at least partially in place before she began copying poems onto the individual sheets that became part of the fascicles.

Just because we do not have access to a large number of poems that Dickinson wrote before she began her fascicle project does not mean that we do not have access to the way that she worked before copying a poem onto a sheet. For instance, we know that a poem could take a variety of paths towards entry on a sheet. Franklin has argued that Dickinson probably made two drafts of each poem, a first draft and an intermediate draft, before copying it onto a sheet, after which she destroyed the earlier drafts.[11] Franklin notes only one extant first draft—of "If those I loved were lost" (F 20)—which Dickinson copied on the inside recto of a small piece of folded paper. She used pencil, did not (for the most part) designate line breaks, and crossed out words, replaced words, and included variant words between the lines. This is a rather controlled process of revision in the midst of writing, and Dickinson recorded the result of this as a clean copy, with choices made, on a sheet that she would eventually sew into Fascicle 1. Of three extant intermediate drafts, only one of these poems—"A Wife—at Day-break—I shall be—" (F 185)—was later copied onto a sheet and sewn into a fascicle. Dickinson copied the earliest extant version in pencil on a leaf of lined stationery that was slightly torn on the right-hand side and that included the abandoned beginning of a letter on its opposite side (the letter reads: "Dear Friends, I bring you so"). There is only one variant word and the line breaks are clearly marked. According to Franklin, about a year later Dickinson returned to this draft and crossed out the penultimate line, wrote a "2" underneath it, and included the line "Eternity—I'm coming sir—" at the bottom of the page. Following this, she did not then copy the revised version onto a sheet, but instead made another draft. She made this draft in ink on a leaf of stationery, incorporated the revision she had indicated on the previous draft, revised a few words, and inserted a stanza break. This is often what a poem would look like if she was going to send it to one of her many correspondents, but for whatever reason this piece of paper was left unaddressed, unsigned, unfolded, and unsent. It was not until 1863 that Dickinson copied this poem onto a sheet of stationery that she would eventually sew into Fascicle 32. What is interesting about the later version is that while it retains the stanza break that Dickinson introduced in the ink draft, it must have been copied from the pencil draft because she maintains some of her earlier word choices.

The compositional histories of "If those I loved were lost" and "A Wife—at Daybreak—I shall be—" make visible the fact that for each of Dickinson's poems that she copied onto a folded sheet that she eventually sewed to other folded sheets there was at least one, but in some cases many more, preceding drafts. They also show that drafts of poems could sit around for years before being copied onto a sheet. In addition to these drafts, we have versions of eight poems that were copied onto paper that was sometimes folded (as if for sending) and sometimes not (as if for retaining) before or around the same time that Dickinson copied them onto formal sheets.[12] And in addition to having initial drafts, intermediate drafts, and other poems at a variety of stages, we know that Dickinson often sent poems or pieces of poems to her various correspondents before copying them onto sheets, a process that I will explore in Chapter 2. I highlight all of this material here as a way of reminding us that Dickinson was actively developing specific drafting and copying methods both prior to making the fascicles and throughout the early years of her fascicle project. These drafts and copies introduce us to writing that occurred outside of the fascicles but was ultimately associated with them. Far from being "like forty locked doors [that] attest to the power of enclosedness and the stimulus of what Dickinson called 'hermetic memory'" or "enclosed textual space in which Dickinson explored the contents of privacy and power," the fascicles are flexible, ever-developing objects whose methods of construction ask us to consider them in those terms.[13]

The fact that Dickinson was a poet long before she started copying poems onto folded sheets of stationery, that she had a variety of ways of getting a poem onto a sheet, and that she thought through her choice of materials indicates that her embrace of the folded sheet of stationery in 1858 is worthy of attention. In order to understand that Dickinson's individual sheets were her primary unit of construction and to allow this insight to bear fruitfully on a reading of her poems, we need to look at some other materials, objects, and practices that were present in nineteenth-century America. In the next section I will explore the materials that Dickinson would have been familiar with and that in some way—visually, experientially, or compositionally—resemble the fascicles, so that we can see how Dickinson was influenced by many of the writing, copying, and gathering practices of her time. In order to be able to read the poems that Dickinson copied onto sheets (as I will do in Section 3) and in order to draw meaning from that practice (as I will do in Section 4), it is important to establish what a sheet is and why it was a significant unit for Dickinson.

VERSE COPYING AND HOMEMADE BOOK MAKING IN NINETEENTH-CENTURY AMERICA

Critical treatments of Dickinson's fascicles as thoroughly unique imply that no one else ever copied and kept her own writings, yet we know that that is not true. There were, indeed, a variety of ways that nineteenth-century women undertook this practice. Recent criticism by Paula Bennett, Mary Loeffelholz, and Eliza Richards has begun to probe the culture in which nineteenth-century American women were deeply absorbed in the practice of writing, copying, preserving, and publishing verse.[14] By presenting some of the specific practices that young women of Dickinson's time had been trained to do in their schools and homes and by placing those practices within their cultural contexts, these critics invite readers to look closely at their materials and processes in whole new ways. In this vein, understanding how Dickinson appropriated and resisted the prevalent methods and materials brings us closer to understanding what the fascicles are and how they might be read.

Many American women of Dickinson's time copied favorite poems, prose passages, morally instructive quotations, sketches of flowers and birds, diary entries, and their original compositions most commonly into what were then and are still now called commonplace books.[15] Kept most often in simple, hardcover, store-bought books, passages of prose and poetry were carefully chosen and copied for the purposes of preservation and referral. The commonplace book has been around since antiquity, but some scholars have argued that in the nineteenth century it took on this particularly eclectic quality, as its contents were most often taken from diverse sources and copied by the owner's hand.[16] This was a pedagogical practice: young women were often taught that copying verses, for instance, would aid in their moral development. It was also a domestic practice: usually a single person sat down to record her compiled material within the privacy of the home. Miss Bradlee, for instance—whose commonplace book dates from 1820 to 1828—includes the compositions of, among others, "Mrs. Hemans," "Percival," "Byron," "L. E. Langdon," and "Mrs. Barbauld," all written out in Miss Bradlee's own hand (fig. 1.2).

While many of Dickinson's contemporaries copied poems into commonplace books, others used autograph albums. Autograph albums originated in sixteenth-century Germany and became popular in the 1830s and 1840s in America. According to Todd Gernes, autograph albums never changed their purpose or format too drastically, as they were always blank books into which the compiler, as well as her friends and family, copied prose, poetry, and drawings.[17] A fancier relative of the commonplace book, an autograph album's cover was often embossed with gold and stamped with a title meant to appeal to its mostly female owners. In some albums, like the anonymous one titled "Flowers of Genius," the owner used the right-hand pages to copy her original compositions and the left-hand pages to produce thematically-corresponding drawings (fig. 1.3). Yet others, like "The Dream," kept in 1846, housed letters, poems, and quotations written to (not by) its owner. Into "The Dream," friends of the album owner, "Ellen"—many of whom she knew at Charlestown Seminary—wrote poems to her, signed their names, and copied important and instructive passages and quotations. Like our present day practice of yearbook signing, these albums often circulated among the compiler's friends and visitors. Entries would often include an opening inscription to the compiler (i.e. "To Mary"), a poem or prose extract (usually without attribution), and the copier's name, date, and hometown. Scholars who have studied the autograph album tend to focus on its communal aspect, arguing that these books are essentially a record of friendships and affections. For instance, while Alice S. Fowler argues that the autograph album "attests to the human need

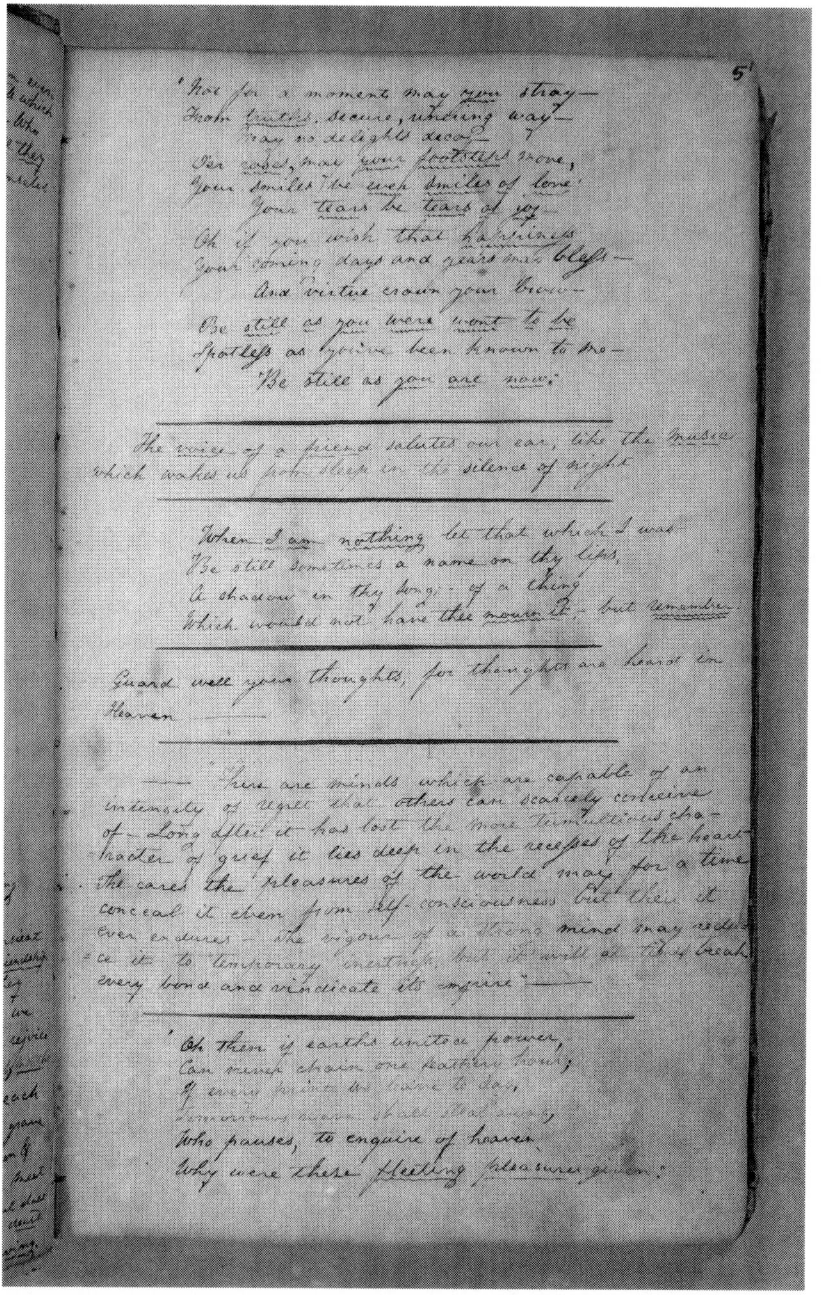

Figure 1.2
Miss Bradlee's Commonplace Book. Courtesy, American Antiquarian Society.

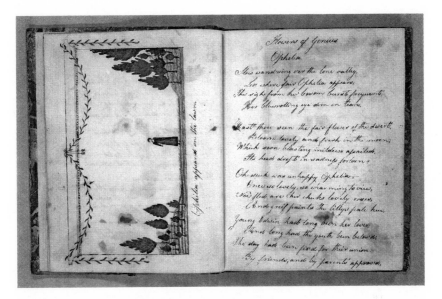

Figure 1.3
"Flowers of Genius" Album. Courtesy, American Antiquarian Society.

to be in a relationship with one another and to be remembered," Gernes asserts that these types of connections provide a resistance to the passage of time, as they "memorialize the present as a stay against the future."[18]

If the boundary between commonplace books and autograph albums sometimes become murky—there are instances in which it is hard to distinguish one type of book from the other, and instances in which the writer, copier, and keeper of the passages are not clear—the third kind of book into which women copied verses—the scrapbook—is wildly different from them at the same time that it threatens to subsume them both. Like the commonplace book and the autograph album, the scrapbook is made out of fragments: of materials, voices, and sources. This fragmentary nature is not a dominant feature of the other two kinds of books. Instead of copying out her favorite poems and prose passages (either for herself or for a friend), the scrapbook maker often varied her process, sometimes copying, but most often clipping and pasting. The clipping process necessarily meant that even more diverse material could be included; thus, all kinds of texts, from long articles to wedding announcements to intricate drawings or engravings, showed up in these books. Thus, the scrapbook engages the world of print. According to Ellen Gruber Garvey, "Readers adapted to [the] proliferation of print by cutting it up and saving it, reorganizing it, and sometimes recirculating it."[19] In this way, "nineteenth-century scrapbook makers were part of an elaborate circuit of recirculation, one that trespassed or found easements across the enclosure of authorship and publication."[20]

Dickinson was surrounded by women who kept these kinds of books. For instance, late in life, Sue kept a book in which she copied some of her own poems as well as the poems of others and gathered clippings that recorded personally important events, postcards sent to her from abroad, and notes written by other people.[21] Additionally, Mabel Loomis Todd, although a generation younger than Dickinson and Sue, kept scrapbooks into which she would one day paste manuscripts of Dickinson's poems.[22] Like these relatives, friends, and neighbors, Dickinson too copied and clipped some of the materials that appeared in print around her. For instance, on the back flyleaf of her Bible, Dickinson copied the poem "The Bible" by Dr. Jacob Holt, which was published in *The Hampshire and Franklin Express*, the local newspaper that Dickinson read, in June 1848, and she added to it the phrase, "Composed by Dr. J. Holt during his last sickness." Along with this poem she also pasted into her Bible two lines from Holt's obituary that she had clipped from a Boston newspaper. Jack Capps has shown that "considerable evidence exists that [Dickinson] habitually clipped and saved many of those items that interested her and sifted through them at later dates in search of materials uniquely suited to her purpose."[23]

While we can assume that Dickinson's own methods for making the fascicles must have been at least partially informed by the presence of such objects and practices—there is, for example, a striking visual resemblance between the dark and distinct lines Miss Bradlee used to mark the end of one entry and the beginning of the next and the lines that Dickinson used between poems in her fascicles—the fascicles are markedly different than these books. For instance, Dickinson did not include poems by others in them, she never (as far as we know) circulated the fascicles, and she did not clip and paste outside materials in them.[24] More to the point, though, these books were all readily-available, inexpensive, hardcover blank books that were marketed to the community of mid-nineteenth-century American women and around which a whole industry had cropped up. By the early 1880s, enough people were keeping albums to warrant the publication of pamphlets like "The Album Writer's Assistant: Being Choice Selections in Poetry and Prose, for Autograph Albums, Valentines, etc."[25] This pamphlet presents a collection of verses appropriate to copy into someone's autograph album, should one be asked to make an entry and not have a text in mind. The "Introductory" essay of the pamphlet expresses the purchaser's need for such a service: "There are few persons who have not at some time in life been solicited by their friends to write in an Album; but how frequently has it been the case that the person asked has found it utterly impossible at the moment either to draw from the well of their own thoughts the sentiment they desired to express or to call to memory any appropriate wishes to make more effective the expression of their own thoughts by introducing a graceful and suitable quotation."[26] Similar commercial paraphernalia also existed for scrapbooks, for, as Susan Tucker, Katherine Ott, and Patricia P. Buckler point out, by as early as 1835 there was a serial called *The Scrapbook* that describes the hobby in detail.[27] Part of what the existence of these pamphlets and serials point to, other than the presence of such practices, is the lack of originality built into their very form. In each of these books exists the ghost of mass production, a quality that is pushed to its extreme in the scrapbook, which, according to Garvey "endorse[s] an ideal not of originality, but of reuse and recirculation, of making the old continually new."[28]

Despite the facts that Dickinson knew women who copied poems into the kinds of books described in this section, that she had probably copied poems into hardcover blank books herself during her time at Mt. Holyoke, and that she lived in a culture that was marketing a variety of containers for women's poetry, she chose not to take up these objects when copying her own poems.[29] Instead of using what had become nameable and definable objects in which to copy her poems, she chose to copy poems onto folded sheets of stationery and sew them together, a practice that had been more common in the eighteenth century, when blank, bound books were rare and expensive.[30] How can we understand this choice and what can it tell us about what the fascicles are? One way of thinking this through is to look at other nineteenth-century instances in which people sewed sheets of paper together.

One type of text that was often stitched or sewn by hand in nineteenth-century America was the diary. For example, between 1827 and 1848, Ichabod Cook made twenty-four volumes of his ongoing diary. He used them to record the events on his farm and his involvement with the local church and he made each entry in verse, most often composing one quatrain per day. For example, the opening entry of the very first volume reads:

> 5 mo. 23 A very rainy day to day,
> And wet attending meeting;
> By that our beasts have stores of hay,
> And we by this have eating.

While there are moments in the diaries when he varies his style, this is the basic form that he maintained for over twenty years. Cook at first made his volumes by taking three large folded sheets of paper, stacking them, and stitching them all the way up the left-hand margin. Although his pages are much larger than those Dickinson used in the fascicles and he stitched all the way up the margin instead of only making two holes, their processes are almost identical. Like Dickinson, Cook copied, stacked, and sewed—in that order. But while the form and content of Cook's entries stayed largely the same, his method of making these volumes quickly changed. For his second volume, he inserted his pages into each other at the center fold in order to create forty-eight surfaces on which to write, placed the title "Memorandums" and the "Volume" number on the cover, and stitched the pages together with fewer, wider stitches.[31] Cook continued to use this method for the rest of the time he was making his diaries, a shift that reveals that, by the second volume, he had clearly decided how long he wanted each volume to be, as he did not limit himself to one volume per year and did not mind starting a new volume in the middle of a year.

Unlike Cook, most diarists who made their own books did use one volume per year. Ruth Henshaw Bascom, for instance, wrote and sewed her diaries between 1789 and 1846, starting each one on the first day of the new year. Like the standard diary or almanac entry, Bascom often marked the day and month on the left-hand side and then wrote a line or two about the day's events. She noted the weather, her activities, and her husband's sermon topics, as well as her travels and the visitors she received. Bascom did not write her entries in rhyme or meter, yet her diaries come closer than Cook's to resembling the fascicles physically—at least, upon first glance. Most strikingly, they are very similar in size: Bascom's diaries vary from anywhere between four to six inches across by six and a half to seven and a half inches long, while almost all of Dickinson's fascicles measure five by eight inches. But like Cook, Bascom did not stack her sheets, but inserted them into each other; unlike Cook, at the end of each year—her marker that a particular volume was done—she sewed all of her groupings together. In other words, even though both the Cook and Bascom diaries were stitched by their authors, each imposed different parameters on their productions. Bascom limited her volumes to the length of the year, therefore producing some often very messy stitchwork (oddly enough, since she was a seamstress), as she attempted to sew very differently sized groups of sheets together. Cook, in deciding in advance on the length that each volume should be (and therefore avoiding the sewing mess that Bascom encountered), limited himself by space; as a result, his diaries fracture the expectation that each year's narrative would be contained in its own volume.

What Cook and Bascom have in common is that they both inserted individually folded sheets into each other, an act that reveals that these writers imagined themselves to be constructing volumes of some sort, adopting and conforming to the standards that printed materials had modeled for them. Dickinson's process of stacking folded pages and then sewing them together created a very different type of object—one that (unlike Cook's and Bascom's and also unlike a printed book) can be unbound and remain readable. In other words, had Cook or Bascom decided to cut the string on their diaries and let the sheets scatter, the texts (and, in their cases, the linear narratives of their diaries) would have been completely disrupted. Yet in the case of Dickinson's fascicles, when Todd cut the string, the poems remained intact. If a poem began on the second side of a sheet and continued on the third, the fact that the sheet was a discrete object into which no other sheet had been inserted made all the difference in keeping that poem whole. This does not necessarily mean that Dickinson constructed the fascicles with an eye to their eventual undoing, but it does mean that she wrote each sheet as a discrete entity, only later connecting it to the others that, with it, would come to constitute a fascicle.

The type of nineteenth-century text that was most often handwritten, stacked, and sewn was the sermon (fig. 1.4). Ministers throughout New England in the early- and mid-nineteenth century wrote their sermons on pieces of folded stationery and, when they were finished, stacked these sheets and sewed them together. By stacking pages, ministers did not need to know ahead of time how long a given sermon was going to be, as they could add more sheets as needed. This way they neither ran out of paper nor wasted it, one or the other of which is almost always the result of inserting pages into each other before the writing had begun. Additionally, the sermon writer could go back and remove or revise parts of the sermon while keeping all other sections intact. If the pages had been inserted, it would have been impossible to remove a section of the sermon, forcing the writer to copy out the entire sermon all over again. In the end, the individual sermon could be taken to where it was being delivered and, upon returning home, the minister could preserve it as part of his group of sermons. Often the date and place appear at the top of the first page of each sermon, marking its difference from the others. Because the writer used sheets, he maintained the possibility for revision, and,

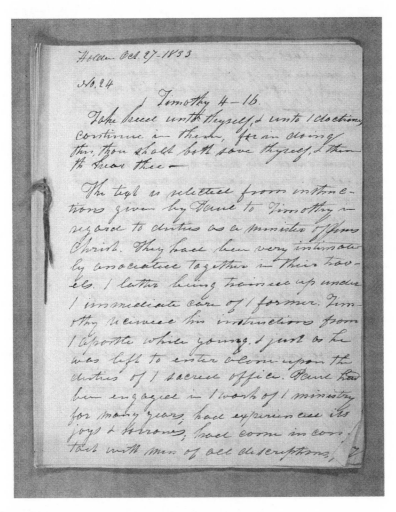

Figure 1.4
William P. Paine Sermon. Courtesy, American Antiquarian Society.

specifically, the kind of revision that can happen in sections. In other words, stacking sheets allowed one to do and undo, organize and reorganize.

How strange it is that the commonplace books, autograph albums, and scrapbooks that contain poetry bear few physical resemblances to the fascicles, while the handmade books look more like the fascicles, but contain (except in the case of Cook's diaries) no poetry. There are very few examples of where poetry and handmade, sewn texts meet, and, of the two examples that I have encountered, neither Caroline Gilman's homemade collection of her original poems nor Emily Goddard's few sewn pages of her copied poems looks exactly like the fascicles. Gilman's manuscript of six folded, inserted sheets, all sewn together at the margin, measures slightly larger than a fascicle. The cover is now missing and the poems inside are marked as such by their titles and dates of composition. She began each new poem on a new page and was content to leave blank space where necessary. These details point to the fact that Gilman clearly intended to make a book of poems.

Emily Goddard's collection is a more complicated case. Her poems appear on loose sheets of various sizes, on folded stationery with two holes at the margin, and on larger sheets inserted and sewn together. Within all of her volumes—which contain original compositions that were handwritten as well as those that were clipped from newspapers—only two sheets of stationery have been folded, written on, stacked, and sewn, like Dickinson's fascicles. But like Gilman, Goddard also presented what she was making as a book in ways that Dickinson did not: she gave each entry a title; she provided a date (of original composition or of copying, we cannot be sure); and, most significantly, even though she stacked these two folded sheets, she began a poem at the end of the first folded sheet and continued it on the second. Either Goddard sewed the two sheets before she began copying, or she knew that what she was making would be larger than one folded sheet. Unlike Goddard, Dickinson did not allow poems to spill over from one folded sheet to another. Dickinson contained any spill-over by inserting a single sheet or pinning in a slip of paper, indicating that she was not—at least initially, as she was copying—thinking about the relationship between sheets or between the individual sheets and the whole.[32]

In summary, while critics have categorized the fascicles as books of poems—in one critic's words, as "attempts at fine, handcrafted bookmaking"—this is not because they resemble nineteenth-century handmade books of poems.[33] Such books are, in fact, rare, as poetry was most often copied into already-bound commonplace books, autograph albums, and scrapbooks. Yet even when authors did sew their own pages together, they did so in a very different way from Dickinson. Because Dickinson stacked her sheets instead of inserting them into each other, she did not necessarily have the unit of the book in mind. Her copying and sewing practices permitted her to construct each sheet individually and allowed the sheets to be unstitched to each other and yet still remain intact.

Arguing that archives are absent of materials that look exactly like the fascicles—objects made by women who directly employed Dickinson's same copying and sewing strategies—is very different from saying that Dickinson's fascicle making process was thoroughly unique. There are, indeed, a few unique aspects of what she did: she did not follow the widely-accepted convention of copying poems into already bound blank books and, once she had decided to use individual sheets, she did not use them to create an object that mimicked the conventions of the book. While these are significant aspects of her practice that I will use to read her poems in the sections ahead, placing them within the larger cultures of verse copying and homemade book making in nineteenth-century America allows us to step back from the all too prevalent conviction of Dickinson's uniqueness. Doing so allows us to see the tension between convention and experimentation, between making a new form and living in the shadow of an old form, that is built into so many nineteenth-century media, including Dickinson's fascicles.

READING DICKINSON'S SHEETS

Both narrative and thematic readings of Dickinson's fascicles have been made possible precisely because critics have made the critical assumption that this chapter has disavowed—namely, that the fascicles are books. This can be seen in Sharon Cameron's assessment that Dickinson was "in effect constituting manu-scripts as if they were books," but it is also present in the criticism that treats the fascicles as book-length sequences.[34] "That Emily Dickinson had something like sequences in mind," write M. L. Rosenthal and Sally Gall, "is the most natural of conjectures."[35] While this might seem to be a logical assumption, the above in-vestigation into the places into which Dickinson's contemporaries copied their verses as well as the ways in which they were most likely to construct homemade books, complicates this classification. Attending to how she made the fascicles reveals that Dickinson's unit is neither the individual poem nor the entire fas-cicle, but rather the folded sheet.

Cameron's groundbreaking analysis of Dickinson's fascicles makes my own possible, for she was the one to establish that the fascicles need to be read and that they allow us to identify larger poetic problems that have to do with boundedness, intertextuality, and identity. While she does produce readings of poems on the same fascicle sheet, our analyses part ways when she insists that critics should extend their readings to the entire fascicle, arguing that rereading "two poems in proximity within the fascicle, poems no longer quite discrete, requires a rereading of all the poems in the fascicle and of the fascicle as a whole."[36] Cameron goes so far as to probe connections between a poem that ends one fascicle and the poem that begins the next, as well as the relations between proximate fascicles. While it may be tempting to read all of the writings in one fascicle as related to each other, as most critics of the fascicles have done, comparative archival research and close attention to compositional method suggest that connections *across* sheets are not Dickinson's primary concern. As Sally Bushell argues in *Text As Process: Creative*

Composition in Wordsworth, Tennyson, and Dickinson: "If we knew for certain that Emily Dickinson wrote each poem in a certain fascicle in relation to the other poems in that fascicle, there would be firm grounds for reading the groupings as a meaningful whole, and other ways of reading the material in different contexts would have to justify themselves in relation to this one. If we do *not* possess such knowledge, then the basis of interpretation becomes speculative."[37] She goes on to assert that readings that treat entire fascicles "adopt a model of interpretation that is out of keeping with the nature of the writing, of the textual material."[38] Instead, paying attention to that material and taking the fascicle sheet as Dickinson's primary unit of construction reveal how Dickinson grouped poems together and allowed them to speak back and forth to each other in non-uniform ways—in effect, how Dickinson used this material unit to register her own resistance to both the static lyric moment and an all-encompassing narrative. In short, when making the fascicles, Dickinson created a space in which she could play with the problems of narrative, sequence, fragmentation, and genre that Dickinson scholars have been struggling with for over a hundred years.

One of the great ironies is that when Franklin first presented the fascicles to a reading public, he stressed the importance of the fascicle sheet. Explaining Dickinson's shift from using half-sheets to using smaller slips of paper to accommodate a poem's spill-over, he wrote, "Her unit, which in one sense had always been the sheet, became more so."[39] In other words, from the very beginning, this idea of the sheet as the unit of construction was present in Dickinson criticism, yet like so much of Franklin's analysis, it has either been misread or disregarded, as critics have attempted to perform readings that span an entire fascicle.[40] While Franklin based his editorial theory on Dickinson's accommodation of spill-over and I do so from an analysis of her method of stacking folded sheets, we both advocate for a return to the fascicle sheet, curious about the sorts of reading options this unit makes possible.

This overlooking of Franklin's important point about the sheet stems from readers' desire to interpret differently based on some larger intertextual context. While this seems like a logical desire, it speaks to the problem with paper with which this book is concerned. Since print preceded handwriting in twentieth-century readings of Dickinson, it has not been possible to trace a genealogy that runs in only one direction between them. Thus, critics have wanted the whole fascicle because they are reading individually printed poems that have always been divorced from their paper. In other words, reading printed poems makes us desire something that resembles a book to which such printed poems might belong. We can see this most starkly in Cameron's analysis, precisely because, unlike other critics who study the fascicles, her analysis actually claims to be invested in the manuscripts themselves. But, as Virginia Jackson has put it most explicitly, "Cameron turns the material context of Dickinson's manuscript books into a limitless opportunity for lyric reading."[41] Instead, when we simultaneously look at manuscripts and resist lyric reading, we can see that handwriting did actually come first, as did the paper onto which that hand wrote words.

While a few sheets contain poems that are thematically similar or can be read as building on each other to create the sense of a story, for the most part, fascicle sheets do not work in either of these ways. Instead, the fascicle sheet offers Dickinson the opportunity to think about and play out what some of the possible relationships between poems might be—relationships that both individually published poems and book-length collections do not permit. Additionally, whereas critical treatments of entire fascicles are often undertaken with the goal of explaining what the individual poems are about, the sheet does not readily provide this interpretive possibility, but instead provides access to how Dickinson manipulates the devices of poetry. In order to fully explore how a sheet can work, I am going to look closely at what eventually became the first sheet of Fascicle 21 and the fourth sheet of Fascicle 17.

In "I—Years—had been—from Home—" (F 440), the "I" of the poem stands before the door of her old home, contemplating what to do now that she has arrived:

I—Years—had been—from
Home—
And now—before the Door—
I dared not open—lest a
face
I never saw before

Stare vacant into mine—
And ask my Business there—
My Business—just a Life
I left—
Was such—⁺ still dwelling there?

I fumbled at my nerve—
I scanned the Windows o'er—
The Silence—like an Ocean
rolled—
And ⁺ broke against my Ear—

I laughed a Wooden laugh—
That I—could fear a Door—
Who Danger—and the Dead—
had faced—
But never ⁺ shook—before—

I fitted to the Latch—my
Hand—

With trembling Care—
Lest back the Awful Door
should spring—
And leave me—in the Floor—

I moved my fingers off, as
cautiously as Glass—
And held my ears—and
like a Thief
⁺ Stole—gasping—from the House.

+ fled + Remaining there + smote—

_____

+ quaked—

In this moment of the past confronting the present, the present confronting the past, and the chaos that ensues from this potential matching up of selves, the poem reveals not simply its skepticism about the possibility of a coherent self, but a deep fear of it. The initial fear is of the moment of disassociation that will occur by, first, seeing a stranger's face and, second, by having to say that a "Life" was left there. The "I" in the poem wonders in clipped, polite language if her "Life" is "still dwelling there," as if she could have been in two places at once, as if she could have been separated from herself (or some part of herself) for this long without ever having to confront this problem. This is established by the fact that she recognizes the passage of time (as can be seen in the opening line), yet she also imagines some sort of temporal loop, one that would allow her former self to have continued to reside in this home while her other self went abroad.

Dickinson opens the poem by having the person figured in this poem refuse to open a door, and in doing so she foregrounds the poem's refusal to force its subject to be made whole by the form in which it resides. Instead of resolving the temporal and emotional conundrum presented at the opening of the poem, the poem embraces a fear of reunion that ends up driving it. The poem is so preoccupied with material boundaries (door, windows, latch, floor, glass) that they actually become a part of this "I," as she acquires a "Wooden laugh." Yet she ultimately refuses to cross into them fully. By boycotting the revelation and connection that might come from confronting this other "Life," she denies the coherence that would come from the closed-circuit reflection she initially sought. The poem ends on an image of wordlessness that has arisen from the possibility of confrontation and potential union with this former self.

What I have just produced is a reading of this poem in isolation from its material context—and, incidentally, from the very different version of it that Dickinson copied ten years later on notepaper that she retained for herself.⁴² We can see how, when read as an individual lyric, we might characterize it, as Alfred Habegger has, as a poem about "the fearsome house of memory."[43] Gary Lee Stonum has looked even more closely, calling it a poem that "featur[es] that volatile and elusive pronoun, the 'I' of the romantic lyric," and "which recounts the I's adventures in an external world."[44] Both of these descriptions use the language of spatial relations, containment, and mystery, as they assume the poem to be an isolated artifact that, in standing on its own, can only relay so much. But when we treat the poem as the first of seventeen poems in Fascicle 21, a very different reading is possible. Eleanor Heginbotham, for instance, in characterizing this entire fascicle as the "serious declaration of the poet," reads this opening poem as the expression of the poet's "terror" and as a poem that is saturated in a "mood of fear" that will change "as the book progresses."[45] In other words, when read in the context of the entire fascicle, this poem represents some beginning (and limited) state from which the "I" (or, according to Heginbotham, the poet) will emerge.

But what happens when we recognize the unit of the sheet as the context with which Dickinson was most directly engaged? What happens when we treat the paper itself as a meaningful context for reading and interpretation? While Dickinson copied "I—Years—had been—from Home—" on the first two sides of this sheet, the poem that begins "You'll find—it when you try to die—" (F 441) follows it on the third and fourth sides:

> You'll find—it when you
> try to die—
> The Easier to let go—
> For recollecting such as went—
> You could not spare—you know.
>
> And though their places
> somewhat filled—
> As did their Marble names
> With Moss—they never
> grew so full—   ⁺ times
> You chose the newer ⁺ names—
>
> And when this World—sets
> further back—
> As Dying—say it does—
> The former love—distincter
> grows—
> And supersedes the fresh—
>
> And Thought of them—so
> fair invites—
> It looks too tawdry Grace

To stay behind—with just
the Toys
We bought—to ease their
place—

This poem, on the one hand, is very much unlike the one before it on the sheet, as it offers instructions to a "you" who will one day find him or herself trying to die.[46] The poem's major warning is that it is easier to go through with death if one doesn't "recollect" all whom have been loved. Yet despite the difference in address and subject matter, this poem is very much like "I—Years—had been—from Home—" in that it ends up performing the opposite of what it set itself up to do. This poem describes exactly why it is so hard *not* to recollect, explaining that the universe and human nature are such that recollecting actually becomes the more appealing option. In the face of this, the "I" experiences a split between what she thinks the "you" should do and what she finds it possible to do herself. In other words, the problem at the core of this poem is very much like the problem enacted in "I—Years—had been—from Home—" as it attempts to recollect and then sabotages this attempt. This poem is not necessarily preoccupied with the particular trauma of the previous poem, but is, instead, more philosophical about the problem of confronting the past.

Recognizing the unit of the sheet allows us to see that "I—Years—had been—from Home—" poses questions about unity and fracture that can be overlooked when it is read either as an isolated lyric or as the first poem in a book. For instance, at the end of "I—Years—had been—from Home—" any attempt to inquire about the "Life" in question is aborted and the poem ends up fracturing and dissolving the self that it initially tried to constitute. Because the poem that comes after it on the fascicle sheet undertakes a different kind of investigation into the problem of the split self, we can see that, while the poems are not articulated from the same position, they learn from and define themselves in relation to each other—an act that, interestingly enough, results in an awareness of the fractures within oneself. We might even read the half page of blank space that Dickinson left at the end of "You'll find—it when you try to die—" as a reflection on the fascicle sheet's simultaneous desire and inability to fill up its own spaces with the texts that will make it whole.

Out of the 218 sheets that Dickinson sewed into fascicles, twenty-seven of them contain two poems. While this only amounts to just over twelve percent of her total sheets, Dickinson included at least one of these sheets of paired poems in almost every fascicle between Fascicle 11 and Fascicle 27.[47] Yet the nature of the relations between the different paired poems is not stable or constant. In order to show that not all sheets that contain two poems work in the same way, I want to return to the summer of 1862 when Dickinson copied two poems of similar length and form onto the folded sheet that would later become the fourth sheet in Fascicle 17. The poem that begins "It was not Death, for I stood up" (F 355) appears on the first two sides and is followed by a line drawn across the bottom of the second side. The poem that begins "If you were coming in the Fall" (F 356) begins on the third side and continues onto the fourth, after which Dickinson drew a line and left the last third of the page blank.

"It was not Death, for I stood up" is a poem that delays revealing its subject, jumps sensory and temporal registers without warning, and attempts to identify things by addressing what they are not:

> It was not Death, for
> I stood up,
> And all the Dead, lie down—
> It was not Night, for
> All the Bells
> Put out their Tongues, for Noon.
>
> It was not Frost, for on
> my + Flesh   + Knees
> I felt Siroccos—crawl—
> Nor Fire—for just my +
> marble feet   + two
> Could keep a Chancel, cool—
>
> And yet, it tasted, like
> them all,
> The Figures I have seen
> Set orderly, for Burial,
> Reminded me, of mine—
>
> As if my life were shaven,
> And fitted to a frame,
> And could not breathe
> without a key,
> And 'twas like Midnight,
> some—
>
> When everything that ticked—
> has stopped—
> And space stares—all around—
> Or Grisly frosts—first Au-
> tumn morns,
> Repeal the Beating Ground—
>
> But, most, like Chaos—
> Stopless—cool—

Without a Chance, or spar—
Or even a Report of Land—
To justify—Despair.

The opening lines reveal that the "I" wants to understand what state she was in, but the lines that follow shift the focus away from an interest in this state of being to that of the surrounding environment. As if the situation can only be understood if rendered through multiple sensory channels, the opening of the second stanza enacts yet another shift, this time to what can be felt by the body. When the "Figures" that are trying to be identified are finally grasped, this is done through the strangest sense of all—taste—and here the poem descends into describing the moment of "Burial." The most striking thing about this scene is the way in which at one moment space becomes "fitted" and time stops and at the next moment the poem is off and running again in a "Stopless" way, without being anchored physically. In this space of chaotic silence, the poem names the "Despair" that is felt; yet, as much as it tries, it cannot "justify" that despair.

"If you were coming in the Fall" is different in that it is hopeful that it will find the thing that it does not have (in this case, a "you") and, even as it registers a greater and greater time span between the present and some future moment of union with that "you," it does not fall into anything like despair:

If you were coming in the Fall,
I'd brush the Summer by
With half a smile, and
half a spurn,
As Housewives do, a Fly.

If I could see you in a
year,
I'd wind the month in balls—
And put them each in
separate Drawers,
For fear the numbers fuse—

If only Centuries, delayed,
I'd count them on my Hand,
Subtracting, till my fingers
dropped
Into Van Dieman's Land.

If certain, when this life was out—
That your's and mine, should be—
I'd toss it yonder, like a

Rind,   ⁺ taste
And ⁺ take Eternity—

But, now, uncertain of the
length
Of this, that is between,
It goads me, like the
Goblin Bee—
That will not state—
it's sting.

The poem is filled with the sentimental and domestic images usually associated with a woman waiting. Even when one might expect anger, desperation, or pathos to rear its head in response to the constant delay of union, the situation is treated with a certain degree of levity—that is, until the "now" of the final stanza, when the length of time cannot only not be measured but cannot be imagined, and therefore the poem's rhetorical strategy can no longer be sustained. At that moment there is the presence of something dangerous, something ominous that might cause pain, although that too is figured somewhat lightly as a "Goblin Bee."

On the surface, then, these are two really different poems: the first attempts to name something through what it is not and the other attempts to bring something closer by imagining all the ways in which it might be far away. One attempts to see the difficult thing for what it is, while the other masks emotional distress with commonplace utterances and images. Such differences are underscored by the way critics have described these poems. For instance, Cameron describes the situation of "It was not Death, for I stood up" as one in which, "unable to order the experience temporally, and lacking relevant outer criteria for it, [the speaker] is imprisoned in the chaos of her feelings as muteness or inexpressiveness is an imprisonment."[48] Vivian Pollak refers to the scene of this poem as one in which "her alienation from the authority of events also signals her negation of a categorical distinction between the living and the dead."[49] Paula Bennett describes this poem as one that depicts a "death-in-life" experience in which "the speaker predicates what cannot be, of a state that nevertheless is, making her body the vehicle through which these paradoxical tensions are expressed."[50] Cameron, Pollak, and Bennett all situate darkness, disorientation, confusion, and negation at the center of their analyses of this poem, terms that we would have a difficult time applying to the romantic mood, earnest longing, and, as Cynthia Griffin Wolff has described it, the denied consummation, of "If you were coming in the Fall."[51] That being said, once these poems were situated as part of Fascicle 17, Cameron redescribed "It was not Death, for I stood up" as one poem amongst many, all of which "similarly represent experiences in excess of the speaker's avowed ability to designate *what is experienced*."[52]

If looking at them as utterly separate poems highlights just how different they are, and looking at them in the context of the entire fascicle produces a very general characterization that can be applied quite broadly, looking at the sheet does something entirely different: it allows us to see how playful Dickinson is with form. Given the major differences in subject and tone, it is quite remarkable to notice that these poems mimic each other as much as they do. They both repeat variations of their opening lines, as the first poem seeks an explanation ("It was not Death, for I stood up . . . It was not Night, for all the Bells . . . It was not Frost, for on my Flesh") and the second poem seeks a result ("If you were coming in the Fall . . . If I could see you in a year . . . If only Centuries, delayed"). Cristanne Miller has commented on the "biblical sparseness" and "overlapping balanced effect" of the repetitions in "It was not Death, for I stood up," arguing that "the short clauses and rapid progression from one unit to the next" in poems like this one "give a feeling of inevitability to the narrative's progression."[53] We might extend this analysis of the poem's syntax and pacing to "If you were coming in the Fall." Like this correspondence, the first lines of both of their final stanzas echo each other rhythmically and syntactically: "But, most, like Chaos—Stopless—cool—" and "But, now, uncertain of the length." While the first poem comes to name the "Despair" that is felt and the second poem ends by admitting all that it does not know, they both achieve these states through repetitions of and variations on a dominant phrase, through a final "But" turn, and through measured, conversational syntax.

The first sheet of Fascicle 21 and the fourth sheet of Fascicle 17 are only two examples of Dickinson's many sheets, but I have used them here to highlight the various kinds of relations that Dickinson sets in motion on individual sheets. Instead of superimposing on these poems a role that they need to play in an entire fascicle's narrative or sequence, I have allowed the boundary of the sheet's edge to guide my interpretive practice. Respecting the breaks that exist between sheets gives them back the identity they once had as Dickinson copied poems onto them and allows us to focus on the relationship between poems that the sheet, as a unit of composition, sets in motion. What we find here is a startling array of Dickinson's experiments with poetic form and relation.

THE PROBLEM WITH PRINT

One of the most fascinating things about Dickinson both to readers who have just encountered her work and to those long familiar with it is that she wrote over eighteen hundred poems but published less than a dozen in her lifetime. Why, they ask, would she do such a thing? Friends, editors, critics, and teachers have all attempted to answer this question. Franklin himself, the person most familiar with Dickinson's manuscripts, even characterizes the reasons why Dickinson may have done this as "reasons unexplained."[54] In this final section I will show how attention to Dickinson's sheets presents us with a possible explanation, one that takes its cues from the paper onto which Dickinson copied so many of her poems.

When Todd and Higginson now famously edited the first collection of Dickinson's poems in 1890, they were faced with the challenge of addressing, in the very first paragraph of the introduction, just what Dickinson must have thought about printing her poems.[55] "It was with great difficulty that she was persuaded to print, during her lifetime, three or four poems," Higginson wrote.[56] The sentence that follows was meant to render even more dramatic such a decision by an unknown woman poet: "Yet she wrote verses in great abundance; and though curiously indifferent to all conventional rules, had yet a rigorous literary standard of her own, and often altered a word many times to suit an ear which had its own tenacious fastidiousness."[57] The contradictions are perplexing: she wrote a tremendous amount, yet she did not print; she was indifferent to conventional rules, yet had a rigorous literary standard; she engaged in an almost obsessive revision process, yet never produced a draft for anyone to read. Higginson's characterization of Dickinson here reveals his desire to simultaneously characterize her as strange and to render her—in all her quirky, contradictory ways—a model for how women's poetry should be written and disseminated (or not).[58] She is the exception who creates a standard, the unique poet who shows how it might be done. Higginson's willingness to be up front about Dickinson's resistance to print and yet his lack of explanation for why this was so gets buried in the tangled portrait he paints of her. One cannot help but read this move as some sort of defensive self-consciousness as he grants her the very existence in print that he claims she did not want. But what, exactly, was the problem with print for Dickinson?

We now know that Dickinson published not "three or four" but at least ten poems in her lifetime. We also know that Higginson, while implying that he had been at the helm of the persuasion effort, did not encourage her to publish and that that encouragement came from a host of other friends and writers, among them Helen Hunt Jackson. Largely in response to Higginson's factual errors, his misrepresentation of himself, and his portrait of Dickinson as so idiosyncratic that it launched many of the myths that remain about her today, critics in the twentieth century rigorously theorized the fact of Dickinson's not printing, giving her back the agency that his portrait seems to have abolished. For the most part everybody acknowledges that Dickinson's poems were surely good enough (and that she was savvy enough) to publish, but that she actively resisted doing so for a number of reasons: according to Martha Nell Smith, the editorial alterations that were made to "The Snake" when it was published in the *Springfield Daily Republican* in 1866 were enough to disenchant Dickinson to future publishing endeavors; according to Cameron, Dickinson did not want to choose between publishing her poems as sequences or as lyrics and because she could not do both, she did neither; according to Marta Werner, Dickinson did not want to subject herself to the demands of the market economy and was "unwilling to make herself over in the image of the printer"; and according to Jerome McGann, Dickinson felt how "restrictive and conventional" the medium of print had become and therefore rejected "the traditional (early capitalist) institution" for achieving the fame that he believes she wanted.[59] In opposition to Higginson's raising of this problem but not speaking directly to it, twentieth-century criticism has positioned Dickinson as a writer who made a conscious choice not to print and whose reasons had been articulated clearly enough to herself that we may now be able to decipher them for ourselves.

While the arguments above speak to the ways in which Dickinson rejected both the idea and the reality of print, I want to add to this conversation by showing that when we look at Dickinson's sheets what we see is something other than flat-out rejection of print. McGann himself has argued that the early fascicles "are being copied to imitate, at their basic scriptural level, the formalities of print," and his analysis of her lines and stanzas is convincing of this point.[60] McGann pushes this analysis one step further when he writes, "Though handwritten, these are poems that have been imagined under a horizon of publication."[61] This is a useful formulation in that it allows us to see that by adopting, borrowing, and appropriating certain conventions of print, Dickinson was necessarily acknowl-edging the world of print. But as we saw earlier in section 2, by copying poems onto folded sheets of stationery, Dickinson was resisting the book as the con-tainer for those poems. What we have, then, is a situation in which Dickinson is activating the tensions that exist within print culture in order to figure out ex-actly what opportunities and limitations that culture could present to her. As we saw in sections 2 and 3, the sheet allowed Dickinson to investigate, among other things, the fluid nature of poetic lines; the relationship between the cultural materials for writing and the texts themselves; different modes of reading made possible by manuscript pages; and the formal, syntactical, and structural rela-tionships that poems copied together have to each other. In other words, by rejecting the narrative of Dickinson as the singular nineteenth-century woman poet who eschewed publishing in favor of either intense privacy (what Higginson seems to want us to see) or a poetics that rejected the conventions and expecta-tions of print (what twentieth-century criticism wants us to see), I hope to show that no less radical is the narrative of a woman poet who, enabled by the public/private elements that manuscript *and* print culture set in motion for her, used the sheet to understand exactly what print would enable and obscure.

What Dickinson's sheets make possible are a poetics that is wholly absent from any version of poems in print that Dickinson, Higginson, or the readers of the 1890 *Poems* would have known. Because, as far as we know, Dickinson owned single-author volumes of male American poets—Emerson, Longfellow, Holmes, and Bryant, for instance—and those of select British women poets—such as the Brontë sisters' *Poems by Currer, Ellis, and Acton Bell* and several collections by Eliz-abeth Barrett Browning—but she did not own any single-author volumes of poems by an American woman poet other than Helen Hunt Jackson, she probably would have been able to conceive of her poems in two print contexts: anthologies and periodicals.[62] Both of these depend on the unit of the individual poem, extracted from its scene of composition and from the other texts with which the writer may have originally surrounded it.[63] We know that the Dickinson household owned, for example, *Gems from American Female Poets*, an anthology published in 1842 and edited by Rufus Griswold, the nineteenth century's famous anthologizer of women's verse.[64] Meant to be stowed in a pocket, this 12-centimeter volume is no larger than a grown woman's hand and contains 192 pages of poems by 40 women, almost none of whom are known today. Brief introductions, written by the editor, give the most basic facts of each woman's life and often include references to her father, husband, and the various trials of her existence. Periodical publication, although not usually accompanied by such introductions, still extracted "gems" from a woman poet's larger body of work and surrounded this singular piece on a page with many other things—sometimes parts of multiple articles or stories, as well as a number of advertisements. In other words, Dickinson encountered the poems of women in places that would render the formal play and generic challenges activated by and within the material context of the fascicle sheet invisible.

Whether Dickinson knew she would not print the poems that she copied onto fascicle sheets and therefore felt free to play all she wanted with the correspondences that I highlighted in the previous section or if the very need to engage such resonances kept her from pursuing the option of print, we may never know. What we do know is that by copying poems on folded sheets of formal stationery (and therefore reproducing certain conventions of print culture), Dickinson was negotiating the limits of print, and one of those limits was its inability to allow the formally playful relationships between poems to exist. Although Dickinson may never have imagined that her poems would eventually be grouped separately under the topical headings assigned by her nineteenth-century editors—"Life," "Love," "Nature," and "Time and Eternity"—she would have known that her poems would probably never appear next to each other, the way they do on a fascicle sheet, if and when they were put into print. And indeed, even in a non-anthology and non-periodical context, even in the single-author book of poems that went into more printings that anyone could have imagined, Dickinson's poems were printed to stand, both each on their own and dozens together under the issues that her editors decided the poems address. What gets lost is the fact that integral to Dickinson's composition of these poems was a material practice that allowed her to think through what poems can do—at the level of pause, of shift, of repetition—when they do not have to stand either all on their own or for something much larger than what they are.

The narrative of Dickinson's radical stance against print not only misrepresents her poetics as defensively private but also, ironically, solidifies the work that Higginson began when he defined the tension between private writing and public dissemination that, by implication, all women poets should embrace if they ever want their poems printed in the kind of simple, classy gift book in which Dickinson's poems could now, at the moment of his writing, be found. What

looks like Higginson's tacit approval of her position on this issue does not necessarily reveal that he believed women's poetry should not be in the marketplace,
for he was both an advocate of young writers and a champion for women's education, but it does remind us that Higginson never really studied the poems in their
fascicle contexts, as Dickinson had sent him poems in letters and Todd had
unbound the fascicles on her own, soon after receiving them and starting work
on the edition of poems to be printed. I would venture to say that Higginson's
awkward silence on this issue of print is a result of his never having understood
the unit of the sheet and the aspects of Dickinson's poetics that she developed
there. For her, the sheet was the very place where Dickinson could feel out the
potentials and limitations of print.

By showing how Dickinson drew on the conventions of a manuscript, textual,
and print culture in order to make her fascicles, this chapter has worked against
three dominant assumptions: that the fascicles represent a spontaneous poetic
project; that when Dickinson made the fascicles she was doing something wholly
unique; and that her poems should be resituated, recontextualized, and therefore
re-read within the context of entire fascicles in order to be understood best.
Indeed, my analysis urges a reexamination of the poems themselves, but that
reexamination must happen as a result of shifting the way we think about the
paper that Dickinson used to make the fascicles. For instance, attending to the
construction of the fascicles, rather than taking them as settled objects, puts into
focus Dickinson's struggle with narration and groupings, with flexibility and
breakage. When we look closely at how she made the fascicles, we can begin to
ask new questions about the relationship between part and whole in her writing,
about the formal territory between lyric and narrative, and about problems of
mobility and duration in the poems themselves.

Yet in order to call attention to the copying practices that Dickinson employed
when making the fascicles and to the sheets with which she was primarily concerned, I have taken them apart in a way that is not wholly unlike Todd's initial
cutting of the string. For Dickinson did eventually make holes along the left hand
margins and sew several sheets together to form distinct groupings. I will attend
to the details of this sewing practice in chapter 3, and there I will investigate the
various modes of relation *between* sheets that such a practice sets in motion. Yet
what we have seen here is that taking the fascicles apart and returning them to
their most basic units reveals that Dickinson did not conceive of the fascicles as
books. Once we can see that the fascicles do not ask to be read like books, then
reading them that way becomes visible as a choice—one that gave editors and
scholars a convenient structure for understanding, interpreting, and producing
readings of Dickinson's texts, but one that Dickinson's material and compositional practices beg us to rethink.

CHAPTER 2

✦

Epistolary Practices
and the Problem of Genre

In the summer of 1858, Dickinson copied the lines that begin "As if I asked a common alms—" (F 14) onto the final side of a sheet that she would eventually sew as part of Fascicle 1 (fig. 2.1):

> As if I asked a common alms—
> And in my wondering hand,
> A stranger pressed a kingdom—
> And I—bewildered stand—
> As if I asked the Orient
> Had it for me a morn?
> And it sh'd lift it's purple dikes
> And flood me with the Dawn!

In light of my earlier analysis of the context that Dickinson's sheets can provide for a reading of her poems, it is interesting to note that these lines have been squeezed between the last stanza of "There is a morn by men unseen—" (F 13) and the whole of "She slept beneath a tree—" (F 15). Read in this context, the moment of wonder expressed in these lines exists as only one of many in which something has been glimpsed or cherished, only to be relinquished in the end. The sheet begins with "I had a guinea golden—" (F 12), a poem that sings of the many things that have been lost—"a guinea golden," "a crimson Robin," and "a star in heaven"—all in an effort to relay a "moral" about "repentance" and "consolation." In the next poem, "There is a morn by men unseen—," other absences are similarly summoned. In this instance, though, the poem draws a picture of a "mystic green" on which the dead live, a place of "dance and game," "a wondrous

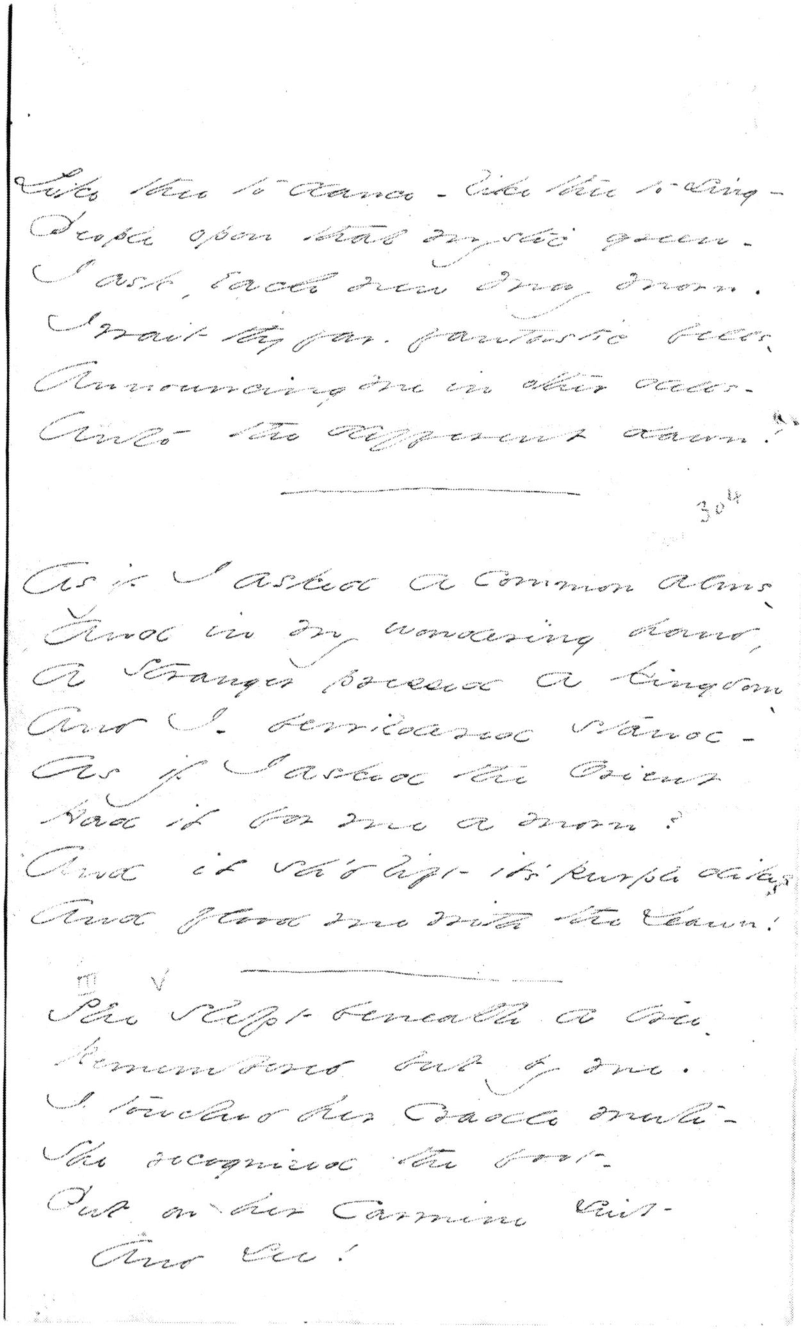

Figure 2.1
"As if I asked a common alms—" (F 14). Copied and sewn as part of Fascicle 1 in 1858. Courtesy, Archives & Special Collections, Amherst College.

scene" of which one longs to be a part. Coming amidst these two poems, "As if I asked a common alms—" need not be read as the tentative imaginings of one who has never before been flooded by the dawn, arguably the most logical reading when encountered as an isolated lyric. Instead, it can be read as one of many reclamations of lost experiences and as an articulation of that reclamation, as a poem that deftly navigates the move between its own sense of innocence and entitlement. The short poem that follows it on this sheet, "She slept beneath a tree—," underscores these recuperative acts, as here, through touch, the poem animates a sleeping (or dead, or not yet born) creature.

But when we read this poem in the context of the fascicle sheet, what gets forgotten, or obscured, is the fact that four years after copying it onto this sheet, Dickinson wrote these lines in a letter that she sent to Thomas Wentworth Higginson. While this might seem very strange to us today, for we are most familiar with Dickinson's poems as either individual lyrics or as pieces of her larger fascicles, an analysis of her compositional methods shows that Dickinson regularly combined her letter writing and poetry copying practices. Dickinson sent many of her correspondents poems that she had either already copied onto sheets or would soon copy there: at least 115 of these were sent to Sue; at least 25 to her cousins Fanny and Louise Norcross; at least 24 to Higginson; and at least 21 to Samuel Bowles. When doing this, she employed a variety of methods: sometimes she copied a poem onto a leaf that she sent in the same envelope as her letter; sometimes she sent a poem on its own, with no letter; sometimes she inserted a poem into the prose of a letter, marking where one ends and the other begins; sometimes she sent what we now call "letter-poems," letters written in the form of poems; and sometimes she embedded a poem so deeply into the prose of her letter that it would not have been recognizable as poetry.

The purpose of this chapter is to explain how and why she did these things; what it means for Dickinson to revisit a poem she had copied onto a sheet or, inversely, to revisit a poem she had sent to a correspondent in order to later copy it onto a sheet; and to deduce what creating a new material context indicates about the relationship between poetry and letters. By looking at the intersection of Dickinson's epistolary practices and poetry-copying practices, this chapter argues that Dickinson was neither an upholder of generic categories nor a great innovator who challenged the distinction between letter and poem—two positions that recent Dickinson criticism has been pulled between.[1] Instead, I will argue that the problem with genre was not Dickinson's problem. Dickinson combined practices, defied conventions, and tapped into the permeability of both modes of writing, but she seems not to have been concerned with the generic issues that later readers have asked her poems and letters to address. In this way, the issue of book history raised by my analysis of fascicle sheets in chapter 1 leads directly into the questions that I pose about genre here, for the problem is not whether Dickinson was writing poems or letters, since our stake in such a distinction was invented by the later protocols of literary criticism. Instead, by focusing on the scene of composition—on the paper itself and Dickinson's process that is made visible by attention to that paper—this chapter argues that the epistolary context provides Dickinson with the perfect medium to think through an instability that is built into both literary modes.

Such a claim challenges the strict distinction between poems and letters that was an integral part of Dickinson's reception and that gained momentum in the subsequent literary criticism, even criticism that argued for Dickinson's intentional blending of the two. Dickinson was first presented to the reading public as a poet, and only later, with the 1894 publication of *The Letters of Emily Dickinson*, as a letter writer. This edition of her letters was primarily intended to supplement the public's knowledge of this mysterious poet. Early announcements for the book, like the one which appeared in the *Boston Herald* on November 27, 1894, present it as something that lovers of her poetry will appreciate simply because it reveals more of her actual life:

> Those who have been interested in Emily Dickinson's poems, and the number is very large, have been eager to see her letters, which contain all the prose she is known to have written. In the poems there was a somber and even weird outlook upon this world and the next. They were written in a mood which was unusual, if not really strange, but they expressed the reality of her life, and it is in their unhackneyed character and strange fervor that they have attracted general attention. These letters have been collected with great difficulty, and it would seem as if some of them were too trifling for publication, but, inasmuch as they contain the only record of her life, they will be received with special interest by the large number of persons who are attracted to her poems.[2]

An announcement in the *Worcester Spy* on December 2, 1894 similarly begins:

> *Emily Dickinson's Letters*, edited by Mabel Loomis Todd, as is the case with the letters of many other unique personalities, are very slightly interesting as letters, and very deeply interesting as reflecting Emily Dickinson.[3]

Early love of Dickinson's poems attracted readers to her letters, but only because it helped them gain access to the woman who had written those poems.

It is only in the last twenty-five years that critics have begun to treat her letters as a mode of writing that offers something other than an explanation for her poems, and several new studies of her letters have established them as a body of text worthy of serious analysis.[4] While recognizing that Dickinson's letters are in and of themselves literary brings the categories of poetry and letters into conversation, critics continue to cite the fact that several of Dickinson's own poems theorize an intense difference between the two. In some cases, her poems have been treated as declarations of what poetry offers that prose cannot. "They shut me up in Prose—" (F 445), for instance, is a poem that likens prose to a "Closet" that her captors place her in to keep her "still." "I dwell in Possibility—" (F 466) pictures "Possibility" and "Prose" as two different kinds of houses, the first of which has more windows, better doors, a sky for a roof, and all the best visitors. While in these cases Dickinson seems to equate prose with structures of containment, champions of her letters are quick to note that she wrote over a thousand letters and often celebrated epistolary prose in such poems as "Going to Him! Happy letter!" (F 277), "This is my letter to the World" (F 519), and "A Letter is a joy of Earth—" (F 1672). Indeed, many of her poems actually address the very kinds of problems inherent in poetic form. For example, "Split the Lark—and you'll find the Music—" (F 905) presents the poem as the site of death, since music can be extracted only once the bird has been killed.[5] Even in "This was a Poet—" (F 446), a poem that celebrates the poet as one who "Distills amazing sense / From Ordinary Meanings," this poet is presented as the one who makes "ceaseless Poverty" felt.

Such analyses make it seem as if Dickinson's letters and poems were discrete and stable categories for her to write in and that they remain so for us to read in. Indeed, even Marietta Messmer's rich contextualization of Dickinson within the "dynamic epistolary culture" of her time turns to nineteenth-century letter-writing manuals to show the "hierarchically inflected differentiation between epistolary and poetic discourse" that was insisted upon.[6] Instead of stabilizing these two literary modes as genres that we can then watch Dickinson dismantle— instead of treating Dickinson's relationship to them as one that intervenes in what Messmer calls "generic hierarchies"—this chapter proceeds from the position that what was being marked in the nineteenth century was convention and not genre.[7] In fact, I will argue that the emphasis placed on these conventions does not reflect a culture that had great stake in the differentiation between letters and poems as genres, but instead one that registered the instability that existed at the heart of both modes of writing.

This chapter tells the story of one poem, "As if I asked a common alms—," as a way of telling a larger story about nineteenth-century American women's epistolary practices, about the ways in which Dickinson addresses the poetic and epistolary conventions available to her, and about the critical tools that we have (and don't have) for understanding these aspects of Dickinson's practices. Because Higginson is more closely allied with the poems that Dickinson sent him as enclosures in her letters, we tend to overlook the details of this specific moment in their correspondence, a moment that, I will argue, allows us to see Dickinson testing the limits of what letters and poems can do for her.[8] Unlike her relationship with Sue, her Norcross cousins, and Bowles, all of whom were active figures in her life, Dickinson met Higginson only twice in the twenty-four years that they corresponded. It was precisely in this state of physical distance that she was able to play with the tension between public and private communication that is activated in both poetry and epistolary correspondence. By investigating the ways in which this text was made and shaped, spliced and remade, overhauled

and reformulated, I argue that Dickinson's act of literal, material recontextualiza-
tion magnifies the possibilities inherent in both letters and poems.

In the first section I will provide the background necessary to understand this
specific moment in the Dickinson/Higginson correspondence, showing the different ways Dickinson had been sending Higginson her poems and distinguish-
ing the embedded poem as a topic for analysis.[9] In the second section I turn to
some of Dickinson's earlier letters, our current editorial and critical methods for
understanding these letters, and the nineteenth-century cultural materials that
point us out of our current critical bind—a bind in which genre gets reified in
spite of our attempts to do the opposite. Throughout, I will refer to different
pieces of writing as "letters" or "poems," and when it becomes unclear what a text
is, I will mark those moments by my inability to use either of these terms. Unlike
many of the critical practices that I describe in this section, I will not aim to find
the "correct" label for these texts, since establishing their generic identity is precisely beside the point. In the final section I explore how the particular technique
that Dickinson used for embedding "As if I asked a common alms—" in her third
letter to Higginson allowed her to use the unstable yet productive platform of the
letter to think through and redefine what happens when she writes "I."

THE DICKINSON/HIGGINSON CORRESPONDENCE

By the time Dickinson sent Higginson the letter into which she copied "As if I
asked a common alms—," they had already exchanged two letters each. Dickinson had read Higginson's article, "Letter to a Young Contributor," in the April
1862 issue of the *Atlantic Monthly* and had promptly written to ask: "Are you too
deeply occupied to say if my Verse is alive?" (L 260). In this opening letter, Dickinson does very little to introduce herself but instead asks, in several ways, if he
would read her poems and offer her some guidance. Since Higginson's article had
done exactly this (offered practical advice to unpublished writers), Dickinson
contacted him, it would seem, in the hopes of receiving a personal response to her
particular poems.[10] With this letter she enclosed five additional pieces of paper:
four poems that were individually copied out on separate sheets of stationery and
a small card bearing her signature. While in the coming years she would continue
to enclose poems in her letters to Higginson, she would not do so with her signature again. Whether she did this with her signature in order to distance herself
from the content of the letter, to imply that her letter can be regarded as an actual
visit from her, or purely as a formality, we will never know.[11]

The first four poems that Dickinson sent to Higginson were "Safe in their Alabaster Chambers—" (F 124), "The nearest Dream recedes—unrealized—" (F
304), "We play at Paste—" (F 282), and "I'll tell you how the Sun rose—" (F 204).[12]
For most of the twentieth century, scholars thought that Dickinson sent poems to
her correspondents only after copying them onto fascicle sheets, since Thomas

Johnson had deduced as much in his 1955 variorum. It was not until Franklin's 1998 variorum that we learned that Dickinson more often sent poems to people *before* copying them onto formal stationery.[13] This shift in our approach to Dickinson's process is important to understanding what she was doing when she sent these poems to Higginson, for, while Dickinson had been sharing her poems with several other correspondents over the previous several years, these enclosures reveal that Dickinson was treating Higginson as a different sort of recipient. In the case of the enclosures of this first letter, three of the four poems had already been copied onto sheets, and one of these had already gone through several drafts in Dickinson's correspondence with Sue.[14]

Dickinson followed a similar protocol in her second letter, although this letter is longer and more substantial, now offering some information about herself that Higginson seems to have requested (L 261). She writes from her "pillow" (as she is alluding either to the fact that she had been literally ill or to her need to recover from his response), thanks him for the criticism of her poems, and states several times that she is in continued need of his guidance. She says that she has been writing "verse" for only one or two years (something we now know is untrue) and that it was spurred on by a "terror." She writes of her books, her old tutor, and her dog. She (now famously) says that she has heard that Whitman is "disgraceful," and that while two editors have asked for her "Mind" (a term she used in her first letter as well), she has been unable to assess her work herself. While Dickinson seems to be providing Higginson with what he must have asked for in his letter (her final sentence reads "Is this—Sir—what you asked me to tell you?"), she does not stray very far from her initial goal, which is to convey her need for his guidance. And just as she had done in her first letter, Dickinson encloses individual poems in the envelope with this letter. This time there are three of them, "There came a Day at Summer's full" (F 325), "Of all the Sounds despatched abroad" (F 334), and "South Winds jostle them—" (F 98), all of which had already been copied into the fascicles and one of which had already been sent to two other correspondents.[15]

In his two-volume biography of Dickinson, Richard B. Sewall presents specific reasons why Dickinson would have included each of these seven poems in her early letters to Higginson. Sewall states that Dickinson was sending "samples of her work, presumably to show its variety and range and something, as in the short poems, of its purpose and method," but he also matches the topics of these poems to those of Higginson's recent essays with which Dickinson would have been familiar.[16] For instance, Sewall argues that Dickinson sent Higginson "We play at Paste—" because it "agreed, on one level, with his emphasis [in "Letter"] on the necessity of constant revision, or practice, in literary composition and, on a higher level, echoed the idea in his final paragraph that the whole human exercise was merely preparation for the divine."[17] Alternately, Cindy MacKenzie has recently suggested that in the act of enclosing certain poems within her letters, Dickinson was implying the letter's "aesthetic contingency by obliquely offering a well-aimed directive that seeks to provide the recipient with a key to under-standing her modus operandi."[18] While it is possible that Dickinson sent Higgin-son these poems because she felt that they matched well with his interests or because she wanted to communicate a specific message, it seems quite likely that she simply wanted to send previously-drafted and fine-tuned poems to the man whom she would soon ask, "Will you be my Preceptor?" (L 265). At some level she must have hoped that Higginson would be a new type of reader for her—one who read, wrote, and gave advice professionally—and it should not be surprising that Dickinson employed a different method for engaging and soliciting his response than she did with her other correspondents.

By the time Dickinson sent that first letter to Higginson, she was primarily situating her poems in three places: onto sheets of stationery that she was sewing together to make her fascicles; in her letters to Sue; and in her letters to Bowles. (We cannot accurately judge what her letters to the Norcross cousins looked like, as they supplied her early editors with transcriptions of these texts.) As Ellen Louise Hart and Martha Nell Smith have meticulously documented, starting in the mid-1850s Sue became Dickinson's primary correspondent. Dickinson sent Sue not only poems but "letter-poems," letters in the form of poems that were often written on small leaves of stationery, usually presented without introduc-tion, and accompanied simply by Dickinson's signature at the bottom.[19] Dickin-son also sent Sue drafts of poems in a way that she never did with any other correspondent, which shows us today that Sue was, in Smith's words, Dickinson's "consultant, collaborator, confidante."[20] Dickinson's strategies for sending Bowles poems was very different, for while she often placed a poem within the text of the letter, Dickinson was careful to mark it as a poem. For instance, the manuscript of her letter of early 1862 (L 251) indicates that Dickinson indented the beginning of each stanza and attempted to hold each line of the "Through the strait pass of suffering—" (F 187) intact, for when she had to turn the line, she left the rest of that line blank. Even in the case of her February 1861 letter (L 229) in which the beginning of "Would you like Summer? Taste of our's—" (F 272) seems to initially be a part of the prose of the letter, four lines down Dickinson begins marking the lines as those of a poem for Bowles to read. In her early corre-spondence with Higginson, unlike in her correspondence with Sue and Bowles, Dickinson kept her poems separate from her letter.

It is interesting to note that when Higginson opened the first two envelopes that Dickinson sent to him, he encountered a variety of kinds of paper. The first letter was written on the first two sides of a folded piece of stationery, but because her second letter is longer, Dickinson was forced to use two sheets of folded stationery. As with the making of her fascicles, Dickinson did not insert these sheets into each other but instead wrote on all four sides of one folded sheet before moving onto the next. While she would have had to stack one on top of the other so that Higginson could follow the narrative of her letter, she did not sew them together. Unlike the fascicles, in which the sewing dictates the order, in a letter, the logic of the sentences tells its reader, should the sheets become shuffled, which sheet comes next. And then there was the paper on which the poems had been copied. Because Dickinson did not share an intimacy with Higginson, it seems fitting that she did not send him "letter-poems" and she did not put poems, even if they were clearly marked as such (as in the ones sent to Bowles), inside the texts of her letter, but instead employed the materials and methods that more closely resemble those that she used to produce her fascicles. "South Winds jostle them—," for instance, was short enough to take up just the front side of a single leaf, but the other two poems that Dickinson enclosed in her second letter were both written on all four sides of a piece of folded stationery, just like those she was sewing together to make her fascicles. Despite the fact that these enclosed poems were written on slightly smaller paper than the sheets she used for her fascicles—this paper is four and a half by seven inches, as opposed to the five-by-eight-inch fascicle paper—they resemble what a sheet would have looked like before it was sewn to other sheets. Yet by not filling the extra space with another poem and by not sewing the sheets together—by not, we might say, sending Higginson a fascicle—Dickinson marks the enclosures of her first and second letters as separate poems in a way that she does not in the fascicles proper.

At this point in Dickinson's life she was conceiving of at least five different yet connected modes of relation between poems: poems copied onto the same sheet of stationery (the topic of chapter 1); poems sewn to each other in the fascicles (a problem I raised in chapter 1 and that I will address in chapter 3); poems *as* correspondence (in the case of the "letter-poems" to Sue); poems copied within the text of a letter but marked as such (in the case of letters to Bowles); and poems as individual enclosures that were sent together in the same envelope (in the case of Higginson). It is the new, sixth form of relation that I will turn to now, one that she instigated in her third letter to Higginson and one that allowed her to challenge the conventions of letter writing with which she was familiar. It is this new form that allows us to see both the letter and the poem as more porous and unstable than her earlier practices revealed them to be.

Agnieszka Salska argues that when Dickinson writes to Higginson, she "separates her artistic concerns from her emotional involvements and attempts to test the response to her poetry of a reader who was personally unknown to her but professionally well established."[21] While this may have been true of her first two letters, Dickinson's emotional involvement with Higginson becomes quite acute by her third letter (L 265), as she now presents herself as someone who is desperate for his attention. Raising the stakes, she writes at greater length about her dead tutor and implies her need for a new one. Using medical terms, she says that her poems relieve her of her "palsy" and refers to the fact that Higginson "bled" her in his earlier letter. This letter is Dickinson's third attempt to get Higginson to sign on as her mentor, as she asks him once again to help her find her way: "The Sailor cannot see the North—but knows the Needle can—."

It is clear from this letter that while Dickinson is being melodramatic in her responses, she had registered (or at least wants to convey that she has registered) an intense reaction to Higginson's response to her poems. (Indeed, we might read the poem "Before I got my eye put out" (F 336) that she will send to Higginson later that summer as another version of what it feels like to receive his criticism.) She writes that his second letter brought her "pleasure," but that it also "surprised me, and for a moment, swung." She addresses his criticisms methodically, in turn revealing to later readers that in his letter he must have suggested that she delay in publishing, that the "gait" of her poems is "spasmodic," and that they are "uncontrolled." (We know from Higginson's letter to James T. Fields the day after he received Dickinson's first letter that he was not pleased with her poems. He writes, "I foresee that 'Young Contributors' will send me worse things than ever now. Two such specimens of verse as came yesterday & day before— fortunately not to be forwarded for publication!").[22] Dickinson gives in to each of his criticisms and plays the role of the deferential student, figuring herself as a small and silent creature asking for his friendship: "Would you have time to be the 'friend' you should think I need? I have a little shape—it would not crowd your Desk—nor make much Racket as the Mouse, that dents your Galleries—." The various stances, reactions, and expressions embodied in this letter have prompted Paul Crumbley to describe it as "Dickinson's famous third letter to Higginson" because it is the one where we begin to see that what Dickinson wanted from Higginson was "for him to save her life."[23] What interests me, then, is that in this letter, she sends no enclosures.[24]

Instead of sending Higginson poems in the form to which he had become accustomed, Dickinson copied the lines that begin "As if I asked a common alms—" near the end and within the body of her letter. Ever since Higginson published this letter in the October 1891 issue of the *Atlantic Monthly*, readers have treated it as one that has a poem inserted near the end. *The Letters of Emily Dickinson* (1894), *The Life and Letters of Emily Dickinson* (1924), and *The Letters of Emily Dickinson* (1931) all set the poem aside, marking it as separate from the letter itself, yet still a part of the letter's overall fabric. Johnson and Ward's 1958 transcription took its cue from earlier publications and has dictated how subsequent readers of the letter have thought about Dickinson's insertion of her poems into her letters. Here is the letter, as Johnson prints it:

265

To T.W. Higginson   7 June 1862
Dear friend.

Your letter gave no Drunkenness, because I tasted Rum before— Domingo comes but once—yet I have had few pleasures so deep as your opinion, and if I tried to thank you, my tears would block my tongue—

My dying Tutor told me that he would like to live till I had been a poet, but Death was much of Mob as I could master—then—And when far afterward—a sudden light on Orchards, or a new fashion in

the wind troubled my attention—I felt a palsy, here—the Verses just
relieve—

Your second letter surprised me, and for a moment, swung—I had
not supposed it. Your first—gave no dishonor, because the True—are
not ashamed—I thanked you for your justice—but could not drop the
Bells whose jingling cooled my Tramp—Perhaps the Balm, seemed
better, because you bled me, first.

I smile when you suggest that I delay "to publish"—that being
foreign to my thought, as Firmament to Fin—

If fame belonged to me, I could not escape her—if she did not, the
longest day would pass me on the chase—and the approbation of my
Dog, would forsake me—then—My Barefoot-Rank is better—

You think my gait "spasmodic"—I am in danger—Sir—

You think me "uncontrolled"—I have no Tribunal.

Would you have time to be the "friend" you should think I need?
I have a little shape—it would not crowd your Desk—nor make much
Racket as the Mouse, that dents your Galleries—

If I might bring you what I do—not so frequent to trouble you—
and ask you if I told it clear—'twould be control, to me—

The Sailor cannot see the North—but knows the Needle can—

The "hand you stretch me in the Dark," I put mine in, and turn
away—I have no Saxon, now—

> As if I asked a common Alms,
> And in my wondering hand
> A Stranger pressed a Kingdom,
> And I, bewildered, stand—
> As if I asked the Orient
> Had it for me a Morn—
> And it should lift it's purple Dikes,
> And shatter me with Dawn!

But, will you be my Preceptor, Mr Higginson?

> Your friend
> E Dickinson—

Because we have already seen that when Dickinson wanted to display her talents in verse to Higginson, she enclosed individual poems, we can also see that in
this case she was doing something different. One way to read the inclusion of this
poem might be as Dickinson's attempt to get Higginson to read one of her poems
without necessarily taking his scalpel to it; if it is included in the letter itself, it
might not be as open to his critique, which, although requested, had been quite
harsh. Its inclusion may also be read as an alternative mode of self-presentation.
For instance, in the letter itself Dickinson presents herself as helpless without
Higginson, going even as far as to say that the language to finish her letter has

failed her, yet we might read her staging of a break into poetry at this moment as a way of highlighting her capacity for spontaneous poetic production, possibly testing out a version of lyric articulation of which she thought Higginson would approve.[25] While Higginson himself might have fallen for this strategy, Dickinson's later readers know that this was purely a performance, as we have access to what Smith characterizes as "Dickinson's pages-long revising strategies in order to make scriptures that appear to be spontaneous pleadings" and what MacKenzie reminds us was a process of "reading and constructing the letter carefully before sending it, anticipating the response of the recipient, yet remaining well aware of the inevitability of misunderstood intentions and gaps in meaning."[26] A third way of reading the poem's inclusion is as a way for Dickinson to abstract her relationship with Higginson. By shifting from the relation between the "I" and "You" in the letter to the "I" and third-person interlocutor of the poem, Dickinson gets to imagine a fictional scenario in which Higginson will present her with the sort of revelation that the poem describes and the letter has implied she desires. In other words, she has asked him time and time again to offer her guidance, and in this poem she generates the concrete images of the "Kingdom" and the "Dawn" that he might bring her.

All of these readings are made possible because of the assumption that Dickinson was inserting a poem here. But what if the letter doesn't mark this shift from prose to poetry as starkly as the printed version does? When we turn to the manuscript of this letter (fig. 2.2), we see that the line between the letter and the poem is less dramatic than the transcription suggests. When we look at the manuscript itself, we can see that each of the previous editors of this letter—Higginson included—has made certain, often inconsistent, decisions about what constitutes a paragraph break, an indent, and a line break. For instance, although Dickinson indents the first line of the first paragraph after the salutation "Dear friend," elsewhere she indicates a new paragraph by leaving space at the end of the last line of the previous paragraph. See, for instance, the spaces after "tongue" at the bottom of the first page, "relieve" at the bottom of the second, "better" in the middle of the fourth, "Tribunal" at the bottom of the fourth, "Galleries" in the middle of the fifth, and "me" at the bottom of the fifth. (Johnson and Ward also think that breaks are signaled by the spaces after "first" in the middle of the third page, "Fin" at the bottom of the third page, "Sir" at the bottom of the fourth page, and "can" at the top of the sixth page, but these spaces are less substantial.) When we reach the part of the letter that includes the lines beginning with "As if I asked a common alms—," these breaks become more obvious and occur more often, leading most editors to deduce that what once signaled a paragraph break now indicates a line break.[27] But Dickinson does not leave any vertical space between what editors are calling the letter and the poem, nor does she indent the lines of poetry, two significant textual markers that the printed versions lead us to believe she indicated.

The point of my return to this manuscript is not to argue that Dickinson did not copy lines of poetry into her letter, but to challenge the idea that these two

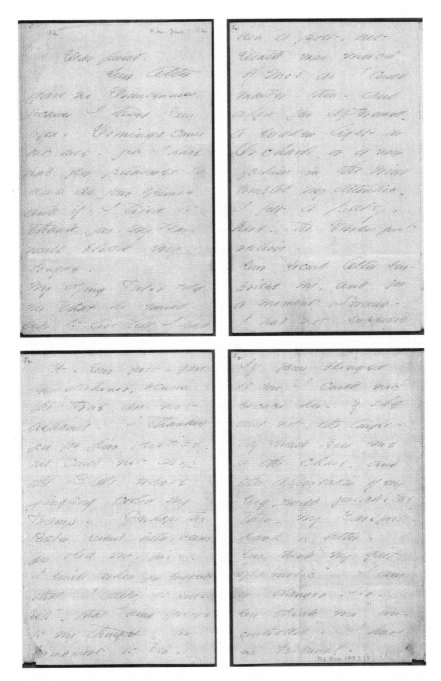

Figure 2.2
Manuscript of Letter 265 sent to Thomas Wentworth Higginson. Courtesy, the Trustees of the Boston Public Library/Rare Books.

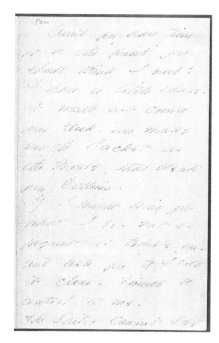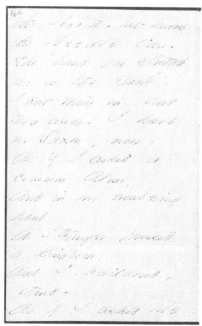

Figure 2.2 *(continued)*

categories—epistolary prose and poetry—are as stable and identifiable in Dickinson's writing as we have thought. The editorial decisions discussed above were, I would argue, all informed by the prior knowledge of this piece of writing as a poem that Dickinson had copied onto a fascicle sheet. I am primarily referring to Johnson, who published it as a poem from the fascicles in 1955, but this is also true of Higginson, who, in preparing the 1890 and 1891 *Poems* with Mabel Loomis Todd, would have come across this poem, either on a then-loose sheet of folded stationery or in the form of Todd's transcription. If Dickinson's editors had not been predisposed to recognize this writing as a poem, they may very well have not marked it as such or have gone in the opposite direction and begun marking poetic lines earlier, as Dickinson dips in and out of regular measure and leaves blank space at the right-hand margin earlier in the letter. In other words, for over a hundred years editors have made the assumption that because this was once an individual poem it must always be one and critics have taken their cues from this, leading a reader as precise as Susan Howe to say that at this moment "the letter became a poem for eight lines."[28] This investment in the solidity of the poem's identity as such positions letters and poems as distinct genres that, while they may come in contact with each other, cannot affect the other. Yet, as we will see in the next section, what was a nineteenth-century convention for marking a shift from letter to poem—a convention that Dickinson is here ignoring, and for good reason—has, over the course of the twentieth century, turned into our own investment in the generically-stable categories that Dickinson must have been transgressing.

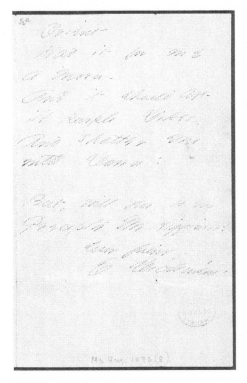

Figure 2.2 (*continued*)

EDITING AND GENRE

Before we begin to tease out what this moment in the Dickinson/Higginson correspondence can tell us about Dickinson's understanding of the relationship between poems and letters, I want to visit a moment in Dickinson's correspondence from ten years earlier. I do this in order to demonstrate that while certain texts raise the question of whether Dickinson was writing letters or poems, this discussion is largely driven by the question of how to print them. The current solutions to this problem—print it as verse or prose—foreclose what an investigation of material context makes visible: that these genres were not stable and distinct in the first place. I take an 1851 letter as my primary text here because, in many ways, it is quite ordinary; it is not, say, complicated in the way that Dickinson's third letter to Higginson is. Why, then, was its generic identity recast so many times over the course of the twentieth century?

In February 1851, Dickinson sent a short letter to Elbridge G. Bowdoin accompanying a lamp mat that she had made for him as a Valentine gift (fig. 2.3). This letter was written in the center of a leaf of stationary and was folded in thirds for sending. It reads: "I weave for the Lamp of *Evening*—but fairer colors than

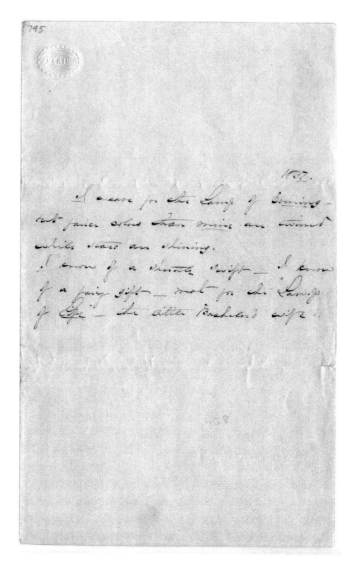

Figure 2.3
Manuscript of Letter 41 sent to Elbridge Bowdoin. Courtesy, Archives & Special Collections, Amherst College.

mine are twined while stars are shining. I know of a shuttle swift—I know of a fairy gift—mat for the "Lamp of *Life*"—the little Bachelor's wife!" (L 41) Research into the circumstance of this letter yields only vaguely interesting things about it: Elbridge Bowdoin was a law partner of Dickinson's father's, was ten years her senior, and, according to a letter that Dickinson sent Austin, was a bit of a bore. But she sent him this Valentine anyway, as well as the one that begins "Awake ye muses nine, sing me a strain divine" (F 1)—Dickinson's very un-Dickinsonian Valentine in hexameters—probably because he had sent novels to the Dickinson Homestead for her and Lavinia to read. One of these novels may have been Ik Marvel's *Reveries of a Bachelor,* which had been published in 1850, which Dickinson had read by 1851, and which may account for the Bachelor reference in this letter.[29] But beyond these minor facts, interest in this letter runs dry. Unlike most of Dickinson's letters, which lead their readers down sometimes unending and circuitous paths of reference and intertext, this letter seems to stop here.

This letter has received very little critical attention because it was produced so early in Dickinson's career, because Bowdoin is of no particular interest to literary scholars, and because the content of this letter does not really tell us anything about Dickinson that we did not already know.[30] But when we look at how this letter has been printed over the course of the twentieth century, it raises crucial questions about how Dickinson navigated the line between epistolary prose and poetry and about the twentieth-century editor's investment in reading everything Dickinson wrote as poetry. Dickinson writes and sends this letter in 1851 and then no one takes notice of it for eighty years, when it is published in Mabel Loomis Todd's 1931 *Letters of Emily Dickinson.* In Franklin's 1998 variorum he tells us that it was published in 1931 "as prose," but a look at the 1931 edition reveals that it is slightly more complicated than this.[31] Todd prints this piece of writing in a section about Dickinson's early Valentines, and given the fact that the texts that precede and follow it are both poems written in formal metrics, these lines seem to be presented, at least visually, as poetry. There is something about the fact that both sections begin with "I," are exactly the same length, are separated by white space, and are indented symmetrically, that would lead one to say that these look like four lines of poetry in two stanzas. When we read them, though, we are left feeling as if they are probably prose, as Dickinson's poetic lines would not have ended on "than" and "for," and the pacing of the sentences pushes the reader to read through the line breaks in each "stanza." It is impossible to say what Todd intended to do here, but what we can see is that what seemed to be prose in the manuscript is subtly, if not yet completely, being transformed into poetry. It is surprising, then, that when it is published again, twenty-seven years later, in Johnson and Ward's 1958 *The Letters of Emily Dickinson,* they present it less as poetry and more as prose. In their transcription, the text reads as two paragraphs, as "are" and "the" are even less likely to be words on which Dickinson would have broken her "lines." When Johnson publishes his variorum of the poems in 1955 and then his reading edition in 1960, this text does not make an appearance. Until this point it has only appeared in volumes of "Letters" and even if within those volumes its generic identity was being questioned, it has not yet been called a poem.

But then in 1993, William Shurr publishes *New Poems of Emily Dickinson,* a collection of what he calls the "prose-formatted poems" that Dickinson included in her letters, and here, for the first time, this letter to Bowdoin is printed as a seven-line poem.[32] Shurr reads this as a poem because of the internal metrics and rhymes that his line breaks then play up. Whether Franklin takes his cue from Shurr five years later we cannot know, but nonetheless he too lineates, this time, *part* of this letter. This text is not included with the other poems, but relegated to the 13th Appendix, which is titled "Some prose passages in Emily Dickinson's early letters and notes exhibit characteristics of verse without being so written."[33] Shurr and Franklin both acknowledge that this letter is prose, but they also print it (or, in the case of Franklin, the second part of it) as poetry. While Franklin is more self-conscious about his choice (relegating it to an Appendix and stressing the text's status as prose), Shurr believes that Dickinson herself *meant* it to be a poem, that she was simply "indifferent as to whether she wrote out her poems in their traditional format or as prose," and that such "poems . . . should be added to the canon and studied in their rightful place there."[34] While the editorial history of this letter reveals that debate about Dickinson's writing practices is alive and well, the current solutions to these questions not only seem inadequate (print it one way or the other), but, in light of Shurr's ideas, foreclose the very kind of analysis that I am trying to open up.

In one attempt to cut through these debates about whether a given text is poetry or prose, Domhnall Mitchell argues that Dickinson consistently marked the difference between the two. By measuring—literally in centimeters—the horizontal and vertical spaces that Dickinson left in her manuscripts, Mitchell argues that Dickinson's writing and copying practices reveal that she was not only aware of these generic boundaries, but upheld them. Additionally, by looking at details of her manuscripts such as capitalization, Mitchell deduces what he considers to be her "generically specific procedures," which we can then use to understand what genre she was writing in when.[35] Mitchell insists that a "rigorous and sustained cross-referencing provides us with a set of procedures, a critical apparatus, by which to measure the extent to which contemporary critical approaches to Dickinson's autograph procedures can accurately be formulated as corresponding to the poet's own purposes."[36] If we apply Mitchell's methodology to Dickinson's letter to Bowdoin, we are able to see that Dickinson does not leave white space at the end of her lines and therefore we can draw the conclusion that she isn't sending him a poem. Similarly, if we go back to the letter to Higginson, Mitchell's method of measurement allows us to recognize, in a way that we wouldn't without his intervention, that Dickinson's method of leaving spaces changes when she gets to the sixth page of her letter to Higginson. But by relying solely on the physical structure and visual layout of Dickinson manuscripts in order to make his assessments, Mitchell misses a crucial point. Why must this mean that Dickinson is or is not copying a "poem" here? Why is that the investment? Additionally, while Mitchell expresses frustration with critics who explore Dickinson's interest in challenging and suspending the boundaries between poetry and prose, his methodology actually enables them to see, especially in the case of the letter to Higginson, that in the new context, the lines beginning "As if I asked a common alms—" are themselves changing.

The inverse methodology is to treat Dickinson's texts as so blended that they deserve a new generic category altogether: for instance, Smith and Hart's "letter-poems" or, more recently, Elizabeth Hewitt's "lyrical letter." What this approach acknowledges is that, in Hewitt's words, "correspondence is a constitutive aspect of Dickinson's poetic discourse."[37] In Smith, Hewitt, and Jerome McGann's treatments of Dickinson's third letter to Higginson, they all use the language of blended genres. Yet within that language still resides the trace of the desire to hold lyric and letter largely separate: While Smith describes this moment in this letter as Dickinson "[weaving] a bit of explanatory verse into her prose," Hewitt describes it as "Dickinson's turn toward lyric."[38] McGann's treatment seems to have wanted to avoid such formulations, as he argues that when Dickinson copies these lines into the prose of this letter she is not simply copying a poem because she "draw[s] its elementary rules of form by an analogy to the writing conventions of personal correspondence rather than to the conventions of the printed text."[39] By acknowledging that "poetical texts flow directly into (and out of) the epistolary texts," and by going so far as to print the parts of the letter that have always been printed as prose as lines of verse, reading what he calls "the metrical subtext of the prose," McGann produces the textual incarnation of what we might think of as the fluid boundary between prose and poetry.[40] Instead of choosing between Dickinson the private poet and Dickinson the social correspondent, then, each of these critics (to varying degrees) treats the two discourses as interconnected in Dickinson's writing.

But these new generic categories, while productively opening up interpretative space in the discussion of Dickinson's poems and letters, still depend heavily on assumptions about what a Dickinson poem is and what it will always be, largely regardless of context. Virginia Jackson articulates this problem as one of circulation and context: "The lyric reading practiced by every editor since Higginson has actively cultivated a disregard for the circumstances of Dickinson's manuscripts' circulation. By being taken out of their sociable circumstances, those manuscripts have become poems, and by becoming poems, they have been interpreted as lyrics."[41] What's at stake, then, in upholding generic boundaries or creating new ones, "is not the existence of Dickinson's writing as either poetic or epistolary but the existence of literary criticism. The reason that the distinction between genres seems an important point of debate for literary critics is that once the genre of a text is established, then . . . protocols of interpretation will follow. In other words, what is at stake in establishing the genre of Dickinson's writing is nothing less than its literary afterlife."[42]

But if we take up Dickinson's manuscripts in lieu of those that have been transcribed, printed, or measured for us by editors who are always at a series of removes and who have particular and often inscrutable agendas, and put them up against the compositional practices with which Dickinson would have been familiar, what we find are Dickinson's own instances of both stabilization and resistance—acts that, I would argue, are not invested in our later questions about genre. As Logan Esdale has pointed out, the sheer number of nineteenth-century books about the epistolary form—"there were letter books . . . for students and secretaries, reprints of eighteenth-century epistolary novels, collections of personal letters, and, above all, life-and-letters biographies"—makes it clear that Dickinson was surrounded by both the presence of epistolary conventions and imaginative ways to reconfigure these conventions.[43] She referred to these conventions within her letters, writing, for example, to Abiah Root in May 1848, "You know it is customary for the first page to be occupied with apologies" (L 23). Countless comments like this indicate that Dickinson may have taken note of what the word was on how to integrate (or not) poems and letters. Nineteenth-century letter-writing manuals such as *The Fashionable American Letter Writer; or, Art of Polite Correspondence*, of which there were numerous nineteenth-century editions, makes it clear that including poems was not a suggested practice. In the introduction, under the section that begins with the sentence "A few things with respect to the style of letters of every class, ought carefully to be avoided," appears the following instruction: "Too frequent quotations is also another error which ought to be carefully avoided; a quotation or happy phrase judiciously introduced, is certainly an elegance in style; but the too frequent introduction of them, or of French or Latin phrases or scraps of poetry, is an unpardonable affectation."[44]

Yet, when we look at the surviving letters of many of Dickinson's female contemporaries—including Abby Cooper, Lucy Putnam, and even Sue—we can see that they were, indeed, copying lines of poetry into their letters. What they made sure to do, though, was to distinguish between poetry and prose. Dickinson herself would have learned about the importance of proper transitions in all forms of composition from Samuel Phillips Newman's *A Practical System of Rhetoric*, a book she studied at Mount Holyoke.[45] It should not be surprising, then, that when Dickinson did break this rule by putting poems in her letters, she often did it in clear way. For instance, a look at the ways in which Dickinson worked before she contacted Higginson reveals that when Dickinson copied poems that she wanted read *as poems* into her letters, she often marked this quite clearly. In her letter to Mary Warner Crowell on April 20, 1856, Dickinson copied verses by Pierpont, indicating their status as poetry by beginning and ending the poem with quotes, by making clear breaks between each of the stanzas, and by leaving significant space between the end of the poem and the beginning of her letter (L 183). When copying her own poems, she employs similar methods. In three early instances in which Dickinson indicates to Sue that what she is sending her are poems, Dickinson marks the shift by leaving space between her prose and the poem, by making each stanza distinct from the next, and by indicating, even when there is no room to keep a line intact, where each line begins and ends. In each of these cases, there is no mistaking what a reader is reading.[46]

In other words, by placing what had been lines of poetry into her third letter to Higginson, Dickinson was not only breaking the rules of fashionable writing, but she was breaking with her own conventions for displaying her talents as a poet to her correspondents. While scholarship that investigates the textual and editorial issues that Dickinson's poems and letters raise tends to handle this situation by either holding the genres of letter and poem stable or by collapsing them entirely, I want to suggest that Dickinson's act of willfully playing with these conventions does not reveal that she was worrying over genre, but instead that she was turning inside out the public/private opposition on which, ironically, much thinking about Dickinson—and nineteenth-century American culture and literature more broadly—has come to depend. In other words, by being preoccupied with how to print Dickinson's poems and letters, we overlook the fact that these moments in her manuscripts probe us to reassess what constitutes public and private acts and what role the circulation of texts plays in this formulation.

Letter-writing manuals from the nineteenth century position women's letter-writing practices, and the texts that they produce, as inherently private. In an effort to define women's letters as domestic in nature (despite their being sent out into the world), these manuals encouraged women to confine themselves to the topics and concerns of the home. As Nan Johnson has written, "The conflation of women's letter writing and the domestic sphere . . . is a deeply grounded assumption in the American letter-writing tradition."[47] Letter-writing manuals of the time not only lay out the various subgenres of letter writing (business, courtship, family, congratulations, social invitations, condolence, etc.) and delineate which were appropriate for women and which were not, but they promote certain characteristics and style for women's letters. Thus, what Johnson calls "the ideological double message of nineteenth-century letter-writing literature" makes itself clear: "Everyone needs to be able to write a good letter, but important distinctions must be made between where and how a man writes and where and how a woman writes."[48]

Such a preoccupation with containing the status of women's letters to the domestic sphere indicates that letter writing in and of itself poses a major threat to such containment. This is only logical, given that letters are a form of communication. As McGann has argued, "If we choose to communicate with written language, we may connect with others through the commerce of publication or through the intercourse of correspondence."[49] In other words, the emphasis on what nineteenth-century women should be writing about and how they should be producing that writing seems to reveal less about the actual status of the genre in historical terms and more about the anxiety around women's letter-writing practices, as they pressed right up against the public sphere and therefore posed a threat to separate spheres ideology. Given that letters naturally straddle this divide—they often contain personal information and yet are by nature shared—they become the natural site for the transgression of a variety of boundaries.

Dickinson recognized this potential for transgression and boundary crossing when she saw it. In the same way that she turned the private/public dichotomy on its head when she took up the conventions of print culture that existed firmly in the public sphere and played with them in the private context of fascicles that, as far as we know, she did not circulate, in her letters Dickinson blurs conventions that would be both inappropriate and incomprehensible in the public sphere, yet these are the very texts she chooses to circulate. Furthermore, by including the same seemingly private poem within different letters to different people—something that we see her doing with Higginson early on and that she will continue to do throughout her life—Dickinson marks the poems within her letters as the more circulated, and therefore more public, objects.[50]

When Dickinson does not simply include poems in her correspondence, but actually embeds them within these letters, turning the letter into both the context and vehicle for the poem's circulation, she changes the status of both the epistolary prose and the lines of poetry. McGann hints at this when he says that Dickinson's third letter to Higginson "is a poetical text that exploits the writing resources—the conventions—of epistolary intercourse," but we have yet to fully understand how this exploitation occurs and, more importantly, what it provides for both Dickinson and Higginson.[51] It is my contention that the instability that is created in these moments is indicative of a larger instability that has to do with the very nature of epistolary correspondence as it uncomfortably straddles the divide between the public and private spheres, an instability that cannot be fixed by labeling it as another genre, but must be understood in terms of its specific components. In the next section I will look precisely at one of these components—at the way in which the embedded lines capitalize on Dickinson's desire to rethink how her "I" is allowed to function in both contexts.

While Dickinson's texts sometimes ask us to measure white space and sometimes demand that we generate new terms to describe them, for the most part the nature of her writing requires that we return to her manuscripts to unravel the problems about context that the texts themselves raise. What we can see there is that, more often than not, they attempt to answer these problems for themselves. In the case of the letter to Bowdoin we have a seemingly inconsequential Valentine, a note accompanying a present, sent to a man she did not really like that much. But upon closer examination, we have an instance in which the metrics and pacing of what will become her later writing are starting to develop, not in poetry proper, but in her correspondence. By turning a short letter like this into poetry, we lose the nuances of her compositional practices, where a formal note of thanks was taken as an opportunity to play with the boundaries between epistolary prose and poetry. When we decide, then, that the lines that had once been a poem copied onto a sheet of stationery are still those same lines of poetry when embedded into a letter to Higginson, we foreclose the opportunity to watch Dickinson taking advantage of and challenging the limits of both modes of writing.

DICKINSON'S "I"

As I hope to have shown, Dickinson was not simply copying the poem that she had once written on a sheet that she sewed into Fascicle 1 as a poem into her letter to Higginson. If she was, she would have marked its presence in her customary ways. That being said, deciding what this text is, or has become, is a way of re-ifying the very assumptions about genre that have nothing to do with Dickinson. Instead, I want to ask: What does a blurring of or shift in modes make possible for Dickinson at this moment in her correspondence with Higginson? What terms get renegotiated when she moves from one type of writing to another, yet with-holds from her reader the markers by which he can register or interpret this move? In order to answer these questions, we need to return to the manuscript of Dickinson's letter, since what she is doing when she sends this letter, what Hig-ginson is doing when he reads it, and what both of their assumptions are about the experiences the other is having are present in the materials of the exchange.

William Decker has argued that "far from being extrinsic to the text, the ma-teriality of the letter exchange is an abiding component in the poetics and narra-tive of epistolary relations."[52] As opposed to the volumes of transcribed and printed letters, then, manuscripts remind later readers of the fact that an actual person, in Decker's words, is made "intensely present to correspondents in the form of hand-inscribed letter sheet that arrives to the relief, dread, ecstasy, an-noyance, or indifference of the recipient, across a vastly variable spatial and tem-poral expanse that contributes its own decided (if often irrecoverable) inflection to the letter's initial meanings."[53] It is precisely the presence of this actual person, and of the "I" that Dickinson creates for herself through the writing of letters and letters that embed pieces of poems in them, that, I will argue, is essential here.

In Dickinson's fourth letter to Higginson she explains that the "I" of her poems is not meant to represent her, a declaration that is now both widely quoted and quickly forgotten. In her words: "When I state myself, as the Representative of the Verse—it does not mean—me—but a supposed person" (L 268). Dickinson states her position quite firmly here, but in doing so she reveals that her letters, on the other hand, *do* present an "I" that corresponds to the actual person at the other end of the correspondence: the very "I" in her sentence of disavowal is meant to be Dickinson and *not* a "supposed person." No matter how much critics want to make of the literariness of Dickinson's letters or of the various masks and personae she assumes when writing them, the fact is that letters hold her "I" more faithfully to her historical personage. Despite the fact that Decker argues that "undoubtedly [Dickinson] recognized that the 'supposed person' spoke in the letters as much as in the verse," his definition of the letter highlights the differ-ence inherent in the "I" of a letter, as he defines letters as "inscribed artifacts . . . that at some point in their history are meant to pass in accordance with some postal arrangement from 'I' to 'you,' and that inscribe the process by which the 'I' personally addresses a specific readership."[54] While Decker calls them "artifacts," we might call them a "medium," one (and maybe the only one, for that matter) by which Dickinson, the actual "I" writing the letter, navigated space and time. I draw such close attention to this issue of the "I" because one of the crucial things that happens when Dickinson embeds "As if I asked a common alms—" into her third letter to Higginson is that she does away with the shift from historical to fictive discourse that an enclosed or even inserted poem implies and, even if self-consciously and imaginatively, embraces the figure of the historical "I" and what it might be able to do for her. Under normal circumstance, the knowledge of who "I" and "you" are in a letter, and how they are positioned in relation to each other, even if that spatially and temporally vexed relationship is the subject of the letter, is held stable. In shifting from epistolary prose to what had been lines of poetry, then, Dickinson challenges within her letter the very structure upon which epistolary relations stand.

The message, tone, and implication of this letter are different depending on whether we read the presence of an inserted poem or the presence of lines of a previously written poem now embedded into the prose. If we read it as an inserted poem, then, according to Dickinson, the "I" of the letter is the particular woman who is answering Higginson's questions and asking for his help, but the "I" of the poem is not this same woman. The new "I" of the poem is distanced from the requests that Dickinson has made in her letter. The conditional "As if" presents the "I" in a state of fictive imagining for which Dickinson the letter writer is not fully responsible. But because the poem is not set apart and because the letter seems to have been built around the incorporation of this poem into its very grammatical and thematic structure—notice the move from "If" to "As if" to "But," as well as Dickinson's reliance on the trope of direction before employing the word "Orient"—the difference between these two "I"s collapses. By allowing these lines to function *as part of the letter*, Dickinson manages to control, if only for a moment, the ground on which both she and Higginson stand. When we read the letter as one that has a poem inserted in it, I suggested earlier that the poem offers up an abstracted version of their relationship by turning Dickinson into a "supposed person" and Higginson into an unnamed interlocutor. But if we read it as part of the letter, this is no longer true, for Dickinson retains her identity as the one who says "I," and she addresses him as a "Stranger." These lines, then, read as a critique of Higginson.

You will recall that Dickinson spends much of this letter both defending herself against Higginson's criticism and asking him for a combination of guidance and friendship. Upon first glance, her desires do not seem to line up, but this is all part of the complex rhetorical strategy that Dickinson employs throughout her correspondence, in which she pulls people close and pushes them away at the same time. In this case, when she embeds "As if I asked a common alms—" into the prose of her letter she activates this push and pull at a formal level. In the context of the letter, these lines now read ironically, for the implication is that all she has asked him for is the equivalent of "common alms" and as a result she has been "bewildered" and "shatter[ed]."[55] Clearly Dickinson wants something different from Higginson, as these lines, especially with their use of the word "should," project her own sense of entitlement. And when she turns, in the final sentence of her letter to write, "But, will you be my Preceptor, Mr Higginson?" her "But" attempts to reorient Higginson precisely around her desires. If we read these lines as part of the letter, we can see Dickinson's frustration with Higginson's response to her poems. By taking lines that were once poetry and embedding them into her letter, Dickinson allows herself to inhabit the "I" of her poem and make its once-abstract critique her very own.

Yet at the same time, and in light of the fact that these lines are almost exactly the same as those copied onto the folded sheet four years earlier, it is important to ask why she used them here instead of critiquing Higginson in new language. I would argue that while this letter expresses frustration with the terms of her relationship with Higginson, the fact that these lines were once poetry and continue to employ regular meter and rhyme tempers this very frustration. In other words, instead of being direct about her disappointment, Dickinson redeploys these lines to express what might be too difficult to express in new language. By turning to what was once a poem, Dickinson manages to level her critique while also pulling back from the force of it. Additionally, this move may have been personally validating for Dickinson, since using a previously written poem to speak to a new situation confirms both the poem and herself as the writer of that poem.[56] Redeploying the poem indicates that there is a lasting truth in it that predates this new and unsettling situation.

While it may seem obvious that a poem enclosed in a letter and a poem embedded into the prose of a letter are different things, this distinction has rarely been made. Most critics have treated the two modes as the same precisely because they have been reading through twentieth-century investments in genre. In other words, if they are both "poems," then they are the same thing. For instance, Messmer argues that "in several instances, the enclosed *or* incorporated poem communicates part of the letter's message, in this way becoming an integral part of its 'letter' context and assuming a function traditionally associated with epistolary rather than poetic discourse."[57] Messmer consistently argues that the poems and the letters participate in "an intergeneric dialogic exchange" with one another; yet, in spite of treating poems and letters as related to each other, she does not differentiate between the ways in which Dickinson's manuscripts reveal the various modes by which she employed poetry in her letters.[58] By collapsing Dickinson's methods, Messmer is able to argue that in the case of Dickinson's letters and poems to Higginson, the two "parts" do very different things: "the 'prose' parts of her letters tend to reinforce Dickinson's gender and power ambivalence, while the 'poems' more frequently acquire a subversive function."[59] Because Messmer treats these parts as two genres that are connected-yet-distinct in Dickinson's practices, she ultimately argues that Dickinson's correspondence "resists any facile alignment with traditional nineteenth-century 'personal' and 'private' women's letters" and that "her letters ultimately appropriate elements of 'literary' and 'fictional-ized' discourses."[60] But as we have seen, it is precisely this "fictionalized" discourse that is suppressed when Dickinson embeds a poem so fully into her prose that her own reader might not register the shift that is taking place.

By looking at this instance in Dickinson's manuscripts, we can see that the conventions available to a nineteenth-century woman writer do not, even as she breaks with them, conform to the protocols of modern literary editing practices and literary criticism that want to read this as genre reformation. Instead, what we see here are Dickinson's experiments with communication. While the desire for intimacy can be felt in the content of so many of Dickinson's letters, especially the letters to loved ones when they traveled out of town, we have yet to recognize how her manipulation of a given text's format contributes to the ways in which she actively controls the distance between her (as "I") and her reader (as "you"). Dick-inson would later articulate (to Higginson, of all people) the tension that exists when people who are at a physical distance from each other must write instead of speak face to face: "a Pen has so many inflections and a Voice but one" (L 470). Twelve years earlier, when she returned to Fascicle 1 to recopy "As if I asked a common alms—" into her letter to Higginson, Dickinson was already experi-menting with several of these inflections by closing down the space between her epistolary "I" and her poetic "I." She was striving after neither the one abstracted lyric voice nor the one intimate voice of the letter writer to her recipient, but instead beginning to harness the potential of all those voices in between, voices that might pull her reader close and push him away at the same time. When we treat these lines as a poem that has been lifted out of one context and inserted into another, we not only misread this letter as one of extreme deference, but we fail to see the ways in which the inclusion of what was once a poem affects both the letter into which it is now being embedded and the identity of the poem itself.

Whereas the many editors of Dickinson's third letter to Higginson simply fore-closed their readers' awareness of Dickinson's compositional practices, what Dickinson did the next time she returned to these lines seems to have caused such confusion that no one has tried to analyze it. Twenty-two years after this instance of thinking about the relationship of the poetic and the epistolary modes—after, we might say, renegotiating how to say "I"—Dickinson returned again to the lines that she had first copied onto the sheet that she sewed as a part of Fascicle 1 and then sent to Higginson. In 1884 she copied these lines as part of a letter that she addressed to an unidentified recipient but didn't send (L 964). Today we have the first two pages of this letter (fig. 2.4) and another, shorter draft of its opening. Whether Dickinson ever sent a version of this letter, and to whom it was addressed, we will likely never know.

This letter begins with a declaration of thanks, indicating that it may have begun as a conventional note acknowledging the receipt of a sent item. In this case, the item is a photograph of a mother and child. While Dickinson seems to

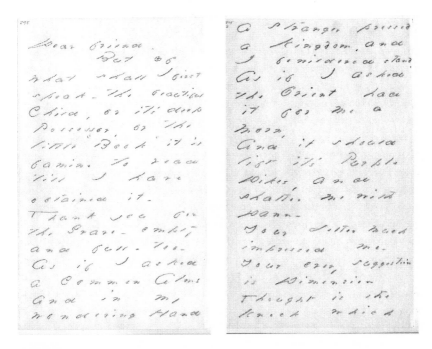

Figure 2.4
Manuscript of Letter 964 addressed to an unidentified recipient and not sent. Courtesy, Archives & Special Collections, Amherst College.

appreciate this gift, she quickly mentions an additional item (a "Book") that has been promised to her by the sender and refers to her state of "famine" without it. In this way, what looks like a note of thanks is also a note meant to remind her friend that a further item needs to be sent. It is not clear what her cryptic next sentence ("Thank you for the Grave—empty and full—too—") refers to, but we can see that Dickinson is balancing her sentences, grateful for one thing and in need of another, acknowledging the presence of a grave both empty and full. The lines beginning "As if I asked a common alms—" go on to further express this balance between gratefulness and critique.

In this case, Dickinson embeds what were once lines of poetry into her letter in such a way that they can no longer be detected as poetry, even if we employ Mitchell's method of measuring white space. Although Dickinson continues to leave horizontal space above paragraph and line breaks, she has become even less concerned with maintaining the integrity of what was once the poetic line. Because Dickinson did not retain earlier drafts of her poems after she copied them onto sheets, she most likely returned to Fascicle 1 in the year before her death in order to copy these words in this order. Yet as she recopied them into this new context, she consciously ignored much of her earlier punctuation and, depending on how we read, she either created new line breaks or did away with them entirely.

I do not raise the text of 1884 in order to say that what is happening at this moment is related to the situation just discussed, for, despite the fact that the same words are taken up again, this act of embedding is almost entirely different. Instead, I follow the story of this poem to its (probable) endpoint in order to show several things: First, that the act of embedding poems into letters is something that Dickinson does not simply do once or twice, but is a practice that she initiated in her correspondence with Higginson and is something that she continues to do over the course of her life and eventually with correspondents other than Higginson. Second, in this act of coming back to the fascicle in order to access these lines, Dickinson shows that the fascicles remained a part of her letter-writing practice throughout her life, revealing that a certain degree of flexibility must have been built into the fascicle context such that she could use these poems in a variety of ways. If the poems had been fixed in the fascicles, Dickinson would not only have been unable to place them in new material contexts, but she would not have been free to alter them in those contexts. Third, and as I will discuss briefly below, the editorial history of this 1884 text reveals that its various editors still have a stake in establishing it as the poem that it was in Fascicle 1, a move that we have seen being made throughout this chapter but which seems particularly bizarre in this instance.

In Johnson's 1955 variorum of the poems, he transcribes this late letter as prose, with no line breaks, but by starting with "As if I asked" and ending with "Dawn—," he divorces these lines from the letter and ends up treating them like a poem nonetheless. Three years later, when Johnson and Ward published *The Letters of Emily Dickinson*, Johnson changed his earlier reading and arranged what he previously considered prose into four long lines of poetry, this time including the rest of the letter around it and, as he did with the letter to Higginson, indenting these particular lines. In Franklin's later variorum of the poems, he includes only the line "Thank you for the Grave—empty and full—too—," deleting all that comes before it and then, like Johnson, reproducing the lines that begin "As if I asked a common Alms and in my wondering Hand" as a poem in four long lines. As with the case of the letter to Higginson, one of the reasons why Johnson and Franklin may have treated this piece of the letter as a poem is that they already knew it as such, and it could therefore be found in among the prose. In doing so, they continue to hold the categories of poem and letter stable, an act that, as we will see in chapter 5, misses the ways in which Dickinson revised, rewrote, and sometimes unmade the texts that were once the poems of her fascicles. The fact is that in this case she went back to an experiment that she had initiated in her third letter to Higginson in order to probe the porous nature of both poetry and letters, an act for which our editorial methods still do not know how to account.

When Dickinson first wrote "As if I asked a common alms—," she could not envision all of the people to whom she would send it and all of the ways in which she would render it. In 1858, when she first copied the lines onto a sheet of folded stationery, she may never have imagined another context for it, for unlike some of the other poems copied onto sheets that she had already sent to various readers, this one, as far as we know, had no other reader. But by returning to it over this twenty-six-year period and copying it out in different ways and with at least two different correspondents in mind, she indicates that something about these lines is both widely applicable and yet particular enough to be used in highly-specific circumstances. As we watch what were originally lines of poetry enter circulation in both private and public ways, we must take notice of their epistolary context precisely because it is the media that made such experimentation possible.

CHAPTER 3

꧀ᘛ

Sewing the Fascicles

Elegy, Consolation, and the Poetics of Interruption

In the opening chapters of this book I called attention to the unstable protocols of reading that govern approaches to Dickinson's fascicles and letters. Whether it is our over-reliance on the unit of the book or our desire to differentiate between letters and poems, these critical practices take their cues not from what Dickinson actually made, but from our later investments in what her work might mean for an understanding of both Dickinson and the history of American poetry. When we do turn to what she made and how she made it, we can see that Dickinson was not just aware of a wide variety of poetic modes, discourses, and strategies, but that she took the opportunity with which writing provided her to confront various literary conventions. In this chapter I will return to her construction of the fascicles—this time looking closely at the way she sewed her sheets together and at the specific kinds of poems she sewed there—in order to probe Dickinson's deep engagement with the most ubiquitous of nineteenth-century poetic genres: the elegy.

This is not to say that Dickinson wrote elegies per se. While there are a few poems that we can attach to the death of a specific person and that employ the conventional tropes and strategies of the genre—the presence of nature, a recitation of the dead person's best characteristics, faith in the fact that the dead person is better off in heaven—Dickinson's engagement with the elegy did not replicate the genre's standard moves. Instead of writing poems about the dead that adopt what appear to be the strict conventions of the elegy, Dickinson wrote hundreds of poems about death from a variety of different perspectives. For example, some of these poems mourn for human and abstract losses; others detail the actual process and aftermath of a loved one's passing; and still others radically fictionalize and fantasize the scene of death. In the face of what seems like Dickinson's very tenuous relationship to the elegy, scholars of the elegy often exclude Dickinson from their studies and Dickinson critics seldom attempt to place her within the genre's historical tradition.[1] In her recent study of eighteenth- and nineteenth-century representations of loss and grief, Desirée Henderson argues for de-emphasizing the generic category in general, by rightly calling attention to the fact that multiple genres—including "elegy, funeral sermon, funeral oration, eulogy, obituary, epitaph, tragedy, tribute, lament, dirge, requiem, monody, threnodoy, encomium, panegyric, obsequies, thanatopsis, and *memento mori*"—saturated American literature of mourning during Dickinson's life.[2] In light of all of this, we might say that we need not limit analysis to this one particular genre.

While we might, then, simply call the poems I will explore here "poems about death" or "poems of loss," I will argue that there is something useful about placing Dickinson's poems in relation to the generic category of the elegy, not because it allows us to read the genre back into them, but because it allows us to expand our understanding of the genre. In the pages ahead I will treat the elegy not as a stable and coherent literary genre, but as a set of malleable and flexible conventions. I can take this approach to the elegy precisely because by nature it embodies a tension that opens it up to revision and transgression. According to Max Cavitch, elegies themselves exist in an in-between space, as they "measure out the distance between emotion and convention, between local disruptions of bereavement and long traditions of resignation."[3] This is precisely why "to this day elegy remains a capacious, flexible, widely practiced poetic genre."[4] Henderson, too, treats the elegy as a "heterogeneous structure" that is open to generic innovation precisely because of the situation it embodies—a situation in which "the unique and individual nature of loss runs up against the dominant conventions that shape memorial traditions and practices."[5] Because elegies attempt to measure loss, because they attempt to articulate what cannot be known or articulated, and because they seek to establish a bond where a bond has just been broken, they are instances of figurative language that always fall short of their supposed goals. In fact, their very identity is based in this failure. In this way, elegy is the genre that reminds us, in Cavitch's words, that "genre is only mistakenly apprehended as a simple fiction of sameness and identity."[6] If we approach the elegy as a genre of complexity, as one that does not simply express tensions and conflicts but is shaped by them, then we can begin to see why Dickinson would have engaged it the way that she did.

While Dickinson would write about death throughout her life, this was a topic that she took up most often during the years in which she was constructing her fascicles. In chapter 1 I asked us to consider Dickinson's unit as the individual folded fascicle sheet—a unit that I still hold is primary—but now I will turn to the fact that after Dickinson had copied these sheets, she sewed them together with string. She did this by stacking the sheets one on top of the other, making two holes along the left hand margin of each folded sheet, and placing a piece of red thread through one set of holes and then through the other, before bringing their ends to meet and tying the string together. Instead of creating a seamless reading experience, this method of construction highlights where each sheet begins and ends. Reading with an awareness of the individual sheets—an experience that is almost impossible to recreate, as even Franklin's facsimile edition blurs these lines—forces us to halt at the edge of each sheet, respecting Dickinson's thresholds and wondering about the nature of these connections and interruptions.[7]

In this chapter I will argue that by writing poems about death and by sewing them to each other, Dickinson investigates the inability of poetry to represent the complicated nature of loss as it exists at the very limits of comprehension. In doing so, she challenges the promise of consolation that the elegy aims to conjure, a consolation that depends precisely on the formal conventions of closure that the stop-again start-again nature of the fascicles makes impossible. Dickinson uses the structure of the fascicles to radically expand time and space, to produce repetitions with a difference, to return to the unreturnable, and to ensure that consolation itself, despite her many attempts, remains impossible. In the act of sewing together sheets on which she delved into multiple and often conflicting experiences with death, Dickinson allows her poems to be saturated in the very issues of breakage, connection, and finality that the fascicle form itself employs and disrupts. It is precisely this understanding of Dickinson's poems about death, and her relationship to the genre of the elegy, that has been obscured by treatments of her individual poems that do not take their fascicle context into account.

In the three sections that follow I will explore these issues as they arise both within Dickinson's individual poems and across the sheets that comprise her fascicles. The first section looks at Dickinson's formal and literary elegy for Charlotte Brontë, analyzing a textual issue that can be seen in the manuscript of this poem—an "Or" that Dickinson included between the third and fourth stanzas—and that I use to inform a reading of the relationship of the sheets of this fascicle to each other. In the second section I consider some of the poems in Fascicles 23 and 27 that perform spatial and/or temporal disruptions while grappling with the topic of death, showing what happens when this strategy is pushed to its extreme and asking what the implications are for the other poems copied on these sheets. In the third section I turn to some of the poems about death written by other nineteenth-century American women in order to show that learning to read Dickinson's approach to the elegy gives us new ways of reading the poems of women whose work has been largely absent from literary histories of the genre.

DICKINSON'S "OR"

In early 1860, Dickinson copied the five-stanza poem that we would come to call "All overgrown by cunning moss" (F 146) onto what would later become the first sheet of Fascicle 7:

> All overgrown by cunning moss,
> All interspersed with weed,
> The little cage of "Currer Bell"
> In quiet "Haworth" laid.
>
> The Bird—observing others
> When frosts too sharp became
> Retire to other latitudes—
> Quietly did the same—
>
> But differed in returning—
> Since Yorkshire hills are green—
> Yet not in all the nests I meet—
> Can Nightingale be seen—
>
> Gathered from many wanderings—
> Gethsemane can tell
> Thro' what transporting anguish
> She reached the Asphodel!
>
> Soft fall the sounds of Eden
> Opon her puzzled ear—
> Oh what an afternoon for
> Heaven,
> When "Bronte" entered there!

Written on or around the fifth anniversary of Charlotte Brontë's death, this poem situates itself squarely within the elegiac tradition: it expresses grief over the loss of a public figure, yet in doing so personalizes that experience; it employs conventional images of nature, figuring the dead person, much as Shelley had done in "Adonais," as a dead bird; and while the poem opens in the enclosure of the graveyard, by the end it has removed the dead from these weeds and moss and has placed her among the angels in heaven. But the most striking way in which this poem does the genre's work is through its references to "Currer Bell" and "Bronte," as they declare the poem's topic to be, at least partially, one of literary inheritance.

While Dickinson's interest in Brontë's novels is evident from her letters, we also know that she had read Brontë's poems, as she sent a copy of *Poems by Currer, Ellis, and Acton Bell* (1846) to Samuel Bowles in 1864 (L 299) and to Thomas Niles in 1883 (L 813a and L 813b). This collection includes many of Brontë's own elegies, and Dickinson seems to have read one, "Mementos," quite closely, as she echoes Brontë's words in her own elegy for Brontë. "Mementos" begins with two stanzas that document the things that a woman, now dead, has left behind for the living to sort through. As the poem takes stock of "this mass of ancient treasures," "fans of leaves," "crimson shells," and "tiny portraits," it pauses on the "green and antique mould" that has grown on top of these "relics old." An explanation follows:

> All in this house is mossing over;
> All is unused, and dim, and damp;
> Nor light, nor warmth, the rooms discover—
> Bereft for years of fire and lamp.
>
> (ll. 21–24)

The opening line of Dickinson's poem, "All overgrown by cunning moss," takes up Brontë's words, "All in this house is mossing over," and in doing so recycles them and pays homage to the poet herself. Dickinson's moss covers a grave and Brontë's moss has grown in a house, but both appear at a site associated with a woman's death. Grammatically, both lines begin with the same "All," yet Brontë's "All" is the subject of her sentence, while Dickinson's subject extends beyond the line, leaving her "all" to function descriptively. This is not Dickinson's only swerve from Brontë's template, though, as Dickinson picks up Brontë's phrase "mossing over," separates these words from each other, cuts the end off of "mossing" to make "moss," extends "over" to make "overgrown," and inverts the order in which they appear. Both lines, as well as Dickinson's process of generating the second from the first, foreground the simultaneous sense of growth and decay that the presence of moss implies. As Dickinson pushes Brontë's more standard subject-verb line by suspending both subject and verb, and as she shifts the victim of the moss from a house to a gravesite, Dickinson performs her own cunning act of poetic competition. As a result of this act, where her words are both the same as Brontë's and different, Dickinson inhabits the position, as writer and elegist, that Brontë once inhabited. This is a typical move for an elegy to make, as the elegist often acknowledges the position newly granted to him or her through the death of a poetic predecessor.

Dickinson's poem was published as a five-stanza poem in *Poems by Emily Dickinson* (1896), *The Complete Poems of Emily Dickinson* (1924), *The Poems of Emily Dickinson* (1930), and *The Poems of Emily Dickinson* (1937). It was not until Thomas Johnson's 1955 edition of her poems that readers learned that there was an "Or" included in the manuscript. It appears that once Dickinson was finished

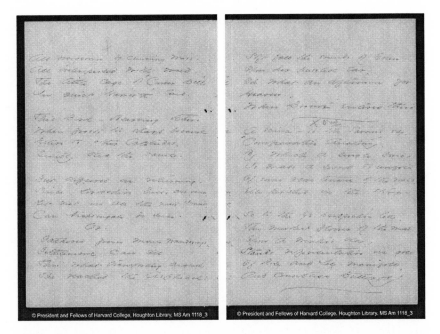

Figure 3.1
"All overgrown by cunning moss" (F 146). By permission of The Houghton Library, Harvard
University, MS Am 1118.3 (5) © The President and Fellows of Harvard College.

copying the poem, she returned to it and inserted an "Or" between stanzas 3 and
4, an assumption we can make because the space that the "Or" fits in is the same
size as the spaces between the other stanzas (fig. 3.1). The insertion of this "Or"
has, since Johnson's publication of it, prompted editors to debate how this poem
should be printed. While Johnson first made us aware of the existence of the "Or"
in the manuscript, five years later, when he published his reading edition of the
poems, he took Dickinson up on the option that he thought her "Or" implied and
printed it as a three-stanza poem, using stanzas 1, 4, and 5. In Franklin's variorum
edition of the poems, he also indicates the existence of the "Or" but printed
stanzas 4 and 5 as a variant to stanzas 2 and 3, a perspective that he maintained
when he printed the poem as stanzas 1, 2, and 3 in his reading edition the following year. Not only are there these competing versions, but, as the manuscript
shows, there is also the option to read the "Or" as indicating a choice between
stanzas 3 and 4, therefore producing two additional options, a poem made up of
stanzas 1, 2, 3, and 5 and one made up of 1, 2, 4, and 5. Additionally, the "Or" can
be read as signaling that stanzas 4 and 5 constitute an alternative poem in its own
right. Finally, one can read the poem as all five stanzas *and* the "Or."

In order to understand the work the "Or" does in this poem, I want to start
with the five-stanza version that Todd printed in 1896. This poem opens in the
present and describes a graveyard scene of natural and artificial containment,
where "moss" and "weed" function much as the "cage" does to hold the subject of

the poem in. In the second stanza a "Bird" appears, seemingly out of nowhere, yet we soon understand that this stanza provides an explanation for the first stanza's grave scene. The second stanza narrates an event that occurred in the past: the bird flew away with the other birds when nature indicated it was time to do so. The third stanza completes this explanation by showing that while nature then indicated that it was time for the birds to return, this specific bird did not, therefore allowing the "I" of the poem to know of its death. In the fourth stanza, the poem undertakes a different, more omniscient explanation, suggesting the "transporting anguish" that this bird lived through in its time between life and death. And the fifth stanza imagines the result of this process: the bird's arrival in "Eden" or "Heaven." In this version of the poem, the graveyard scene of the first stanza is explained by the four stanzas that follow it, as they narrate the totality of the bird's experience.

Whether one understands the insertion of the "Or" as an impulsive gesture at revision, as a result of Dickinson's intentional playfulness, as an indication that she may be marking different versions to be sent to different correspondents, or as a notation of a variant, I want to argue that Dickinson's interruption by means of the "Or" is deeply linked to the subject of her poem, as it forces the poem to grapple with the problem of narrating the experience of loss. This manifests most obviously in the way that the "Or" disrupts the temporal ordering of the poem's experience, a disruption that both Todd and Franklin avoided when they published the poem as stanzas 1, 2, 3, 4, and 5 and as 1, 2, and 3 respectively. Every possible reading that takes the "Or" into account fractures this narrative movement. If we read the poem as stanzas 1, 4, and 5, we are denied the figure of the bird, nature's cycle of death and rebirth, and the "I." Additionally, choosing between stanzas 3 and 4 to make a four-stanza poem either denies knowledge of the bird's failure to return or of the transporting anguish through which it lived. While one could argue that Dickinson employs closure when she moves the bird to heaven, the central work of "All overgrown by cunning moss" is achieved by the "Or"'s refusal of formal closure and by its destruction of the possibility of a coherent reading experience, for, in every case, the temporal wholeness created by the five-stanza form is disrupted.

In her recent study of nineteenth-century grief and mourning, Dana Luciano argues that, contrary to the prevailing sense that nineteenth-century Americans were required to compartmentalize and soldier through their grief for the dead, in reality there was a "tenderness toward prolonged sorrow that was not only permitted but positively encouraged."[8] According to Luciano, people took pleasure in the disruption that death caused, precisely because it was a way of resisting the increasingly "mechanical and impersonal" time of modernity.[9] Death calls linear time into question, as mourners enter into and then linger in what Luciano calls the "slow time of deep feeling," a temporal order very different from the one they are required to perform in under all other circumstances.[10] This tension between the drive to move forward and the impulse to stand still that Luciano has located within a culture saturated by grief is crystallized by the form of not only the elegy, but of poetry in general, for critics have long theorized that as linguistic objects that are uttered either in the minds of their readers or out loud, poems exist in time, that their form itself is a temporal one. Herman Salinger, for instance, has argued that "poetry, along with but also over and beyond all forms of language, is rhythmic in essence, is of the very stuff and matter of Time."[11] Yet what occurs within poems is often described, most notably by Sharon Cameron, as a departure from time—as time standing still or the arresting of time—and poems become an articulation of experience ripped out of time.[12]

Dickinson herself was keenly aware of both the poem's temporal form and its ability to halt time, and in this poem she disrupts both the temporal progression and the timeless moment that poetry is thought to embody. In other words, the "Or" works to dislodge the temporal order to which the poem might otherwise succumb. For instance, while the image of the bird might otherwise create the sense of a timeless moment (in the sense that the image reduces time and action to a still point), the formal indeterminacy created by the "Or" fractures the potential for this.[13] For, just after the image has been solidified, the "Or" provides the alternative route that the bird had not been allowed. While she "differed in returning" (in other words, she was denied the choice to return) within the story that the poem narrates, the form produces an alternative ending. The "Or," in essence, provides the bird with a way out of the stasis that the poem might have otherwise produced for it.

By producing a formal alternative to the stasis and timelessness that can be regarded as both pleasurable and deathlike in itself, Dickinson questions the notion that a poem—and especially a poem that takes death as its subject—can ever really make time stand still. Even as this poem is uttered in time and draws attention to sounds as they occur in the poem itself, Dickinson is challenging the notion that either stopped time or temporal movement are representable in poetry. First, and as is clear when one reads the poem out loud, the insertion of the "Or" asks the reader to enter into a temporal loop, where she must hold the past and present sounds in mind, while simultaneously placing the future sounds next to (and not in front of) her. This mimics the experience of return, the very thing that is denied to the bird in the poem, and allows the reader to undergo a revision to her own temporal order, where the beats within poetic language are normally meant to carry her forward. Additionally, the poem declares itself to be preoccupied with sounds themselves: the quotes around "Currer Bell," "Haworth," and "Bronte" at least partially ask to be regarded as spoken. The poem also draws attention to issues of quietness: "Haworth" is "quiet" in the first stanza; the bird retired "quietly" in the second stanza; and, most interestingly, when the poem seeks out the bird in the third stanza, the aural dimension of the scene has disappeared and the bird is described as that which cannot "be seen," a strange move given the way a bird normally makes its presence known. In the fifth stanza, sounds have returned—"Soft fall the sounds of Eden"—but now it is the bird who is the listener, and this is clearly a new role, for it has a "puzzled ear." In other words, throughout the poem there is a rejection of the very sound that might otherwise provide it with the aural dimension that implies temporal movement.

"All overgrown by cunning moss" is absorbed by these temporal issues and by the ways in which poetic form and experimentation with that form necessarily disrupt them. The result of these disruptions is that the poem cannot produce the consolation that would otherwise emerge at its end. Consolation had long been the defining marker of the elegy, since it occurs as the closing move that allows the mourner to emerge into the place the dead person once inhabited. Peter Sacks proposes that such consolation occurs through reattachment to another object, yet elegies written in different historical moments and out of different cultural and religious traditions have varying requirements.[14] In pastoral elegies, for instance, this sense of closure was promised by the form of the poem, as both the singer of the elegy and the listener knew that the poem would end in a way similar to how it began. Milton famously broke this convention in "Lycidas" by employing an opening frame without returning to it in the end. He did not turn his back completely on the genre's expectation of consolation, however, but shifted it into the content of the poem when he wrote, near the end, "Weep no more, woeful Shepherds weep no more, / For Lycidas your sorrow is not dead." The image of resurrection with which "Lycidas" ends became the central trope in Puritan elegies but was later abandoned by the Romantics, whose poems, according to Abbie Findlay Potts, rely on the trope of "anagnorisis," or revelation, in order to produce consolation.[15] These poems attempt to discover meaning where it has not yet been revealed, and consolation occurs when this new knowledge is embraced. Yet the devices that produce consolation in Romantic elegies are weaker than those that came before, and in this period elegies begin to struggle to achieve consolation. According to Luciano, it is not entirely clear that by the nineteenth century consolation is still the elegy's endgame, since during this period "grief had become something to be cherished rather than shunned."[16] If we read Dickinson's disruption to the consolation that might have occurred in this poem within the history of the elegy, we can see that she is not radically departing from the genre's conventions, but is engaging with its evolving form.

If Dickinson had copied this poem on a piece of paper all by itself, our analysis might end here. Instead, though, she copied it as the second entry on the first sheet of Fascicle 7, a fascicle that includes several poems that take up the issue of death. What we can see by looking at these poems in their fascicle context is that Dickinson not only embraced the disruption that occurs within the individual poem but compounded this by employing a larger structure of connection, interruption, and breakage. "She went as quiet as the Dew" (F 159) and "She died— *this* was the way she died" (F 154)—poems that Dickinson copied on two other sheets in this fascicle—deepen, revise, and contradict the work done in "All overgrown by cunning moss," as both take up the subject of loss in ways that the first poem initiated. Both poems rewrite the moment of a dead one's departure, rethink how to articulate absence, and stage their own "Or" moments. Much like the "Or" that Dickinson placed within "All overgrown by cunning moss," an implied "Or" can be read at the edge of each fascicle sheet, an "Or" whose function it is to revise what has come earlier, multiply the possibilities, forestall closure, and produce the experience of reliving the same dark moment over and over again. These redeployments, modifications, and iterations across the sheets of a fascicle perform the unending nature of grief as it is felt within the same or similar occasions.

I am not the first to argue that poems in the fascicles might be read as related to each other through repetition. While Cameron primarily reads the relations between proximate poems on the same sheet, between a poem that ends one fascicle and the one that begins the next, and between two proximate fascicles, by extending her analysis of the variants within a poem in order to show the ways in which poems in the same fascicle might be read as variants of each other, she also argues for "associations within fascicles where poems are not physically proximate," specifying that these poems often "repeat and modify aspects of each other."[17] Domhnall Mitchell also argues that poems in the fascicles "endlessly revise each other."[18] But by looking closely at the kinds of poems that get repeated—namely, poems about death, mourning, and grief—I hope to situate this repetition as not simply a textual idiosyncrasy, but as one that is tied to the experience that the poems themselves attempt to articulate. In other words, while Cameron and Mitchell have drawn attention to the presence of repetition within a fascicle, neither allows that observation to inform a reading of Dickinson's approach to genre, since for both of them, the fascicles are simply collections of lyrics.

Whereas many of Dickinson's individual poems about death, such as "Over and over, like a Tune—" (F 406) and "It dont sound so terrible—quite—as it did—" (F 384), address, according to Faith Barrett, "the role of repetition in the survivor's attempt to come to terms with that loss," I will now show that Dickinson extends this strategy beyond the boundaries of the poem proper.[19] While Dickinson figures the subject of "All overgrown by cunning moss" as a bird who "Retire[d] to other latitudes," the third poem on the second sheet—"She went as quiet as the Dew" (F 159)—presents another way of rendering this death:

> She went as quiet as the Dew
>   a familiar
> From an Accustomed flower.
> Not like the Dew, did she return
> At the Accustomed hour!
>
> She dropt as softly as a star
> From out my summer's eve—
> Less skillful than Le Verriere
> It's sorer to believe!

In this poem, the dead woman has again departed and not returned when expected, but the poem has narrated the experience differently. This poem begins with the woman's death, with her going, as it were, from nature in the most natural way: in the same way that the dew leaves the flower, so the woman has left this world. But in the next two lines, this sense of natural process is disrupted by the recognition that were she actually the dew, she would have returned, a structure that echoes the bird's departure and non-return in "All overgrown by cunning moss." Additionally, the repetition of "Dew" and "Accustomed" as well as the words "a familiar" written above the first "Accustomed," produces disruption at the level of form.

Just when the reader has registered the formal disruption that occurs because of death, the poem switches gears. Whereas the dead woman was imagined as "Dew" in the first stanza, she is figured as a "star" in the second, therefore presenting a metaphorical variant, an option to see her in one or both of these ways. Through reference to "my summer's eve," the poem positions either itself or a person as the owner of the summer's eve from which the star/dead woman departs, an act that situates a mourner and elegist who, in this case, has a hard time believing that this woman is gone. The two stanzas present a choice, much like the choice that the added "Or" of "All overgrown by cunning moss" implied, as this poem also allows two options to exist simultaneously.

The implication at the end of "She went as quiet as the Dew" is that this mourner, while cognizant of the facts, struggles to accept that the woman is dead. It might not then be surprising that on the third sheet of this fascicle, we find a poem that reimagines and rearticulates, once again, a similar moment of death. The first two treatments of death are concerned with the process by which someone has died and perform how one might make sense of that leaving. This third attempt, "She died—*this* was the way she died" (F 154), the fifth poem on the third sheet, employs an entirely different perspective:

> She died—*this* was the way she died.
> And when her breath was done
> Took up her simple wardrobe
> And started for the sun—
> Her little figure at the gate
> The Angels must have spied,
> Since I could never find her
> Opon the mortal side.

As if all other considerations have not gotten it right, this poem attempts it this time in plain, straightforward language, closing the opening line uncharacteristically with a period. What occurs in the first line, "She died," is blunt, yet what happens after that first dash wraps meaning back into the form of the poem. "This," in its italicized state, can be read as a reference to the written document, and through it we are able to recognize that "this"—the story and our access to it—is a secondhand account that can never be the actual process of death itself. Dickinson intensifies this sense of belatedness in the second line, which does not narrate "the way she died," because now she is already dead: "And when her breath was done." As in the other two poems, the dead woman takes her leave of this world and heads up, towards a heaven where the angels live and that the mourner—again, the "I" is revealed late in the poem—realizes she can only imagine.

With the exception of the opening line, this poem can be read in the tradition of some of the sentimental elegies written by Dickinson's female contemporaries in that it celebrates the simplicity and bravery of one who now resides, as she should, with the angels. But Dickinson added two variant lines to this poem after she had copied it onto the fascicle sheet, a move that, as we have seen, can work to defer closure and undermine whatever consolation the poem might otherwise have produced. Inserted between the leaves of this sheet and eventually sewn into the fascicle when sewing time came was a slip of paper carrying the words:

> Or
> "Bernardine" Angels, up the hight
> Her trudging feet Espied—

Not only is Dickinson's method for including this "Or" different from that in "All overgrown by cunning moss," but these two lines are variants for lines that occur in the middle of the poem. The effect, then, is not the same as that of the "Or" in "All overgrown by cunning moss." Dickinson's use of more sophisticated diction and syntax in this variant creates a tension between the simplicity of the earlier lines and the complexity of the later option. While this "Or" does not revise the narrative movement of the poem, it does create a visual interruption as the slip literally sticks out, initially leaving readers unclear about its status, about where it should be applied, and about how it should be read. Only after reading all of the poems on the interior of this sheet can we figure out where these two lines are meant to fit. Once situated, these lines puncture the tightness of what we might consider to be the poem proper.

What we have seen in this examination of Fascicle 7 is a variety of treatments of death, all of which interrupt the temporality built into poetic form and upon which elegiac consolation depends. By dispersing these poems across the sheets that she then sewed together, Dickinson compounded these disruptions, reiterating the fracture in the form of the fascicle itself. As I move even further away from what we might identify as elegies in the next section, I will press on both the textual and temporal disruptions that continue to mark Dickinson's diverse considerations of death, loss, and grief.

INTERRUPTING THE JOURNEY

The opening poem on the first sheet of Fascicle 27, "There's been a Death, in the Opposite House" (F 547), neither mourns a dead person nor stages an "Or" moment that interrupts and loops time. Instead, it narrates the experience of observing a house in the aftermath of death. Unlike elegies, which usually focus on the specific aspects of the human who has died, this poem represses the dead person and instead highlights the space in which the death has occurred:

There's been a Death,
in the Opposite House,
As lately as Today—
I know it, by the numb
look
Such Houses have—alway—

The Neighbors rustle in and out—
The Doctor—drives away—
A Window opens like a Pod—
Abrupt—mechanically—

Somebody flings a Mattrass
out—
The Children hurry by—
They wonder if it died—on that—
I used to—when a Boy—

The Minister—goes stiffly in—
As if the House were His—
And He owned all the
Mourners—now—
And little Boys—besides.

And then the Milliner—
and the Man
Of the Appalling Trade—
To take the measure of
the House—

There'll be that Dark Parade—

Of Tassels—and of Coaches—
soon—
It's easy as a Sign—
The Intuition of the News—
In just a Country Town—

Each stanza is concerned with a different aspect of how to know that a death has taken place. The opening stanza focuses on when the death occurred and on the position of the onlooker: she is "Opposite" to the scene of death, in that she is across from it but also in that she is living. The second stanza presents the relation of inside and outside, of the space in which death occurred versus the world around it: the neighbors move between these two spaces; the doctor leaves the inside for the outside; and an unseen person opens a window from the inside, thereby allowing air to flow between the two spaces. In the third stanza we finally encounter a reference to the dead person, but only for this person to be referred to as an "it." Whereas everybody else in this poem has a profession ("Doctor," "Minister," "Milliner," and "Man of the Appalling Trade") or status in relation to others ("Neighbors," "Mourners," and "Boys"), this dead person has no identity. The fourth stanza addresses the issue of ownership as it positions the minister as the one who owns the house, the mourners, and the boys. If the minister owns, the auctioneer measures, and between the fourth and fifth stanzas everything is accounted for and ready to be assigned to the highest bidder. In a closing move to formalize its knowledge of death, the poem addresses the "Dark Parade" that will "soon" occur. Each of these aspects of the house and town exists as a "Sign" of the very incident that has been largely kept out of the poem.

While the poem is preoccupied with illuminating each of these signs, two moments disrupt the poem's desire for clarity and seamless move to the graveyard. The first is the unsettling line at the end of the third stanza: "I used to—when a Boy—." This line can be read in several ways: the "I" is a man who is referring to what happened when he was a boy; an actual boy (as well as, but not with, the minister) is going—across the stanza break—into the house; the "I" is mocking the minister by referring to him as a "Boy," as if in the space of the dash the boy becomes a minister; or the "I" sees a boy, but the presence of the minister interrupts the thought and attention is turned to him. There is no correct way to read this strange line and thus all of these explanations exist simultaneously. The second disruption occurs in line 20 ("There'll be that Dark Parade—") as Dickinson set this line off by itself, thereby breaking the pattern of not just quatrains, but topically discreet quatrains, that she had established for the poem. In both cases, Dickinson unsettled the ease with which the rest of the poem attempts to communicate the knowledge of death that can be gained through attention to the mundane material signs of it.

I want to pause on the "Dark Parade" for a moment because, as with the editing problems caused by the "Or" in "All overgrown by cunning moss," this line created difficulties for early readers and editors of the poem. When Todd published this poem in 1896, she printed this line as the last line of the fifth stanza, thereby creating a six-stanza poem. Linda Grimes has noted that anthologists who include this poem often make this alteration, one that, in Grimes's opinion, "weakens the total impact of the poem."[20] Besides just "regulariz[ing] that stanza," and therefore giving the poem "a uniform appearance," Grimes argues

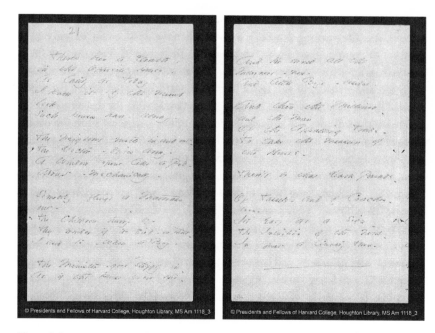

© Presidents and Fellows of Harvard College, Houghton Library, MS Am 1118_3

© Presidents and Fellows of Harvard College, Houghton Library, MS Am 1118_3

Figure 3.2
"There's been a Death, in the Opposite House" (F 547). By permission of The Houghton Library, Harvard University, MS Am 1118.3 (113a) © The President and Fellows of Harvard College.

that this editorial practice erases Dickinson's "specific reason for the separation . . . eliminat[ing] the special nuance of meaning that Dickinson achieved in her original."[21] In Grimes's view, "the funeral procession, 'that Dark Parade,' will occur after the measurement of the house and will literally separate itself from the house."[22] Grimes's attention to this line alerts us to the fact that by setting "There'll be that Dark Parade—" apart from the other lines of the poem (fig. 3.2), Dickinson interrupts the poem at the very moment when it moves from present to future ("There'll") and when it does away with the distinction between inside and out (all, even the dead body, are now outside).

Paraded across, among, and between the opening poems on the next five sheets, all of which begin with a poem about death, are a variety of Dickinson's approaches and resistances to writing about such a topic, resistance that, I would argue, is crystallized in the way that Dickinson both lingers on and halts the final movement in "There's been a Death, in the Opposite House." If that poem attempts to make the "Intuition" of death concrete by relaying the details that are visible to an outsider, then "I measure every Grief I meet" (F 550), the first poem on the second sheet, does a similar thing but from a different position. This poem enacts the very measuring that is disdained in "There's been a Death, in the Opposite House," and the possibilities of measurement and comparison of the various sources of grief, of which death is only one, are weighed. Unmoored to any particular story of grief, this uncharacteristically long poem looks at a variety of kinds of grief, questioning their nature and speculating about their relationship to the unnamed one that is the poem's focus. When it comes to the topic of death in the seventh stanza, Dickinson writes: "The Grieved—are many— / I am told— / There is the various Cause— / Death—is but one— / and comes but once— / And only nails the Eyes—." What is confusing about this characterization of death is the implication of death's effect: it comes only once, which implies it is final, but at the same time it "only nails the Eyes." When the eyes are nailed, the subject becomes blind, but, oddly enough, the other senses continue to function.

While "I measure every Grief I meet" speculates on the various causes of grief and is not conclusive in its assessment of death as one of them, the first poem on the third sheet, "There is a Langour of the Life" (F 552), narrates the actual process of death. In this poem, death is the thing that comes after pain, "When / the Soul / Has suffered all it can—." The second stanza makes concrete what it feels like to be in this state and drifting toward death: "A Drowsiness— diffuses— / A Dimness like a Fog / Envelopes Consciousness— / As Mists— obliterate a Crag." By the end of the poem this "it" is dead, as the "Surgeon" declares "There's no Vitality." Again Dickinson comes right up against the idea of death as final, but the stanza of fog and mists allow the dead one to continue existing in the image of the crag.

To summarize: The first poem on the first sheet narrates what happens after someone in a small town has died; the first poem on the second sheet wonders, in philosophical terms, how one can see the effects of death on the living; and the first poem on the third sheet narrates the process of death, from the per-spective of the dying person and the surgeon who is present. What we have here is a variety of ways of approaching the topic of death, as each one exists in a different relation to the event. In the first poem of the fourth sheet of this fascicle, Dickinson provides yet another approach. "It's Coming—the post-poneless Creature—" (F 556) figures death as a creature and narrates its jour-ney to the person it will take with it. In other words, this poem provides a prelude to all the experiences of death that we have already encountered across the sheets of Fascicle 27. And just when we think there are no other ways to address this subject, we read the opening poems on the two final sheets. The first poem on the fifth sheet, "Did Our Best Moment last—" (F 560), antici-pates death without making it concrete, as it addresses the topic only inciden-tally by way of wondering why we are not "given" ecstatic moments in life. The answer follows: "'Twould supersede the Heaven," and through this the poem imparts the belief that death will bring with it the joy we lack in life. The first poem on the sixth and last sheet of this fascicle, "She hideth Her the last—" (F 564), does not directly address the issue of death, but in its references to "The Closing of Her Eyes" and "low apartments in the / sod," implies just how close death is to the living.

Reading across the fascicle sheets in this way, with an eye to the topic of death that is foregrounded in the very first poem, we are left with a better understanding of the "Dark Parade" that interrupted the experience of the opening poem. Embedded in the image of the "Dark Parade" and in its status as a broken-off piece of poetic stanza is the knowledge of what will happen in the future, of the predictability of death rituals, and of the poem's desire to turn time around and resist the expected movement to the grave. As the interruption registered at the formal level in the opening poem is deployed over the course of the fascicle, the other sheets take up the invitation to think about different ways of rendering the experience of death.

By opening every sheet with one of these poems, Fascicle 27 presses to its extreme the poetics of interruption that I highlighted at work in Fascicle 7. But, as one might expect, the fascicles are not forty instances of the same thing. During the years in which Dickinson sewed fascicles, she worked in a variety of ways, developing and altering her relationship to what writing about death raises. Instead of showing how more of the fascicles work along these lines—see, for example, Fascicles 3, 9, 13, 16, and 20—I want to turn now to one of Dickinson's most famous poems about death to show how it employs these interruptions inside and outside of its frame.

"All overgrown by cunning moss" is concerned with the death of another, and "There's been a Death, in the Opposite House" declares in the very first line that a death has occurred, but in other poems it is often not clear who or what is dead. Sometimes without clarifying their subjects explicitly, Dickinson's poems tackle the possibility or impossibility of death, present various figures for death, and employ the perspectives of the already dead.[23] This happened in 1862, when Dickinson wrote the lines that begin "Because I could not stop for Death—" (F 479) on the first two sides of the first sheet of Fascicle 23:

Because I could not
stop for Death—
He kindly stopped for me—
The Carriage held but
just Ourselves—
And Immortality.

We slowly drove—He
knew no haste
And I had put away
My labor and my leisure
too,
For His Civility—

We passed the School,
where Children strove
At Recess—in the Ring—

We passed the Fields
of Gazing Grain—
We passed the Setting Sun—

Or rather—He passed
Us—
The Dews drew quivering
and Chill—
For only Gossamer, my
Gown—
My Tippet—only Tulle—

We paused before a
House that seemed
A Swelling of the Ground—
The Roof was scarcely
visible—
The Cornice—in the Ground—

Since then—'tis Centuries—
and yet
Feels shorter than the Day
I first surmised the
Horses' Heads
Were toward Eternity—

Whether the "I" of the poem did not have time to stop for death, possibly because of her "labor," or whether she was physically or emotionally incapable of it, this "kindly" civil figure stops for her, an action that one might see as a strange one to open both a poem and a fascicle sheet. But this stopping is the very thing that sets the action in motion, as the three figures of "I," Death, and Immortality huddle together in the carriage and begin their journey.[24] The two stanzas that follow are structured by the movement of the carriage through space and time: as it "slowly drove," it passed the school with its children, then the fields, and then the sun. Just as this tour of this town at dusk is getting started, Dickinson interrupts the linear progression of time by inserting, once again, although this time very differently, an "Or."

By the time we get to this poem's "Or" in its crucial fourth stanza, the journey has begun and a variety of landmarks have been passed. Having already passed the "Setting Sun," Dickinson revises the poem's narrative: "Or rather—He passed / Us—." At this moment we realize that the poem is grappling with the memory of how the events occurred, of how both space and time were ordered in this death scene. The pause at "Or" brings the carriage to the stopped position with which the poem began and allows the sun to move past it. While the "Or" in "All

overgrown by cunning moss" is a more drastic insertion that changes the structure of the poem, both "Or"s reveal crucial hinges in their poems, moments when
temporal progression is disrupted.[25]

While the journey seems to continue in the very next stanza, as the poem
returns to using the "We"s that opened so many earlier lines, Dickinson retains
the stasis temporarily achieved by the "Or," as the earlier anaphora "We passed"
is modified to "We paused." Now the passengers in the carriage encounter a grave
(whose we do not know), and with the repetition of "Ground," attention is drawn
downward and away from the horizon toward which the carriage had before been
moving. In a final, dizzying temporal move, the last stanza reveals that this journey occurred in the distant past, yet the time between that past moment and the
moment at which the poem is articulated feels shorter than the day in which the
actual journey took place or, we might say, shorter than the length of time it just
took to read the poem. Because of this, the poem is recast in this time warp, as it
is clearly uncertain about what register of time is most accurate. Dickinson's interruption of temporal progression halfway through the poem by means of the
"Or" sets the stage for this later sense of circular time.

In *Poems by Emily Dickinson* (1890), *The Complete Poems of Emily Dickinson*
(1924), *The Poems of Emily Dickinson* (1930), and *The Poems of Emily Dickinson*
(1937), Dickinson's editors left out the fourth stanza of this poem. In excising this
problematic stanza from the poem, not only is the confusion over who passed
whom as well as that unnerving chill deleted, but the journey continues in a
seamless manner: after passing the setting sun, the travelers pause in front of the
house. This route to (or through, or after) death is an easier one, as the poem
never stops to question the way in which the journey took place. As we saw in the
handling of "All overgrown by cunning moss," editors have been quick to treat
Dickinson's "Or"s as an editorial choice for them to make. Even here, in a poem in
which the "Or" is clearly the first word of a line and not a later addition between
stanzas, Dickinson's editors have chosen to read it as indicating a variant stanza.[26]

Starting with Johnson, it is obvious to later editors who had access to Dickinson's
manuscripts that this is not simply a variant stanza (for instance, which stanza
would it be a variant of or for?) but an integral part of the poem. The "Or" in
"Because I could not stop for Death—" is crucial in that, like the space that sets
"There'll be that Dark Parade—" aside, it interrupts the forward movement of the
poem, thereby challenging the notion of a journey toward death that occurs
unproblematically in time. By looping time back on itself in order to revise the
story of this journey, the poem halts. This stasis anticipates the final stanza's grappling with time, and, together these two moments work to distract us from the
fact that this journey does not seem to end. The "I" of the poem never exits the
carriage, and it is never made clear whose body is in the ground. In the final lines,
Dickinson alludes to the beginning of the journey when "the / Horses' Heads /
Were toward Eternity" and therefore avoids the deathlike finality that would be
implied by the journey's—and the poem's—terminus.

Throughout the rest of Fascicle 23, Dickinson renders a variety of death scenes. Across all six of the sheets, Dickinson copies poems that narrate the process of death, wonder about the nature of the afterlife, and present the figure of death: "He fought like those Who've nought to lose—" (F 480), "Wolfe demanded during Dying" (F 482), "Most she touched me by her muteness—" (F 483), "The Whole of it came not at once—" (F 485), "Presentiment—is that long shadow—on the Lawn—" (F 487), "You constituted Time—" (F 488), "The World—feels Dusty" (F 491), "The Day undressed—Herself—" (F 495), and "The Beggar Lad—dies early—" (F 496). As I have shown, we can read the dispersal of these poems across sheets and then the sewing together of these sheets as Dickinson's way of prolifer- ating and repeating the scene of death, an act that reveals the conundrum over the impossibility of consolation that resides at the heart of any rendering of death. But what do we make of the poems that appear on these sheets that seemingly have nothing to do with death? How are they affected by and how might they be read in relation to Dickinson's preoccupation with death as she copies and sews sheets?

In the last poem on the second sheet of Fascicle 23, "From Blank to Blank—" (F 484), Dickinson narrates a journey toward an "end," but it is not clear that this end is death. In a series of stunning echoes of her earlier poem that begins "After great pain, a formal feeling comes—" (F 372) and in a list of "or"s, "From Blank to Blank—" contemplates how nearing even an abstract end can only be rendered in multiple and conflicting ways:

> From Blank to Blank—
> A Threadless ⁺ Way + Course
> I pushed Mechanic feet—
> To stop—or perish—
> or advance—
> Alike indifferent—
>
> If end I gained + reached
> It ends beyond
> Indefinite disclosed—
> I shut my eyes—and
> groped as well
> 'Twas ⁺ lighter—to be Blind—
>   + firmer

This poem undertakes a journey, but this time there is no subject and no guide, and thus it follows "A Threadless Way" or, as the variant states, "Course." Without any organic sense of where to go, the poem has to push its own feet. The feet have been rendered "Mechanic," but so has the action of pushing them. The poet at some level declares her own poetic feet and her process of making them "Me- chanic," and the poem opens into a creative wasteland, with "Blank" and "Blank" existing as stand-ins for the language that would be present under other circum-stances. Where the poem is going and how it will get there no longer matter and, as we learn in the next line, getting there doesn't really matter either. The poem states that "To stop—or perish— / or advance— / Alike indifferent—," and with these "or"s Dickinson highlights a situation in which what looks like choices are actually not choices at all. To stop would be to stop the present movement; to perish would be to stop this movement and any further movement; to advance would be to move forward. What the poem is doing at the moment is not clear. From the outside, these actions seem to be anything but "Alike," as each one pro-duces a different outcome. But as we will see in the second stanza, none of these ways of approaching this journey will bring it to its close. The journey exists only as the movement around the options: "To stop—or perish— / or advance—."

In the second stanza, the poem addresses the issue of ending directly: "If end I gained / It ends beyond." It doesn't matter which option presented in the first stanza is taken, as none of them will lead to any true end. The poem blindly gropes along and, absent any desire to reach the end, the journey itself becomes the point. Without the landmarks encountered in "Because I could not stop for Death—," this poem is unable to chart its own progression or, paradoxically, to mark its own stasis. In this way, "From Blank to Blank—" narrates a different kind of journey, one that the end of "Because I could not stop for Death—" projects as a possibility. Whether the "I" of "From Blank to Blank—" is already dead or is groping towards death we cannot know, but we can see that the poem rejects the temporal markers that go along with any narration of experience. In being neither stopped nor in motion, and in light of the knowledge of death that surrounds this poem, this poem rejects both stasis and narration.

As I hope to have shown, Dickinson interrupts and sometimes halts individual poems from moving sequentially from their beginnings to their ends by creating a formal and temporal loop both inside and outside the poems themselves. By then re-creating the indeterminacy established in the individual poem over and between the poems on the sheets, Dickinson raises further questions about time, progression, and endings as they are raised by any consideration of death. In thinking about the many ways Dickinson addresses the subject of death, we see that in the same way that a literal death often confuses our sense of time, a poetic rendering of this experience can grapple just as profoundly with these questions. In other words, Dickinson's poems about death take their formal cues from the very disjunctions that death poses. In doing so, they end up using (and often rejecting) the expectation of both narrative movement and time stopped that poetry is thought to capture in its form. What we find in the fascicles—within the individual poems, in the spaces between them, and in their accumulations—is such a deep engagement with the questions of time that it causes time itself to loop, therefore foreclosing the possibility of closure and consolation that we often see as intrinsic to the very poems that rely on them most.

READING NINETEENTH-CENTURY WOMEN'S POETRY

While the poems discussed in this chapter are not elegies proper, I hope to have shown that when Dickinson writes about death she engages this flexible and malleable genre. By creating interruptions within these poems, she performs the impossibility of consolation that comes from temporal progression and tidy closure. By dispersing such treatments of death across sheets of paper that are themselves both connected to and broken from each other, she multiplies and magnifies the problem of consolation for poetic renderings of loss and mourning. By treating these strategies as Dickinson's engagement with the genre of elegy, I hope to have provided one way of placing her poems within discussions of this tradition. In this final section I will turn to some of the poems that Dickinson's female contemporaries were writing about death, in order to situate her work in the context of a widespread nineteenth-century preoccupation with the elegy. Reading Dickinson's generic interventions can, in turn, inform the way we read nineteenth-century American women's poetry of death and mourning.

Because the elegy has traditionally been a genre taken up by men, often on the eve of their entrance into the literary profession, how to read women's elegies—and, as I will explain, particularly nineteenth-century American women's elegies—is still up for debate. It is my contention, though, that reading Dickinson's poetry as critically engaged with the problems that writing elegies raises allows us to see her as neither the isolated, disenfranchised woman mourning privately for another nor as a radical social advocate who existed, by choice, outside of her culture's norms. Instead, by reading Dickinson as actively engaged with this literary genre, we can see that she was a woman poet who took her role as a poet seriously, interrogating the genres she had inherited and grappling with how she might reinvent them. This kind of analysis can provide us with new ways of thinking about how the elegy itself works and, by extension, how we might begin to incorporate women's writing into critical discussions of the genre. In other words, if Dickinson allows us to track the development of poetic genres differently—in this case identifying the temporal fracture at the heart of elegy, a fracture that she utilized in the structure of her poems and the making of her fascicles—then how might this change the way we read other nineteenth-century women's elegies?

The critical work on gender and elegy has largely centered on discussions of whether there is a defineable "male elegy" and "female elegy," for which there may be distinct and opposing characteristics.[27] While it is undoubtedly useful to understand how male and female writers have approached the genre differently, and many theorists of the elegy have weighed in on this debate, it seems to me that another way into the question of the relationship between gender and genre is to see what happens when we insert a poet like Dickinson into our understanding of the genre. In other words, instead of asking how she did it differently than her male contemporaries, instead of setting her aside or asking her to head up a counter-tradition, I want to ask how seeing what she did with and within the parameters of the genre she had inherited can allow us to situate other women's elegies in relation to that tradition. In order to do this, I am going to look at two very different poets, both of whom were Dickinson's contemporaries: Amelia Welby and Sarah Piatt.[28] While I do not mean to position these two poets against each other, I will stress the differences in their approaches to the genre, differences that Dickinson's interventions allow us to contextualize.

Unlike the disruptions to generic conventions that I have argued the fascicles undertake, many other elegies of Dickinson's and many of those by her female contemporaries work to produce the very consolation through closure that is required by the genre. For instance, when Dickinson sent an elegy to a friend or neighbor who had just lost a loved one, she often did not challenge the genre's conventions in the ways I have just discussed. Lines such as those that close "There came a day—at Summer's full—" (F 325), which she sent to the Reverend Edward S. Dwight upon the death of his wife, or those that begin "She sped as Petals from a Rose—" (F 897), which she sent to Sue upon the death of her niece, provide their readers with the consoling assurance that death is simply the beginning of a new journey. A look through mid-century anthologies of American women's verse yields hundreds of examples of the conventional, culturally-sanctioned elegies that women were writing and by which Dickinson was surrounded. For instance, in the gift book of women's verse that I mentioned in chapter 1, *Gems from American Female Poets*, we find Elizabeth Margaret Chandler's elegy for dead Revolutionary War soldiers in "The Battle Field"; Emma Embury's "Stanza: On the Death of the Duke of Reichstadt"; Amelia B. Welby's "On the Death of a Friend"; Julia H. Scott's poem about the death of her child, "My Child"; Mary E. Lee's "Lines to the Dead"; and Caroline M. Sawyer's "The Warrior's Dirge."[29] These poems all uphold the conventions of the genre in which they are working.

Take, for instance, Amelia B. Welby's "On the Death of a Friend," which is representative of the elegiac verse contained elsewhere in this anthology. The poem, which consists of six tightly woven stanzas of twelve iambic tetrameter lines, begins by looking toward certain elements of nature—the star that the dead friend loved best and the waves of the "shadowy-mantled seas"—that make the deceased present in the mourner's thoughts. It is these elements of nature that instigate the remembering and that produce the awakening of feelings:

> For never does the soft south wind
>   Steal o'er the hushed and lonely sea,
> But it awakens in my mind
>   A thousand memories of thee.
>
> (ll. 21–24)

Throughout the poem the dead friend is securely situated in heaven or, as the poem puts it, "in purer air." It meanders back through their time together on earth and bemoans the separation of their "kindred hearts," recalling the June in which they shared a particularly intimate moment. In the final stanza, Welby calls on the cycle of the seasons to provide her with the reassurance that June will return, allowing her once again to be filled with the memories that allow her to mourn:

> There are some hours that pass so soon,
>   Our spell-touched hearts scarce know they end:
> And so it is with that sweet June,
>   Ere thou wert lost, my gentle friend!
> Oh! how I'll watch each hour that closes
>   Through Autumn's soft and breezy reign,
> Till summer-blooms restore the roses,
>   And merry June shall come again!
> But ah! while float its sunny hours
>   O'er fragrant shore and trembling sea,
> Missing thy face among the flowers,
>   How my full heart will mourn for thee!
>
> (ll. 61–72)

Welby cannot resurrect her friend, but she still provides herself and her reader with a sense of consolation that comes from her mastery of time. Each year June will return, her heart will become full, and the dead friend will be remembered. This system is as tight as the poem's form, or at least the poem makes it appear this way. No alternative is proposed, and the poem ends with the consolation that comes from formal closure.

Dickinson's various "Or"s that this chapter has discussed suggest that she is particularly eager to fend off the closed-circuit, fully-explainable world that the strong sense of closure evoked in a poem like Welby's retrospectively produces. By interrupting temporal progression, Dickinson fractures the cycle within which most poems about death exist: in the case of "All overgrown by cunning moss," for example, while the seasons fulfilled their cycle of death and rebirth, the bird did not. Instead of explaining away the grief that emerges from this fracture, Dickinson embraces the fracture that death produces, as she forces us to return, time and again, to the scene of death. Yet it is attention to Dickinson's fractures and interruptions that allow us to see the very ways in which Welby is upholding the conventions of the genre that she has clearly been taught. Welby's poem may not radically alter the way in which we map the development of the genre through nineteenth-century America, but her highly conventional participation in it allows us to see the ways in which those conventions thrived.

Whereas Welby performed the very kind of elegiac closure that Dickinson's poems not only resist but actively challenge, I briefly want to look now at two poems by another woman poet of Dickinson's time, Sarah Piatt, one who, like Dickinson, took up the problem with consolation that exists at the heart of the genre.[30] While Piatt was a contemporary of Dickinson's, she led a very different kind of life as a poet, as the publication of her poems spanned the years between 1854 and 1911 and consisted of eighteen volumes of poems and the appearance of individual poems in thirty-seven literary periodicals and children's magazines.[31] Although the recent publication of *Palace-Burner: The Selected Poetry of Sarah Piatt* implicitly makes the case that she is a nineteenth-century American woman poet deserving of recovery, Piatt is still often read—when she is read—as one of the many sentimental female poets of her generation whose work would add very little to a literary history of the time. I turn to her poems here not to argue one way or the other, but instead to suggest that if we take Dickinson's desire for non-closure seriously and allow it to return us to nineteenth-century women's poetry with a keenness of eye for their potential formal interventions and generic preoccupations, we can read Piatt's own poems about death as participating in the development of the genre.

Take, for instance, "An After-Poem," a poem that Piatt published in 1871, and that, like Dickinson's "Because I could not stop for Death—" and "From Blank to Blank—," is not an elegy, but is a poem that mines the temporal problem that writing about death makes central:

> You will read, or you will not read,
> > That the lilies are whitest after they wither;
> That the fairest buds stay shut in the seed,
> > Though the bee in the dew say "Come you up hither."
>
> You have seen, if you were not blind,
> > That the moon can be crowded into a crescent,
> And promise us light that we never can find
> > When the midnights are wide and yellow and pleasant.
>
> You will know, or you will not know,
> > That the seas to the sun can fling their foam only,
> And keep all their terrible waters below
> > With the jewels and dead men quiet and lonely.

The title of this poem draws attention to time, and this preoccupation is compounded by an interest in the way that time shifts. This is conveyed in the opening line of each stanza: "You will read, or you will not read," "You have seen, if you were not blind," and "You will know, or you will not know." While the syntax of these lines is parallel, the unnerving move from future and negative future (in the first stanza) to past and conditional past (in the second stanza) and back to the future and negative future (in the third stanza) supplies the poem with a way of leaving open all we do not know about the state of those dead men on the sea floor. The first two stanzas, despite their opening lines, are filled with clichés about nature, and therefore do not prepare us for the "quiet and lonely" dead men that we encounter at the end. They are trapped under the surface of the ocean's foam and not in a settled way, for the many temporal shifts that occur within the poem allow it to rock and sway, threatening to bring those dead men up.

In a later poem, "At the Grave of a Suicide," published in the *Atlantic Monthly* in 1886, Piatt again tackles the problem with consolation, but this time by boldly addressing the circumstances under which consolation can be most challenging. Whereas many nineteenth-century elegies invoked the comfort provided by the knowledge that God has called the dead one away—a powerful poetic strategy inherited from Puritan elegies—here Piatt describes the grave of a person who, in his act of suicide, has made such comfort impossible:

> You sat in judgment on him,—you, whose feet
>   Were set in pleasant places; you, who found
> The Bitter Cup he dared to break still sweet,
>   And shut him from your consecrated ground.
>
> Come, if you think the dead man sleeps a whit
>   Less soundly in his grave,—come, look, I pray:
> A violet has consecrated it.
>   Henceforth you need not fear to walk this way.

While the final two lines might look like a consolation to this "You" in terms of both the suicide's death and the behavior that occurs in response to it, the poem's abrupt shift in temporal register with "henceforth" supplies it with neither an ending nor a way of quelling the issue of suicide. Instead, this is the beginning of the time when these two very different types of men will meet. Like Dickinson's poems, Piatt's poems that were written in response to the deaths she encountered and imagined defer closure through manipulations of the temporal journey that their inhabitants take.

The elegies of Welby and Piatt exist on opposite ends of a spectrum of women's poetry that was written in nineteenth-century America, poetry that often took up the topic of death and the grief that is generated from those deaths. Welby upholds a convention of the elegy that may already be on its way out, while Piatt takes every opportunity to challenge that convention, but both reveal that all elegies have to decide what to do with the problem of time and consolation. When we look at how dynamically and creatively Dickinson took up this problem and when we treat it as central to the genre, then the women poets who we thought had nothing to add to the genre's narrative suddenly become crucial participants in and innovators of it.

This chapter has recorded the story of a poet whose themes, materials, and concerns converge on the scene of her copying and sewing. My analysis of this process has focused on the poems in Fascicles 7, 27, and 23 and how the moments of interruption within and between them shed light on Dickinson's relationship to writing about death. By drawing attention to the specific way in which Dickinson approached this topic, I aim to provide new ways of thinking about how elegy itself works. Whether they embrace, break, or alter the move toward consolation that occurs in poetic time, elegies have the potential to rethink radically the very closure that is meant to give them their identity. It is, of course, impossible to say whether Dickinson consciously undertook the generic intervention that I have laid out here. What we can say is that Dickinson intended to make clusters of poems and she intended to place these clusters in relation to each other. What emerges from these acts is a picture of Dickinson in the act of rethinking what it means to write about death—a picture of a poet who, in constructing her fascicles, was at some level guided by her sense of the poetic traditions that she was engaging.

When read as printed lyrics, "All overgrown by cunning moss," "There's been a Death, in the Opposite House," and "Because I could not stop for Death—" not only appear stripped of their formal complexities, but they appear without the materials surrounding them that might instruct a reading of those complexities. Even when read in the context of their fascicles, where connections between and among poems become available, these poems will most likely continue to be read as if they were printed lyrics. While turning from the individual poem to the sheets that were sewn together does not do away with this hermeneutic circle—for one can imagine a theory of the sheets that is just as closed as a reading of the lyric—attention to Dickinson's sewn sheets reorients the discussion toward the materialities of Dickinson's writing. Attention to the sheet entails engaging Dickinson's poems on their own terms, probing the details of her process, asking what work her temporal and spatial interruptions are doing, and attempting to place this work within the historical and material contexts in which they were written. As Dickinson's poems reveal themselves to be engaging specific traditions, and as these traditions are taken up and modified through her choice of medium, Dickinson's poems become more than lyrics without histories.

CHAPTER 4

✧

Dickinson's "Sets"
and the Rejection of Sequence

In early 1864 Dickinson copied the lines that begin "I felt a Cleaving in my Mind—" (F 867) onto the second side of a sheet of folded stationery:

> I felt a Cleaving in
> my Mind—
> As if my Brain had
> split—
> I tried to match it—
> Seam by Seam—
> But could not make
> them fit—
>
> The thought behind, I
> [+] strove to join
> Unto the thought before—
> But Sequence ravelled
> out of [+] Sound—
> Like Balls—opon a
> Floor—
>
> > [+] tried [+] reach—

The figure of the split self, in this case imaged as the split brain, is one that Dickinson often played with, and this poem's attempt (and subsequent failure) to match up these corresponding units is typically where such investigations led. In "The first Day's Night had come—" (F 423) and "I—Years—had been—from

Home—" (F 440), for example, the knowledge of who one is in the present versus who one was in the past creates a kind of identity crisis. What is different about this poem is that, while it does address the disorder that comes from such a crisis, it does not linger on these feelings. Most readings of this poem argue that it is interested solely in the internal coordinates of its own making—its temporal disorder, its fractured logic of matching—but I want to suggest that by naming the rupture as a "Seam," this poem does three things: it imagines the sides of the brain as material that can be sewn together to become the thing that would halt the cleaving; it predicts the result of the cleaving/splitting as the unraveling of "Sequence"; and it directly addresses the material onto which it was copied.[1] It is this literal material context—the loose sheet of stationery— and the ways in which Dickinson uses it to interrogate the limitations of the kinds of sequences that her fascicle project set in motion, even as it resisted them, that will be my focus here.

Dickinson copied "I felt a Cleaving in my Mind—" onto the second side of a loose sheet of folded stationery that would later come to be known as "Set 2." After six years of methodically copying already-drafted and often already-sent poems onto sheets of folded stationery and then sewing those sheets together with string, Dickinson stopped sewing. I begin this chapter about the loose sheets that Dickinson copied between 1863 and 1865 and then again between 1871 and 1875 with this particular poem in order to highlight the relationship among this change in Dickinson's methods, the development of her post-fascicle poetics, and the material quality of the loose sheet with which she would now be engaged.[2] It is not simply that her use of the word "Seam" makes legible all of the different kinds of sewing that Dickinson must have done (including that of sewing her sheets together) or that her reference to "Sequence" names a logic by which a poet might order a large group of poems, but that this poem is copied onto a loose sheet at the very moment when it had become clear that matching her sheets "Seam to Seam," as it were, was no longer working. In the act of sewing depicted in this poem—or, more precisely, in its impossibility—we see Dickinson questioning the very modes of relation that the sewn fascicles had inadvertently yet quite logically set in motion.

Although Dickinson used the language of stitches, sewing, threads, strings, and seams throughout her poems, I will argue that Dickinson does not simply linger longer on this language at this moment, but that the actual poems that she was writing during this period (and the way that she was writing them) required her to abandon the very practice of sewing sheets that she references inside these poems.[3] Whereas the first chapter introduced the sheet as the principle unit of Dickinson's poetics, and chapters 2 and 3 pursued readings of her paper as readings of the relation between media and genre, this chapter will argue that at this point in Dickinson's practice, the logic of the sheet becomes the logic of the poem. As the material quality of the paper determines the form of her poems, and as her developing poetics requires a new material form, we enter upon a scene in which, we might say, the poems *are* the paper.

In this chapter we will see that the move to loose sheets was a gradual move and one that her earlier sewing practice eventually required her to make. What had previously been a compositional practice grounded in the potential relations of poems to each other in space (both on an individual sheet and, in more complicated ways, between sheets that Dickinson had sewn) now became a practice that actively confronted the limitations of such relations. Looking closely at the ways in which these poems were made will allow us to see that what might seem like an arbitrary or personal decision to alter her methods can be read as a reflection on the fact that Dickinson's fascicle project was, from the beginning, a way of thinking through the limitations of these relations. While we might think that this shift in Dickinson's practices simply returns her to the individual sheet, we will see that treating poems copied onto loose sheets only in relation to the sheet on which they are copied is limiting because it assumes that in ceasing to connect poems, Dickinson returns to an earlier poetics. Instead, it is my contention that Dickinson learned from the strategies she deployed in making the fascicles and that these late, loose sheets are the literal manifestation of the very boundaries of what a fascicle can and cannot do.

In this chapter I will look at a variety of material and textual details that radiate out from "I felt a Cleaving in my Mind—": the poem as it was copied onto the loose sheet we now call "Set 2"; an earlier draft of this poem's second stanza that was sent to Sue; several other poems that Dickinson made in similar ways and copied onto other loose sheets; the other poems that share the sheet with "I felt a Cleaving in my Mind—"; and the fascicle into which this sheet could have been sewn but was not. By calling attention to and separating out the problems of time (in regards to a poem's history) and space (in regards of a poem's physical placement) as they relate to this one poem's various drafts, manifestations, and histories, I hope to show how the poems copied onto loose sheets take up and reimagine sequence's time and space coordinates in this new material context, initiating a post-fascicle poetics that required a shift in Dickinson's compositional practice.

WHAT ARE THE "SETS"?

Before we look at the materials that reside at the center of this investigation, it is important to articulate a methodological break that I am making with almost all Dickinson scholars who have considered this subject: I will question, and ultimately reject, the term "sets" to describe Dickinson's loose sheets of fascicle stationery. This break is a result of my time in the archives, when I saw what Dickinson's loose sheets actually looked like. In some ways they look just like what one might imagine they would look like: fascicle sheets before the holes had been made in them. Indeed, for the most part, they are described by this minor difference. But because scholars call them "sets" and because Franklin reproduces them in groups that resemble the fascicles, someone visiting the archive at which they are housed is prepared to encounter loose sheets that are somehow related to each other, even if this mode of relation is unclear. Because few people have taken the time to describe these materials, I had the disorienting experience of calling up these "sets" and then not knowing what I was looking at.

In contrast with the fascicles, it is impossible to call up a "set" at the archive, as these are Franklin's regroupings of loose sheets that Todd had placed together and that still remain together. For instance, if you want to look at "Set 2," you have to call up Folder "87" at the Amherst College Archives, a folder that contains the seven loose sheets that Franklin later distributed among Sets 2, 5, 6a, 6b, and 7. Only once you cross-reference with *The Manuscript Books of Emily Dickinson* and extract the single sheet of folded stationery that has "I felt a Cleaving in my Mind—" copied on the inside verso, are you then looking at "Set 2" (fig. 4.1). This folded sheet looks just like a fascicle sheet that all four sides have been written on (in this case one poem appears on each side). The single-sheet quality of this "set" most obviously calls the terminology employed to describe it into question ("set" of what?), and it is worth noting that seven of the nineteen "sets" present this conundrum, as six of them are composed of one sheet and one is composed of one leaf.[4] On the opposite end of the spectrum, once you reconstruct "Set 5" you are faced with a multitude (ten, to be exact) of folded sheets of stationery, and it is entirely unclear (especially since you just did the shuffling of sheets) if there is an order to them.

Why do we call these different reconstructed objects "sets"? Why is this misnomer imposed on single sheets and why are multiple sheets placed together instead of being treated separately? Franklin tells the readers of his facsimile edition of the fascicles and sets that he groups unbound fascicle sheets "by similarity of paper and date."[5] While it may be true that similar paper is used for sheets in each of these reconstructed groupings and that the poems on these sheets were copied around the same time, Dickinson did not group these poems together. In other words, it has yet to be made explicit to present day readers and scholars that while the fascicles are Dickinson's groupings, the "sets" are the twentieth-century textual scholar's.[6] Further, I would argue that while by grouping together these sheets Franklin takes his cue from Dickinson's method (in that he respects her earlier practice of placing sheets in relation to each other), this is actually a misreading of that method in that he groups by paper and date, a methodology that Dickinson never employed and that undermines the idea that she may have imagined a variety of organizing principles for her sewn sheets.

This chapter proceeds from the position that we have retrospectively imposed order on these materials, going so far as to give them the misleading name "sets," when in reality these loose sheets bear no significant relation to each other beside the fact that they contain poems that were sometimes copied at a similar moment. One reason for this misleading designation may be that some scholars who know Dickinson's fascicles well could not abandon the idea

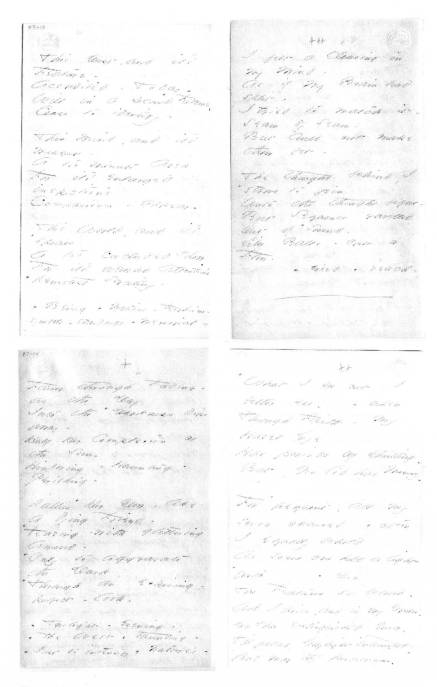

Figure 4.1
"Set 2." Courtesy, Archives & Special Collections, Amherst College.

of her methodically-planned and well-orchestrated poetic project and therefore continued to read organizing logics where there were none. In other words, scholars have found it impossible to read Dickinson's manuscripts as anything other than fascicles. Domhnall Mitchell, for example, describes these objects as "unbound collections," therefore acknowledging their unbound state but also still relying on the coherence that "collection" implies.[7] He even goes so far as to refer to them as part of Dickinson's "fascicle form of bookkeeping," with the simple qualification that they were "collated" but not "bound."[8]

While Mitchell makes the difference between fascicles and sets into something more minor than it is (and therefore claims the poems in the "sets" as those that we might read along whatever lines we establish for reading the poems in the fascicles), others acknowledge the difference as major and are left with a different conundrum. Sharon Cameron, for instance, declares "the importance of a different understanding of those poems intended to be bound than of those for which no binding appears to have been intended."[9] The result of acknowledging that "the sets have many of the characteristics of the fascicles except that they were not stab-bound and tied" is that Cameron leaves them out of her consideration of the fascicles.[10] Because they are so different from the fascicles, they cannot be considered alongside them in her study. But just because there is no obvious structure to these materials (and that whatever structure might exist is complicated by the existence of the fascicles to which they are related but are not the same as), does not mean that Dickinson's loose sheets—the term I will use instead of "sets"—are incomprehensible. But how are we to understand these materials that are connected to, even if almost entirely different from, the fascicles?

Current critical approaches to this stage in Dickinson's writing invite us to treat the change in her practices as the result of an exterior pressure, one that is often rendered as some event that took place in Dickinson's life—for instance, her mother's stroke, Dickinson's own vision trouble, or the end of the Civil War. Along the lines of these explanations, Dickinson found herself in a changed position in relation to her writing, copying, and sewing processes.[11] Other explanations, both of which Franklin suggests, are that Dickinson came to find the sewn fascicles difficult to use and that at this point in Dickinson's life "her need for self-publication declined, and with it the desire to leave an organized legacy for the world."[12] Habegger supports the second of these explanations when he calls attention to the issues of self-editing and preservation that these materials bring into focus: "From 1871 to 1875, resuming her practice of 1865, Dickinson made clean copies of her poetry on folded sets of stationery. This self-editing, however, was more selective and sporadic than the systematic preservation of 1858–1865, when she preserved the vast preponderance of her work in manuscript books and sets. In the seventies the proportions were reversed, two-thirds of her poems never being collected."[13] Both theories are faulty because Dickinson continued to write an enormous number of poems and letters during these years, and although she altered this specific element of her process, she maintained her customary drafting and copying process. While it may be true that Dickinson wanted to be able to browse and find poems more quickly, it remains entirely unclear why this would have been initially easier to do when sheets were sewn together but then eventually easier when loose.

For Dickinson, most processes were gradual and, as she declares in "Crumbling is not an instant's Act" (F 1010)—a poem that is copied onto a loose sheet in 1865—never actually the result of a single, drastic event. According to Cameron, in fact, this poem tells us "that the beginning of a process contains and predicts its conclusion."[14] Indeed, Dickinson had the loose sheet in mind for a long time before she started leaving them this way. For instance, during the first four years of making the fascicles, Dickinson often copied poems onto sheets and then held onto them until she was ready to sew them into a fascicle.[15] Between copying sheets that were eventually sewn together, Dickinson was copying and sewing many other sheets that now belong to other fascicles entirely, and in this way she was constantly making and retaining loose sheets. While this strategy was temporarily abandoned (as far as we know, all of the fascicles after Fascicle 15 were copied without these kinds of interruptions), she returned to it two years before fully ceasing to sew sheets together when she left "a few miscellaneous or leftover fascicle sheets unbound"—the sheets that Franklin tells us eventually became Sets 1–4.[16] In other words, Dickinson had been experimenting with loose sheets much earlier on in her fascicle-making process in ways that have yet to be recognized because these sheets were eventually absorbed into the fascicles themselves. Seeing this move as a gradual one allows us to see the sheets as both the units that make up her fascicles and the units that develop a resistance to being sewn together.

If we read the loose sheets as a material that has always been present and that Dickinson comes to embrace more fully after an extended engagement with sewn sheets, then we can see that there is something about the poems themselves and about Dickinson's sense of their relation to each other that both produces and becomes most fully realized in the loose sheets. Returning to "I felt a Cleaving in my Mind—," then, we can see that this poem is largely about its inability, in the face of seams not matching, to maintain a balance between the most crucial coordinates of a sequence, those of time and space. "I felt a Cleaving in my Mind—" identifies the problems of sequence by confusing and compounding its own temporal and spatial registers in such a way that the final move to unravel sequence seems only natural. What, in the first stanza, is figured as the physical splitting of the brain is, in the second stanza, presented as both a spatial and temporal disjunction. It is no longer simply two sides that need to be matched up, but it is the emotion, cognition, and language that reside inside "the thought behind" and "the thought before." But by using these terms—"behind" and "before"—Dickinson creates a problem, albeit a productive one, for her poem. "Behind" is a word that is associated with space, and because of this, its opposite would be something like "in front." But instead of using this term, Dickinson uses the word "before." If we read "before" spatially, then it is easy to match "the thought behind" to "the thought before," and even if this seems slightly off, we understand that maybe in Dickinson's vernacular these things were opposites or maybe Dickinson simply needed a two-beat word here. But given the fact that "before" is primarily a temporal designation, coupled with the fact that this stanza will ultimately not allow for the joining that the poem declares itself to be initially after, "the thought before" can be read as requiring what would be its opposite in time—something like "the thought after"—which, of course, is not present in the poem. In other words, in the midst of reflecting on the matching of seams that she is literally faced with, Dickinson mixes spatial and temporal terms in a way that not only, as Jed Deppman has put it, "opens up the ambiguity of the 'Cleaving' event itself," but suggests a continuity and rupture between space and time, conflates the planes on which such knowledge can be experienced, and imagines a matching process that is ultimately revealed to be impossible.[17]

The final lines of the poem press even deeper into this problem. Whereas the first variant indicated in this poem ("tried" for "strove" in line 5) provides a benign synonym, Dickinson indicated "reach" as a variant for "Sound," a option that allows us to read "Sound" as a designation of space (as in, out of earshot, or off in the next room). It is not surprising that in the 1896 *Poems* this variant was adopted, as it makes it much easier to grasp the meaning of this line. But if "reach" allows for a spatial reading, then "Sound" produces an understanding of the scene that exists on an aural level: once "Sound" loses its "Sequence," it just becomes noise, and noise can only be registered temporally. The beauty of the variant here is that depending on which word you read, the final line of the poem means something different. The notion of "Sequence" raveling out of "reach," coupled with the final line's reference to "Balls—upon a Floor—," conjures up a very concrete visual image of actual balls rolling, say, around a corner. If it is "Sound" that you read, then the balls upon the floor come to represent, in aural and temporal terms, an irregular, disorderly, unmeaningful utterance. And if you subscribe to Cameron's suggestion that we read the variants as "non-exclusive alternatives," then we need not choose between these words and are faced with a crystallization of sequence's time/space conundrum.[18]

In the face of this time/space imbalance a disorder ensues that demands Dickinson make a change in her compositional practices. As a result, poems on the loose sheets are largely unbalanced, albeit in highly productive ways, precisely because they confront the temporal and spatial problems of sequence. This is not to say that poems copied onto sheets that were sewn together are not also unbalanced, but there was a strong enough emphasis on the relations of poems to each other on the sheet and between sheets that these imbalances were supported by the surrounding poems. As Dickinson confronts the limitations of sequence as a structuring device, the unit of the sheet is itself thrown into question. Dickinson's interrogation of the coordinates of sequence is a reaction to the ways in which the fascicles, in being sewn together, were made to function like sequences even if, as we saw in chapter 1, they resist this designation by being sheets that were stacked as individual clusters instead of nested to make books.[19]

COMPOSITIONAL TIME

If we think about how "I felt a Cleaving in my Mind—" was made in time we are led to the fact that an earlier version of the second stanza had been sent to Sue shortly before the whole was copied onto the loose sheet.[20] These words were copied on a leaf of paper that was torn from a sheet down the right side and was eventually folded in thirds before being given to Sue:

> The Dust behind
> I strove to join
> Unto the Disk
> before—
> But Sequence
> ravelled out of
> Sound
> Like Balls opon
> A Floor—

The most striking difference in content is that in the version sent to Sue, Dickinson writes "Dust" where she will later write "thought," and she writes "Disk" where she will later write "thought" again. In this transition from one set of terms to another we can see Dickinson playing with her uses of figurative language. On the one hand what we might read as material, physical, and tangible ("Dust" and "Disk" as things of this world) in the version to Sue becomes a cerebral abstraction ("thought") in the longer poem. On the other hand, what we might read as theological ("Dust" as body and "Disk" as Sun/Son) becomes domestic and commonplace (everyone has a "thought"). In other words, we can read her later revision as either a move to intensify the metaphorical or a move away from the metaphorical, but either way it allows us to see how the poem grew from some earlier confrontation with unmatchable things. Given the complexity of the version of "I felt a Cleaving in my Mind—" copied on the loose sheet, we might say that the single stanza sent to Sue was a less developed version of it. Even if we treat "Dust" and "Disk" as terms that are related in a vaguely theological way and therefore read Dickinson as pointing out their relation as potentially productively incoherent, her revision of this stanza shifts the emphasis away from this preoccupation and places it within the spatial/temporal and visual/aural dynamics that I highlighted in my earlier reading of the entire poem. In other words, the later version of this poem embeds the problem of the earlier draft by addressing (albeit theoretically) that which comes "before" it in time.

When Dickinson sent Sue "The Dust behind" she was engaging in what would become the well-honed practice of sending Sue fragmentary pieces of poems that would eventually become longer ones that she would then copy onto loose sheets.[21] This was a practice that emerged during Dickinson's process of copying loose sheets, was specific to her post-fascicle process for drafting poems, and was part of her correspondence with Sue in particular. Many more poems went to Sue before being copied onto loose sheets than went to anyone else (Dickinson sent at least thirty-six poems to Sue before copying them on loose sheets, whereas a total of twenty-six poems were dispersed among all of her other correspondents, six of which were also sent to Sue) and at least a third of the ones sent to Sue were sent as early fragments of what later became longer poems, whereas this only happened in two of the twenty-six instances of texts sent to other correspondents. One might argue that we cannot know for sure that Dickinson had not already drafted the longer versions of these poems before sending Sue their final lines. While we cannot rule out this possibility entirely, it seems highly unlikely to me. If they had been sent to Sue, and Sue and Dickinson were corresponding about the final stanzas of longer poems, much in the way they had about "Safe in their Alabaster Chambers—" (F 124), then it is very odd that none of these would have survived. It also seems unlikely that Dickinson would have drafted longer versions and only sent Sue the final lines, out of the context of their longer poems. Lastly, the manuscripts show that the leaves on which Dickinson copied these texts to Sue indicate that she did not simply forget to copy the earlier stanzas of these poems, or that her later editors misplaced earlier pages of longer notes, but that Dickinson meant for Sue to have these lines and only these lines, in these forms. For these reasons, I read these situations as ones in which Dickinson wrote the final lines first, sent them to Sue, then wrote the longer poems to which these lines eventually served as concluding lines, finally copying them onto loose sheets. I will now turn to two other examples in order to explore what the specifics of this drafting and sending practice can tell us about this stage in Dickinson's poetics and what it has to do with the loose sheets.

In 1864 Dickinson sent Sue four lines that would later become the last stanza of the four-stanza poem "This Consciousness that is aware" (F 817), which she copied onto a loose sheet. Addressed "Sue" on the back side and signed "Emily" at the bottom, these four lines read as a cryptic (maybe because private) definition of the soul:

> Adventure most unto
> itself
> The Soul condemned
> to be
> Attended by a single
> Hound
> It's own identity—

In these lines Dickinson attempts to articulate her definition of the "Soul" as that which is tangled in its own solitariness, with its "identity" as its only companion. A year after producing this definition, Dickinson wrote the poem that sets these lines up, copying all four stanzas onto a sheet that is now considered part of "Set 6a":

> This Consciousness that
> is aware
> Of Neighbors and the Sun
> Will be the one aware
> of Death
> And that itself alone
>
> Is traversing the interval
> Experience between
> And most profound
> experiment
> Appointed unto Men—
>
> How adequate unto itself
> It's properties shall be
> Itself unto itself and None
> Shall make discovery—
>
> Adventure most unto
> itself
> The Soul condemned to be—
> Attended by a single
> Hound
> It's own identity.

In this later poem, "Consciousness" is the subject, but instead of attempting to define what "This Consciousness" is all about, the poem simply posits it as the being that is "aware of Death." While one can read the "itself" of "And that itself alone" as a reference to "Death" (as in, consciousness is only aware of death), the enjambed nature of the poem's fourth and fifth lines lead me to read "itself" as "Consciousness" (as in, consciousness, with its knowledge of death, is traversing alone). Consciousness travels through life (or, as Dickinson renders it, "the interval," "experience," and the "most profound experiment"), and it does so in a state of extreme aloneness. Consciousness requires nothing external to it for its existence, and this is stressed by the circular phrase "Itself unto itself," as it crystallizes the two earlier uses of "itself" by now placing them in the same syntactical unit. In the internal space of "Consciousness," the emphasis is not on "discovery" but on "Adventure." Although Dickinson uses the negative word "condemned" to describe the "Soul" (which we can now read as another manifestation of "Consciousness"), there is the sense that this state in which process is valued over product is being at least partly celebrated here. While the poem ends by again holding out the idea that company might be had on this journey and then ripping away that hope and leaving "Consciousness"/"The Soul" in a state of utter isolation, the poem's tight phrasal circuits make this state seem both inevitable and powerful.

Given that the first three stanzas provide a different figure for the "Soul," some of this figure's backstory, the context for understanding what Dickinson means by "Adventure," and several of the linguistic and rhetorical patterns that the last stanza will employ, it should seem strange that the last stanza could have once been just four lines sent in a note to Sue. Yet here we see Dickinson's process of making a poem: what begins as a cryptic attempt at a definition of the "Soul," sent to Sue for sharing or for feedback, becomes a more extended description of that "Soul." The formal stationery that Dickinson eventually copied it on requires that the poem not be fragmentary, but we can see Dickinson also pushing against this expectation as each stanza creates a tightly internal world that is right on the cusp of not needing what comes next.

Dickinson employed a similar strategy when, in 1861, she sent Sue a note containing what would, in this case, four years later, become the final lines of the two-stanza poem, "'Tis Anguish grander than Delight" (F 192), which she copied onto an loose sheet:

> Dear Sue—
>   I'm thinking
> on that other morn—
> When Cerements—let
> go—
> And Creatures—clad
> in Victory—
> Go up—by two—and
> two!
>   Emily.

When Martha Dickinson Bianchi published this note in *The Single Hound* in 1914, she printed it as a four-line poem. Franklin, on the other hand, reads it as three lines of poetry "preceded by a sentence, itself in iambic tetrameter."[22] What both of these printings of the note speak to is that, as I argued in chapter 2, once we know that parts of Dickinson's letters and notes either were or later became poems in other contexts, we read that knowledge back into earlier incarnations of that language that is not marked as such. For, in the case of this note to Sue it makes no sense to separate "I'm thinking on that other morn—" from "When Cerements—let go—," given that the syntax (specifically the way that the "when" clause depends on the opening statement) pulls them together. It also makes no sense to print it as a four-line poem, given the fact that the note opens with both a personal address and the articulation of what can be read as a casual thought. By 1861, Sue was accustomed to receiving notes that read both like epistolary musings and that scan as lines of poetry, in alternating iambic tetrameter and trimeter, and therefore probably knew how to read this.[23]

Four years after having sent this note to Sue, Dickinson wrote the following poem on the last side of a loose sheet that is part of what we now call "Set 7":

> 'Tis Anguish grander
> than Delight
> 'Tis Resurrection Pain—
> The meeting Bands
> of smitten Face
> We questioned to, again—
>
> 'Tis Transport wild
> as thrills the Graves
> When Cerements let
> go
> And Creatures clad
> in Miracle
> Go up by Two and
> Two—

In the note to Sue it is not clear if the "other morn" is a casual, domestic, and private way of speaking about some shared time in the past or if it is a reference to the Resurrection, but it is clear that Dickinson is thinking about the dead body's release from the things of this world (namely, the "Cerements," or graveclothes) into a state of being clothed by the abstract notion of "Victory." In the later poem, the casual "I'm thinking on that other morn" is now replaced by the more formal set up of three descriptions of what this process of re-clothing oneself, as it were, in what is now rendered as "Miracle," is like: it is an "Anguish grander than Delight," it is "Resurrection Pain," and it is a "Transport wild as thrills the Graves." It is exactly these kinds of metaphors that Dickinson has spent the four years between the note to Sue and the copying of this poem developing, as we can see from this poem's compositional history that she had the core of the poem from the very beginning. Even though she gives a taste of what will come in the first stanza's final lines ("The meeting Bands of smitten Face"), the reader really only knows what the withheld subject/action of this poem is at the very end.

What does it mean to write the end of a poem first? What does a poem look and sound like when the core of its revelation is drafted before the rest of the poem is copied out in full? What does it mean that these poems have known their seemingly spontaneous revelations for longer than we think they have? Why do the longer, more formal, and more fleshed out versions of these earlier lines and notes get copied onto loose sheets of stationery instead of being sewn into fascicles? First, the general impression is that Dickinson's poems often make their readers feel as if they do not always know where they are heading. This is a strategy that results in the reader's sense that she has stumbled upon revelation, a feeling that David Porter gestures at when he refers to her method as "a knowing how to start but without a goal in view."[24] Noting that the final stanzas of these poems were both written first and sent to Sue radically changes the way we approach their internal logics. Additionally, it is my contention that this strategy for making poems developed in conjunction with Dickinson's move to loose sheets, for it was not a method that Dickinson had used when she was sewing fascicles.[25] Because many of the poems copied onto loose sheets grew out of the process of fragmentary sending and of being made from back to front, they embody a complicated relation to issues of how lines, letters, fragments, and poems evolve in compositional time. I would also like to suggest that copying poems onto loose sheets of stationery after what I am reading as their earlier existence in partial form can be read hand in hand with Dickinson's poetics of this period, even when it comes to poems that we do not know were made this way. Poems copied onto loose sheets between 1863 and 1875 depend less on the poems that surround them on the sheet, and because of this, poems from this period both contain their own narratives more fully and at the same time are always on the brink of re-becoming the fragments they were. They are, we might say, more preoccupied with "the thought before" in compositional time than they are with the relations between poems in physical space. As Dickinson deemphasizes the relationship that her poems have to each other in space, the poems themselves register a greater dependency on their interiors, as they are often the result of a starting-at-the-end process. In being made backwards, they stop up their own revelations, which in turn makes them more self-contained at the same time that they figure the unraveling of which they are a part.

LOOSE SHEETS V. SEWN SHEETS

If sewing sheets together established a certain degree of finality to the poems written on those sheets—I say "certain degree" because, as we saw in chapter 2, Dickinson was often returning to these texts and rethinking them—the decision not to sew keeps poems in some sort of extended intermediate state. This is not to say that the sewn fascicles do not embed an internal resistance to this finality in their form—chapter 3 was largely an exploration of this resistance to closure—but that the move from copying poems onto sheets that are sewn to copying poems onto those that are not can be read as a reflection on the limitations of the relations that the fascicles had set in motion. Before we can make such an assessment, though, we need to look at the sheet onto which "I felt a Cleaving in my Mind—" was copied, so as to understand how the identity of this sheet differs from the identity of the sheets to which it might have been sewn in a fascicle proper.

Dickinson copied the lines that begin "This Dust, and it's Feature—" (F 866) on the first side of this sheet:

> This Dust, and it's
> Feature—
> Accredited—Today—
> Will in a second⁺ Future—
> Cease to identify—
>
> This Mind, and it's
> measure—
> A too minute Area
> For it's enlarged
> inspection's
> Comparison—appear—
>
> This World, and it's
> ⁺ species
> A too concluded show
> For it's absorbed Attention's
> ⁺ Remotest scrutiny—
>
> + Being + Nations—Fashions—
> symbols—standards + Memorial—

The repeated pointing that this poem engages in ("This" . . . "This" . . . "This". . .) makes what might be read as the increasingly abstract concepts of body, mind, and world more physical and present. By starting with "Dust," Dickinson begins with a reflection on the materials that both surround and constitute the writer (remember that "I felt a Cleaving in my Mind—" began as a meditation on such "Dust" as well), calling attention to the physical world in which our bodies and the particles of life in which we live are "Accredited—Today" but will eventually "cease to identify." The future is bleak, and each of the two subsequent stanzas reinforces this. Both the "Mind" and the "World" do not have the necessary characteristics to prevail in the face of time: the mind is "A too minute Area" and the world is "A too concluded show."

To read "I felt a Cleaving in my Mind—" in relation to "This Dust, and it's Feature—" is to highlight the literal material context of these poems as the sheet and to engage, at some level, in a spatial reading. "This Dust, and it's Feature—" comes first on the sheet and there might be good reason to think that it functions to initiate a concern with some distant future for which the structures of the present are not prepared. The "Cleaving" and "splitting" might be read, then, as reactions to the impenetrable nature of the prior poem's conceptual frame. If we read the sheet this way, then it is also important to look at what comes after "I felt a Cleaving in my Mind—." But unlike what we might expect, the two poems that follow it on the sheet do not model an alternative to sequence that the end of "I felt a Cleaving in my Mind—" rejects, nor do they enact the raveling out that it posits in some future time and space. Instead, they experiment with form and with resemblances in ways that we might say the unmatching performed in "I felt a Cleaving in my Mind—" makes possible. This is different from riding the sequence (or the impossibility of sequence) out, as the poems that follow in space find new ways to crystallize the problem of sequence's time and space coordinates.

The third poem on the sheet—"Fairer through Fading—as the Day" (F 868)—reads unlike Dickinson's other poems, as it is written in iambic tetrameter with a consistent trochaic first foot, an a-a-b-c rhyme scheme, eight words ending in "ing," and a variant in each of the lines of the second stanza (creating almost what looks on the manuscript page like a third stanza):

> Fairer through Fading—
> as the Day
> Into the [+] Darkness dips
> away—
> Half Her Complexion of
> the Sun—
> Hindering—Haunting—
> Perishing—
>
> Rallies [+] Her Glow, like
> a dying Friend—
> [+] Teazing, with glittering
> Amend—
> [+] Only to aggravate
> the Dark
> [+] Through an expiring—
> perfect—look—
>
> + Twilight—Evening—
> + the West + Taunting—
> + Just to intensify + Nature's—

Not only does the form of the poem walk the thin line between upholding and challenging order (what sounds like a lack of meter is really quite a strict metical form, with only three of the poem's thirty-two feet varying from the pattern that is quickly established), but the logic of the poem's content and meaning is hopelessly circular. While we might read the initial "as" as a word denoting motion (as a synonym for "while"), the initial "Fairer through Fading" implies that the unidentified subject of this poem (the one who is "Fairer through Fading") is, most likely, human, as this is a commonplace way of describing someone who is dying. A comparison is therefore established between this unnamed person and "the Day," in both of their acts of "Fading." But at the beginning of the second stanza the unnamed dying person/fading day is now compared (this time through a "like" instead of an "as") to "a dying Friend." In other words, the dying person is like the fading day, which is like the dying friend. Instead of saying that Dickinson has lost track of her initial comparison or that all sense breaks down in the face of the grief associated with a situation that would call for such a comparison, I want to argue that the loose sheet allows, to some extent, for a situation to be described in unmatchable comparisons and ultimately faulty resemblances. It should come as no surprise that immediately after entering the second (and, as we have seen, ultimately nonsensical) comparison, the poem is dominated by ⁺'s and the corresponding words that they signal at the bottom of the page. We might say, then, that once inside the part of the poem where the combination of similes does away with the possibility of matching, everything becomes variant and doubled. Not only are there different ways that each of the subsequent lines can begin, but in the case of the final variant ("Nature's" for "Through an"), there is a completely different syntax for the final line of the poem.

This poem's sites of formal mismatching are anticipated by the move towards some greater chaos that is depicted in "I felt a Cleaving in my Mind—." But it is not as if Dickinson had figured this out already, or had mastered just what the "Balls—opon a Floor" are going to look and sound like, in all their disarray. This is made clear by the fourth and last poem on the sheet—"What I see not, I better see—" (F 869)—which attempts to establish connections between itself and the poems that have come before it while foregrounding a different version of the unmatchable:

> ⁺ What I see not, I
> better see— + when
> Through Faith—My
> Hazel Eye
> Has periods of shutting—
> But, No lid has Memory—
>
> For ⁺ frequent, all my
> Sense obscured + often
> I equally behold
> As some one held a light
> ⁺ unto + opon
> The Features so beloved—
> And I arise—and in my Dream—
> Do Thee distinguished Grace—
> Till jealous Daylight interrupt—
> And mar thy perfectness—

While we might feel initially inclined to draw meaning from the fact that this poem looks so strange on the page, with the interlined variants and what seems to be a very bottom heavy form, those characteristics can be explained by the fact the Dickinson was trying to get the whole of this poem (with its variants) on this sheet, and she was quickly running out of room. It is not that we need to imagine the variants at the bottom and imagine a stanza break before the line that begins "And I arise," for we are faced with the way Dickinson copied it here, but this is simply to say that it would be shortsighted to draw too much meaning from what looks like a shift in her methods and an experimentation with a longer, clunkier final stanza.

Suspending those features for the moment, though, does not regularize this poem's content or structure. Dickinson indicated a variant for the very first word of the poem, which was something she did only very rarely, and in this case the variant indicates the difference between reading this line as about some unseen/ seen thing (as implied by "what") and about the time in which such nonseeing/ seeing occurs (as implied by the "when"). In other words, what is an emphasis on the object itself can, it seems, just as easily be shifted to an emphasis on the temporal frame in which an object might be viewed. The rest of the stanza orients itself more towards the emphasis on subject instead of on time, as it compares two different ways of seeing. The first line implies that the poem's "what" is probably God: she can't see God with her eyes, but she can see God when her eyes are closed and she calls on her "Faith." This comparison turns "Faith" into an alternative way to see, one that the poem declares even allows for "better" seeing. Just when we think that all factors line up here, we encounter the strange fourth line ("But, No lid has Memory—") which, with its use of "But," pulls back from the alternative way to see a God not present to human eyes by introducing the unaccounted for remainder of this over-simplified equation: "Memory." Even if God can be seen in the dark, the "I" gets no memory of this.

At the opening of the second stanza it is not just sight that is in question but now all of the senses are involved. What the "I" could see "better" in the first stanza she can now only see "equally," and this change can be understood in light of the fact that all senses have been "obscured." This notion of multiple obscured senses is soon abandoned as the poem returns to sight as the primary one by which the "beloved" can be seen. It is here that the poem declares itself to be describing a "Dream" that "Daylight" somewhat violently interrupts, which is an odd move, given that the poem has been preoccupied by what can and can't be seen both in the dark and in the light. The poem's final move makes visible, as it were, all the comparisons, resemblances, opposites, and matchings that the poem's logic rests on but ultimately can't unite: seeing/not seeing, seeing/remembering, sight/other senses, one kind of light/another kind of light.

The poems that surround "I felt a Cleaving in my Mind—" on the loose sheet problematize space as an organizing structure by continually performing unmatchableness at the level of both form and content. In order to understand the difference between this poetics and that which is employed in the fascicles, as well as the role that Dickinson's compositional practices and material contexts play in this difference, I want to look at the fascicle that the loose sheet that has become "Set 2" could have been copied into but was not. In *The Manuscript Books of Emily Dickinson*, Franklin states that "Set 2" was copied onto the same stationery that Dickinson had used to make Fascicle 38, but that while Fascicle 38 was made in 1863, "Set 2" was copied in 1864.[26] Franklin eventually revised his thinking about this timing when editing his variorum, as he dates both Fascicle 38 and Set 2 as coming from 1864.[27] While his earlier assessment would point to the fact that Dickinson may have copied "Set 2" at a later date onto a sheet left over from the making of Fascicle 38, Franklin's later assessment indicates that this sheet was probably copied at the same time that Dickinson made Fascicle 38 and for whatever reasons was left out of it.[28]

When I say that Dickinson "left it out" I am making the assumption that she did not simply misplace this sheet, but that she made the conscious decision to withhold it from the sewing of Fascicle 38. As I have already shown, Dickinson's move to loose sheets was a careful and gradual one, and by the time she came to make Fascicle 38 she had already copied the two sheets that are now known as "Set 1." She then made seven more fascicles before copying the one sheet now known as "Set 4a" and the one sheet now known as "Set 4b." After then copying and sewing Fascicle 38 and copying the sheet that is now known as "Set 2," Dickinson only copied and sewed one more fascicle (Fascicle 39).[29] In other words, when we look at Fascicle 38, we are looking at the very end of her fascicle-making process, at the final instances when Dickinson was doing both things—copying sheets to sew and copying sheets to leave unsewn—at the same time.[30] What, then, is happening on the loose sheet that makes it unable to be sewn as part of Fascicle 38? Does the loose sheet assert itself as unconnectable or do the sheets sewn into Fascicle 38 require that the loose sheet be external to it? Are the poems in Fascicle 38 already displaying or manifesting their own desire to not be sewn? Do the sheets in Fascicle 38 attempt to navigate the issues of time, space, sequence, and matching/mismatching in the same way that the poems on loose sheets do? In order to answer these questions, I am going to sketch out some of the ways that I see the six sheets of Fascicle 38 working and then look closely at one poem. By identifying where, in particular, we can see Dickinson anticipating the act of not sewing that she is already practicing and that she will soon embrace, we can identify the ways in which this fascicle and, by extension, the entire fascicle project, is consumed by the problems of sequence that it raises.

In chapter 1 I addressed some of the modes of relation that exist between poems copied on the same sheet. What I have shown in this section so far is that the sheet that eventually becomes "Set 2" does not embody those forms of relation but actually resists them. This can be made even more explicit if we look at the sheets that eventually comprise Fascicle 38. Let me characterize each of the sheets that were sewn into Fascicle 38 briefly, in order to provide an overview of what is going on in this fascicle both as a fascicle and in relation to the loose sheet that is called "Set 2." My reading will underscore the fact that fascicles at some level present poems ordered in space (in other words, we read side 1, then 2, then 3, then 4 of a sheet) and we will see that even though we cannot read unproblematically across sheets, there is something about the fact that these sheets were sewn that compounds the idea that the poems copied and sewn in this manner are texts deployed in space.

On sheet 1 we can see the connection to the poems on the loose sheet most clearly, and this provides additional evidence that the loose sheet was copied at the same time. The obvious connection has to do with the presence of "Dust" in the opening poem, "A Drop fell on the Apple Tree—" (F 846). When Dickinson copied the first poem on the loose sheet, she had only used the word "Dust" in twenty-five poems at this point, and yet here—in the moment of copying Fascicle 38 and the loose sheet—we encounter three instances.[31] It seems clear that, for whatever reasons, Dickinson is consumed with thoughts of "Dust" and goes at this topic/concept in several different ways. In addition to this, the death of a woman referred to in the sheet's second poem, "Her final Summer was it—" (F 847), can be read as related to the third poem on the loose sheet, "Fairer through Fading—as the Day." As I discussed in chapter 3, the fascicle was often a place to render the experience and apprehension of death, mourning, and grief in myriad ways across the sheets. This occurs across the loose sheet and the sheets of Fascicle 38, as each one presents a different way into a woman's death and the experience of understanding it in the context of all that was unknown about her life.[32] Seen in this light, we might think that there was not just room for the loose sheet amongst this fascicle, but that it may have actually been copied with sewing in mind.

While this sheet might be seen to make the case for the loose sheet being closely enough connected that it might have been sewn, there are poems on other sheets that speak to the possibility of leaving it loose. This happens most dramatically in the first poem on sheet 2, "By my Window have I for Scenery" (F 849), which I will discuss at length below, but it also happens, to a lesser degree, in the first poem of sheet 3, "It was a Grave—yet bore no Stone—" (F 852). This poem describes a grave that has not only not been marked by a stone, but because it was not "enclosed," the space that it takes up is described as "A Consciousness," and what it holds is no longer a body but "a Human Soul." While we might say this is a common reaction to an unmarked grave—this is a scene that Whitman, for instance, renders time and again in *Drum-Taps*—the fact that this poem addresses the identity of that which is inside when the normal markers or boundaries are not present is what I would argue is the very thing that allows Dickinson to copy it into what we now call "Set 7" the next year.

Sheets 4 and 5 of this fascicle work very much the way Dickinson's earlier fascicle sheets work, in that poems are cast roughly in relation to the others on the same sheet. In the case of "Time feels so vast that were it not" (F 858), which is on sheet 4, and "They say that 'Time assuages'—" (F 861), which is on sheet 5, poems across sheets posit the problem of measuring time. In "Time feels so vast that were it not" it is a matter of time's vastness and, in essence, the need to name it as vast, that is at issue, while in "They say that 'Time assuages'—" there is a certain calling into question of the cliché that time will heal pain. We see Dickinson theorizing time in relation to the experiences and emotions that are related to mourning, death, and grief that are figured all over this fascicle. Time (in, as she renders it, all its boundary-less vastness) does not make any of it any better and we might say that it is in the face of realizing that there is no way to manage or harness time that a poem like "I felt a Cleaving in my Mind—" took shape on a sheet that had to remain separate from the others.

By looking closely at the ways in which Dickinson made the poems on sheet 6 of this fascicle, we can see another mode of connection to the loose sheet. The first poem on this sheet, "On the Bleakness of my Lot" (F 862), was made backwards, as the second stanza was sent to Sue before the entire poem was copied onto this sheet. We know from my previous analysis of this strategy that Dickinson did this most often with her loose sheets, and this allows us to see the sixth sheet of Fascicle 38, and by extension the whole fascicle, as sheets that, at certain moments, declare themselves to us retrospectively as, we might say, just barely bound.

In other words, this fascicle does several things that feel very fascicle-like (sheets 4 and 5 read like related-yet-closed units; there are poems across all of the sheets that address the death of a woman), but there are also things about this fascicle that already anticipate Dickinson's move to stop sewing. We are not looking at a case where the loose sheet is so different from the sheets in Fascicle 38 that it obviously had to be left out. On the contrary, there are certain sheets in Fascicle 38 that display qualities that might lead them not to be sewn. In order to explore this further, I want to look at the sheet, and the poem that takes up most of that sheet, in which this tension surfaces most dramatically.

In early 1864 Dickinson copied the lines that begin "By my Window have I for Scenery" (F 849) onto the first three sides of a folded sheet of stationery:

> By my Window have
> I for Scenery
> Just a Sea—with a Stem—
> + If the Bird and the
> Farmer—deem it a "Pine"—
> The Opinion will + do—
> for them—
>
> It has no Port, nor
> a "Line"—but the Jays—
> That + split their route

to the Sky—
Or a Squirrel, whose
giddy Peninsula
May be ⁺ easier reached—
this way—

For Inlands—the Earth
is the under side—
And the upper side—is
the Sun—
And it's Commerce—if
Commerce it have—
Of Spice—I infer from
the Odors borne—

Of it's Voice—to affirm—
when the Wind is within—
Can the Dumb—⁺¹ define
the Divine?
The Definition of Melody—is—
That Definition is none—

It—suggests to our
Faith—
They—suggest to our
Sight—
When the latter—is
put away
I shall meet with
Conviction I somewhere met
That Immortality—

Was the Pine at my
Window a "Fellow
Of the Royal" Infinity?
Apprehensions—are
God's introductions—
⁺ To be hallowed—accor-
dingly—

⁺¹ Grant ⁺²<u>serve</u> + Ply between
it, and the Sky + Better

attained— easier gained—
+ divulge + Extended
inscrutably—

While the sheet on which this poem was copied would eventually be sewn as the second sheet of Fascicle 38, the very sprawling nature of the poem across multiple sides, the way it sets up a comparison that it never follows through with, and its faulty system for indicating variants signal that even in the case of a sheet that was sewn, Dickinson was pressing against the seams that had, until now, helped to establish a certain degree of order.

In many ways this poem rests on a premise conventional to poets, which is that they see things differently than other people. In this case the object in question is a pine tree, but the "I" of the poem establishes her take on it as a "Sea" even before she reveals that others (in this case "the Bird and the Farmer") "deem it a 'Pine'." Having set up this equivalence (what is a Pine to them is a Sea to me), the poem goes on to describe this "Sea," what it does not have ("Port," "a 'Line'"), and the relation that the animals ("Jays" and "a Squirrel") have to it. When setting this sea in its larger context, the earth and the sun are positioned as the lands on either of its sides, and even though the "Commerce" that is intrinsic to it cannot be seen, it is named as "Spice" because of the odor it emits. Up until now the parallel holds up, and even in the beginning of the fourth stanza when the "Voice" of the Sea/Pine is described as present in the company of the "Wind," we are struck by how numerous the equivalences the poem has constructed are. But in the second half of that fourth stanza, with the lines "The Definition of Melody—is— / That Definition is none—," the poem, much like the poems on the loose sheet, comes up against the limits of its own ability to describe one thing in terms of the other.[33] While there is some sort of "Divine" presence inside the Sea/Pine that is partially attributed to the presence of the "Wind" inside, the "Divine," much like "Melody" to which it is implicitly compared, cannot be defined.

What results is an unraveling of logic and form. In the fifth stanza sight is "put away" and the poem breaks out of the stanzaic form that it had established and produces an extra line, "That Immortality." In addition to this, the metaphor of the Pine as a Sea seems to have been forgotten, as the identity of the Pine is now cast in relation to "a 'Fellow / Of the Royal' Infinity." In shifting to ask if that was God in the tree, the poem leaves the sea comparison behind and instead undertakes a whole different set of equivalences. If, as the final lines of the poem assert, "Apprehensions—are God's introductions—," then the question becomes what to do with this. In the last line of the poem we are instructed that they "be hallowed—accordingly," but the variant here instructs otherwise, in saying that they are "Extended inscrutably—." In the face of attempting to set up an equivalence between the pine and the sea, the poem's final move is to address that which is neither named nor written. In essence it not only lets its own comparison unravel, but it calls into question the very process of trying to name that equivalence. Turning to the absent-yet-present, heard-but-not-seen presence of God instead underscores the fact that the poem can no longer see a way out. The long list of confusing variants that follow—Dickinson included superscript numbers that, while maybe an attempt to clarify references and positions, actually make it harder to do so—speaks to the poem's imbalances of form and logic.

In terms of how the sheets of Fascicle 38 look visually and how the poems on them are laid out, it is interesting to notice that sheets 3 and 6 each consist of four poems, one on each side. Sheets 4 and 5 are also quite regular in this way: on sheets 1 and 4 the first poem takes up the first two sides and then there is one poem on each of the remaining sides; on sheet 5 the first side has one poem, the second and third sides are taken up by one longer poem, and the last side has one poem on it. Only sheet 2 varies from this way of treating sides, as "By my Window have I for Scenery" is so long that it and its variants take up almost the first three sides. It is followed by three short lines at the bottom of the third side and then a single poem on the last side. I discuss sheet 2 as the sheet in which we can see Dickinson pushing away from sewing, but that being said, it is important to note that the loose sheet that becomes Set 2 has one poem on a side, and it is therefore not simply a matter of visual excess or irregularity that makes this sheet unable to be sewn. In other words, if it were a matter of regularity of layout, the second sheet in Fascicle 38 would have been left out.

It is not my intention to make hard and fast rules about the difference between poems on loose sheets and poems in fascicles, as Dickinson worked in both modes and we know that those modes overlapped in time. Additionally, as this analysis has shown, loose sheets often exhibit characteristics of the fascicles and fascicle sheets are often pressing against the limitations of the sewing process that they are always on the brink of rejecting. That being said, one of the ways in which sequence is contained and deployed in the fascicles is through the emphasis that the materials themselves (both the sheets and the string) place on order in space. In the fascicles, Dickinson attempts to harness sequence even if she is coming up against its limitations all the time. The loose sheets, by doing away with the string that would join the poems in space and by thematizing and embodying all the ways that order, matching, and resemblance can be broken down, reject sequence as an organizing principle. What happens with the shift to loose sheets is that relations that used to occur in space now get embedded into the poems as problems for them to embody.

Both "The Dust behind" and "This Dust, and it's Feature—" are preoccupied with what will happen to the material remnants of our bodies and our work in the future, but they render these consequences very differently: "The Dust behind" attempts to "join" ultimately incommensurate terms and is left in the midst of the unraveling that occurs as a result. "This Dust, and it's Feature—" is composed of three densely-packed and highly-enigmatic stanzas, each of which meets its own distinct and neat end. What we have here are two paths through which we can read "I felt a Cleaving in my Mind—" and which we need to see in relation to each other in order to understand the work that "I felt a Cleaving in my Mind—" is doing. When we approach this poem through its compositional history in both time (it is written after "The Dust behind" is written and sent to Sue) and space (it is copied on the page following "This Dust, and it's Feature—"), we can see that Dickinson was creating a web of connections between multiple poems (some of which are not present on the sheet) that address (even in the case that they antic-ipate) the conundrum that loose sheets produce. By identifying the "Dust" that exists (both as she retains it and lets it go) in both contexts, we can see how Dick-inson was working with ideas of joining and unraveling. By moving to "thought" from "Dust" and by setting up the poem's second stanza with a reflection on the very "Seam" that she was actually faced with, Dickinson turned "I felt a Cleaving in my Mind—" into one of her most pointed reflections on the relationship between her materials and her compositional process.

I have highlighted this poem's compositional history and its material context in order to show how this loose sheet interrogates the problem that sequence poses. In light of this, I want to make two concluding points about the loose sheets that we call "Sets" and the poems that Dickinson copied there. First, poems copied on the loose sheets figure, theorize, and address the problem of sequence as a time/space issue, and this results in constant unmatchableness at the level of metaphor and form. Dickinson used the loose sheets to deploy her worries over what happens when time and space stop working and when unmatch-ableness takes over. This characteristic of the poems makes them rich for a study that they have not yet had, and one might look at "I could not prove the Years had feet—" (F 674) in "Set 1" and "Split the Lark—and you'll find the Music—" (F 905) in "Set 5" for two of the most striking examples of this. Second, as Dick-inson disrupted the connections that sewing permitted, allowed the loose sheets to scatter, and theorized both the disruptions and the scattering in the poems themselves, she emerged into a phase of her career where her individual poems became her prominent concern. Because poems copied on loose sheets do not depend on each other, they are inherently more self-contained. Yet what defines these poems is not the lyric wholeness we might expect (where poems become less dependent on their surroundings and context), but is their immersion in thinking through the very materials and strategies of composition that make them possible.

CHAPTER 5

⟣

Methods of Unmaking

Dickinson's Late Drafts, Scraps, and Fragments

Throughout this book I have presented examples of many of the ways that Dickinson used paper to compose, preserve, and circulate her poems. From copying poems onto folded sheets of stationery that she sewed together or left loose, to drafting poems as notes to friends and embedding poems in her formal correspondence, Dickinson engaged in a process of committing her poems to paper of all different kinds. By taking her choice of material seriously—not simply as containers or repositories from which a poem can be extracted and lose nothing—I have introduced the idea that we can read Dickinson's poems (and her developing poetics) in relation to her material and compositional practices. The social life of paper that this book has explored now comes to a stunning conclusion as we watch Dickinson take up ads, memoranda, fliers, labels, and countless other scraps of paper in her final years.

After 1876, Dickinson stopped copying poems onto formal sheets of stationery and her primary materials became the fragments of different papers that surrounded her in her household. Few critics have paid attention to Dickinson's writings in her last decade, as they consider them incomplete scraps and drafts—a disappointment to readers of her earlier poems. As recently as 1998, R. W. Franklin referred to them as "a proliferating disarray of scraps of paper," and in 2001 Alfred Habegger described the writing from this period as "a quantity of inferior work, some of it sketchy, repetitive, obscure," asserting that "like other explosively original writers, Dickinson couldn't avoid a certain loss of energy and freshness."[1] Additionally, studies of Dickinson's manuscripts to have emerged in the last twenty years do not extend their analyses to these late materials. While there are a number of potential factors that may contribute to the critical oversight, and subsequent rejection, of these poems—among them that there is no absorbing narrative of Lavinia finding *these* poems in a secret box and that readers have become wedded to the fascicles as Dickinson's primary (and authorized) texts— this chapter proceeds from the position that, for the most part, we still do not know how to read (or even whether we should try to read) lines of poems that were cop- ied onto scraps of household paper. For instance, what do we make of words (almost always with marks of revision all over them) written on envelope flaps, recipes, shopping lists, and advertisements? What about words set down on torn pieces of paper, often no larger than the palm of a hand, and then pinned together? Who is the imagined reader of such things and how could we ever, as much-belated readers, approximate that stance? In order to disentangle the problems of readership, mate- riality, and genre that these texts raise, I want to point us, once again, to the scene of composition. By looking closely at the ways in which Dickinson radically altered the materials on which she wrote, we will be able to navigate a new relationship to them, one which will allow us to see two things: the ways in which these late poems require a less formal and more fragmented material context than her earlier poems; and how the poems, in turn, develop in relation to this new context.

While it is true that these poems were written amongst a devastating series of losses—in 1874, Dickinson's father died; in 1875, her mother had a stroke from which she would never fully recover; in 1878, Samuel Bowles died; in 1882, both her mother and Charles Wadsworth died; in 1883, her nephew, Gib, died; and in 1884, Otis Lord died—and that they are shorter and more fragmented—for instance, the sustained journeys and reflections of poems like "Because I could not stop for Death—" (F 479), "I started Early—Took my Dog—" (F 656), and "My Life had stood—a Loaded Gun—" (F 764) are nowhere to be found here— this does not mean that Dickinson was past her prime or that she had abandoned her desire to make poems. For the few critics who have engaged with Dickinson's late poems, part of the pleasure comes from precisely the unexpected shifts that she made at this point in her writing career and from figuring out how to read and understand these shifts. While Mabel Loomis Todd may have been invoking the sense of discardability that she saw as intrinsic to these texts when she first called them "scraps," critics who have chosen to take up these materials have done everything to avoid reading this assumption back into the work itself.[2]

While recent work by Jeanne Holland, Melanie Hubbard, and Susan Howe takes up these late texts for serious critical attention, Marta Werner has been the most dedicated editor and reader of Dickinson's late manuscripts.[3] Werner locates the most radical move of Dickinson's career in this late stage when, in her words, Dickinson had a "desire to inscribe herself outside all institutional ac- counts of order."[4] Rejecting "institutional accounts of order," though, does not mean that Dickinson descended into disorder, and it is the "multiple or contin- gent orders" that Werner's various analyses (in her book, in multiple articles, and on her website that is devoted to these manuscripts) attempt to articulate.[5] As Werner sees it, at this moment in Dickinson's career, she "abandoned even the minimal bibliographical apparatus of the fascicles, along with their dialectical structure, to explore a language as free in practice as in theory and to induce the unbinding of the scriptural economy."[6]

Werner's attention to these texts not only positions them squarely within our critical sight, but invites us to ask certain questions about Dickinson's late process that have not yet been asked. For instance, what does a language "as free in practice as in theory" look like? And, even more to the point, what happens when Dickinson's "scriptural economy" comes unbound? One assumption might be that whatever happens at this stage and whatever that happening looks like, we will need a new critical apparatus to understand it. Yet in her recent consideration of the history of twentieth-century readings of Dickinson, Virginia Jackson has argued that even the most attentive and sensitive readers of Dickinson's late manuscripts have refused to make such a move and have continued to treat them as (or, more to Jackson's point, turn them into) lyrics. Jackson's point seems to be that it is not simply that the legibility of Dickinson's manuscripts (which in the case of the late texts is dubious at best) depends precisely on the prior existence of these poems in print, but that the bind of reading manuscripts as if they are lyrics can, ironically, get intensified when those manuscripts look nothing like lyrics. Jackson goes on to argue that even Werner is engaging in "an emphatically lyric reading" of texts that not only do not position themselves as lyrics, but actually anticipate and worry over the idea that they might one day be read as lyrics.[7]

By looking at the manuscripts in order to understand the process by which these late poems were made, we are able to situate ourselves, as closely as possible, within the moment of composition and therefore ask what about Dickinson's relationship to making poetry is visible in her move to scraps, drafts, and fragments. Doing so allows us to see that at this moment Dickinson turns to a very different kind of material on which to copy her poems—to the fragments of paper, often from her household, often torn and irregular, often containing some other kind of text—that by its very nature interrupts her process, keeps her poems from ever feeling finished, and places emphasis on the material remnant itself. By approaching these late texts this way, we are able to see that they are neither scattered missives nor settled (if disappointing) lyrics. Instead, the paper on which these poems were copied reveals Dickinson's continued and painstaking attention to the problems of closure, relation, order, and logic that writing poetry raises.

In this chapter I will highlight several of Dickinson's late compositional methods in order to show that what happens at the end of Dickinson's life is worthy of our attention and is not simply a descent into chaos; instead, it is a sustained exploration of what happens when Dickinson took poems apart, when she no longer placed value on them as finished products, and when she sought to preserve the literal, material site of this process. Here we will see just how highly dependent Dickinson's poems have become on their own documentary status. In the first and second sections I look at the way in which Dickinson was drafting poems during these years, drawing particular attention to the relationship between her variants and subsequent drafts, as well as to her uneasiness about letting a poem come to its end. In the third section I turn to the domestic materials— recipes, advertisements, wrappers—on which Dickinson often copied poems, questioning how we might read the relation of these materials to the poems themselves. In the final section I look at the tiniest scraps on which Dickinson wrote and at the pins she sometimes used to keep these scraps together, arguing that even at this latest of late moments, Dickinson was placing emphasis on the material object itself.

THE TROUBLE WITH ENDINGS

Because Dickinson rarely produced final copies of her poems during this late period and therefore did not destroy drafts in the way she had become accustomed to doing, we have unprecedented access to her drafting, editing, and revising processes. While one may argue that what is visible to us at this point must have existed in some form earlier as well (and therefore we cannot say definitively that the compositional practices of this period are any different from earlier ones), I will show that Dickinson initiated a new set of practices during this time, ones that reflect her trouble with the way her poems were ending and with her competing desires to both explode and tighten the texts she was writing. It is a practice that no longer has the formal, finished, fascicle sheet in mind. What we will see in this section is how ending manifests itself (sometimes productively and sometimes not) as a textual and material impossibility. While this is related to the issues of closure that I discussed in chapter 3, there we saw Dickinson working across and between poems; here the emphasis falls on them individually.

Dickinson's manuscripts from this period show that she was absorbed with issues of drafting and revision, as so many of them include a vast number of variants, sometimes copied in multiple directions on the page, often making the lines difficult to decipher. The lines that begin "Fortitude incarnate" (F 1255), for example, were copied in 1872 in pencil on a very lightly graphed fragment of paper that had been torn at the left hand side. The page is filled with variants (both interlined and included at the bottom of the page) that consume over a third of the space of the page. In this case, Dickinson made cross marks that indicate her choices between variants, turning these lines into a text that could be translated into the tidy three-stanza poem that it was first published as in 1945. In other manuscripts from this period Dickinson simply allowed the variants to stand as multiple viable options. For instance, in 1875 Dickinson copied the lines that begin "Crisis is sweet and yet the Heart" (F 1365) in pencil on a leaf with many variants and revisions, all of which she left as viable ways for rendering the poem.[8] Whether Dickinson included variants that she then chose among or that she allowed to remain as possibilities, the paper on which she drafted these poems bears the marks of the very messy process of generating multiple words and phrases for a given set of lines.

One of the things that both of these examples reveal, and that proves to be true of many of her late, drafty manuscripts, is that Dickinson tended to include many variants towards the end of the poems she was writing.[9] This is particularly interesting in the case of the lines that begin "Contained in this short Life" (F 1175), as Dickinson copied three drafts of this poem on the same piece of paper (fig. 5.1). The first draft was written on the front side of a leaf of lined stationery, and the other two were written, in different directions, on its back side. By looking closely at these three versions we can see how this poem that starts as one about decipherability and friendship and becomes one about the soul and the tension between containment and freedom evolved in relation to the existence of the variants that Dickinson generated towards the end of each subsequent draft. The first draft on this piece of paper reads:

> Contained in this short
> Combined
> Comprised Life
> Were wonderful extents—
> Are magical
> > Terrible
> > miraculous
> > tenderest—
>
> Discernible to not a friend
> Except Omnipotence
> A friend too straight
> to stoop
> > subtle
> Too distant to be seen
> Come unto me enacted
> how   accomplished
> With Firmaments between—
> > Centuries
>
> The soul came home
> > to sleep
> at night from trips
> That would towns
> > scenes
> Un   to sense—
> have dazzled
> As doth the tired sense
> > unmanifest to sense
> Unwitnessed of the sense
> [up the right side of the page:"Were exquisite extents"][10]

Figure 5.1
Three drafts of "Contained in this short Life" (F 1175). Courtesy, Archives & Special Collections, Amherst College.

Attention to this manuscript shows that while Dickinson was making room for the many interlined variant words that she copied at the same time that she copied the poem, the poem is ultimately consumed by this variant-making process, in that there are four different versions of what seems to be the poem's final line at the bottom of the page. It is interesting that in a poem that is about what is containable and uncontainable, Dickinson ultimately is not able to contain the multiple ways of rendering this description. Dickinson had some control over the tidy listing of variant words that she included in the first several lines (notice the six adjectives that might modify "extents"), and she even maintained this control once "Omnipotence" had been named as the friend that is "too straight" and "too distant," such that it can discern the "extents" that are referenced, if unspecified, in the lines. But as soon as she changed the subject to "the soul"—whether by way of analogy or next step or shift, it is hard to tell—it is as if the poem falls apart into its variants. One might say that it is this explosion of variants at the poem's end that allowed Dickinson to go back and include a variant for the second line up the margin of the now full page. It also allowed (or forced) her, as I will show next, to start the poem again.

When Dickinson turned the leaf over to start again, she retained only the first two lines of the poem that she had written on the other side:

```
                          plain
             Contained in this short Life
                    exquisite
             Are magical extents    loth
             The soul returning soft at
             night    slily           ly Home
             To steal securer        thence
                       at sunrise    strictest
             As Children strictly kept
             turn        est    er
             Take sooner to the sea
             Whose waters are the brawling
             Brook                   nameless
             To think infinity
                    Beside Infinity
                    Whose nameless fathoms
                    slink away
                    Beside infinity
```

In this draft, Dickinson abandoned the "Omnipotence" that the friend could decipher and that was central to the earlier draft, and instead focuses more closely on the issue of containment. In this version, the "soul" is more fully realized as one of the magical extents that are contained within life. But with the addition of the new lines starting with "As children," Dickinson introduced an analogy that reorients the poem's message. The final lines of this draft assert the cliché that those undergoing forced containment are the very ones who will love their freedom most. The logic, though, seems off here, as the word "contained" is working in different ways at once, as a marker of both expansiveness and confinement. As a result, then, of an analogy that isn't really working, Dickinson once again struggled with the logic and making of the poem's final lines. While seemingly at ease with the inclusion of variants early in the draft, she ended by tinkering heavily with the two final lines, as here she presented three different options for them. In describing the water/fathoms that these children turn to, the poem is clearly troubled by their relationship to infinity.

The creases that run horizontally across the page and the placement of words in relation to these creases indicate that at this point Dickinson folded the paper in thirds and began another version on one of the panels made by this folding. At this point Dickinson made choices, ignoring all of the variants she had written in the second draft except for those relating to the final lines, and writing a version of the poem without variants:

```
             Contained in
             this short Life
```

Are magical
extents
The soul returning
soft at night
To steal securer
thence
As Children
strictest kept
Turn soonest to
the sea
Whose nameless
Fathoms slink
away
Beside infinity

What we can see here is more than the making of a Dickinson poem, but the process by which a poem becomes so encumbered by the variants at its end. It is the variants themselves that force Dickinson to stop, start, stop, and start the poem again. We might think that because Dickinson eventually worked her way towards a variant-less version of the poem that articulates a clean analogy and a palatable moral that she was still committed to achieving a finished product. But returning to the making of the poem allows us to see that, as early as 1870, Dickinson was struggling with how to end her poems and that producing variants was part of the way she navigated that problem.

Werner reads Dickinson's variants as the "leading formal problem" of her work that can be seen, retrospectively and once we study the fragments, as having been the "problem" the whole time.[11] Her impulse to see in these late texts what has been there all along, and to do so by way of the variants, proves just how present and powerful the variants are at this moment. It is by being weighed down with variants that these late poems reveal themselves to be encumbered by Dickinson's preoccupation with what to do with their endings. But what might it mean that Dickinson (either intentionally or unintentionally) was troubling her poems right as they come to their ends? Or maybe more precisely, what does it mean that she opened them up right at the moment when she could close them down and tie them up? Before we can answer these questions, I want to look at an entirely different, albeit related, way that Dickinson registered her trouble with endings.

In the midst of thinking about the ways in which her individual poems should or might or cannot end, Dickinson embraced a whole new kind of revision process that troubles the notion of ending by turning what had been clean copies of "finished" poems back into drafts. This happened in two ways: she went back to some of her fascicle poems, sometimes revising right there on the fascicle paper and sometimes copying them out on different paper, and she began taking new poems apart as they were being made. When returning to the fascicles she sometimes revised in order to send a piece of a poem to one of her many correspondents; in other cases she seemed to want to reimagine the situation or emotion conveyed in the poem in order to render it slightly differently; in still other cases she seemed to simply want to play with the language of an old poem again. In many cases she revised by extracting a stanza or two.[12] When revising poems that she was writing for the first time, she tended to drastically cut and shorten what she had written. While the extraction and shortening that happened at this stage seems closely tied to Dickinson's practice of sending people parts of her poems, we can also see that certain instances of extraction happen as a result of the kind of explosion of variants that I have just discussed. Both the explosion of variants and this shortening process are attempts to destabilize the structure of the poem by questioning just how finished it can ever really be.

In 1882 Dickinson wrote the lines that begin "Echo has no Magistrate—" (F 1569) on a small piece of lined stationery, and, as in the manuscripts of "Contained in this short Life," there is an accumulation of variants towards the bottom of the paper that bleed out from and back into the poem itself (fig. 5.2). The first stanza is

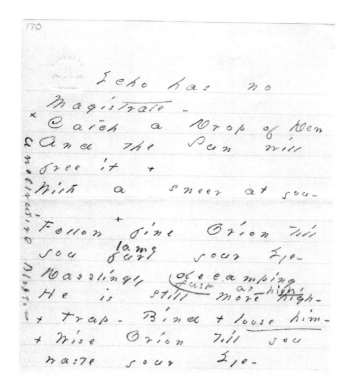

Figure 5.2
"Echo has no Magistrate—" (F 1569). Courtesy, Archives & Special Collections, Amherst College.

relatively unencumbered by these variants, as it is set apart from the mess below it by a line of white space and Dickinson neatly marked two crosses that correspond to variant words below. In the case of the second cross (the one after "free it"), Dickinson seems to have expressed her preference for the variant ("loose him") by underlining it. It is in the second stanza where things start to get messy: Dickinson included a variant for most of a whole line ("Wise Orion till you waste your Eye" for "fine Orion till you furl your Eye") and interlined two variants ("lame" above "furl" and "just as high" above "still more high"). The words "Unobtrusive Blossom" were written along the margin of the piece of stationery and Franklin reads this as a variant for the first line of the poem.[13] Regardless of whether this is the line that it corresponds with, it is clear that it was written after the rest of the words on this page, since Dickinson placed it here because there is no more room. We might read her going back to create a variant for the opening line once she had finished writing the poem as a result of the way in which the poem itself has suc- cumbed to the many variants at its end. When Dickinson then copied out just the second stanza on a single leaf torn on the left hand side, folded this in thirds, wrote "A 'Pear' to the Wise is sufficient—" at the top, "Susan" on the back, and "Emily" at the bottom, she isolated the final stanza, making choices between its variants, and extracting it from its longer, drafty version.

If in the case of "Echo has no Magistrate—" Dickinson unmade the poem by taking the first stanza off, in "A Drunkard cannot meet a Cork" (F 1630) she did the opposite, but for what I would argue is a similar reason, in that she was engaged in a process of rethinking how these poems end. In this case, the lines were copied on a leaf torn (quite messily) along the left-hand side. While most of the lines were written on the front side of this leaf, the last line was written upside down on the back. It is clear that this is a very early draft of this poem, as the variant for "Remembrance" (which is "Prospective") is written in the midst of composition, Dickinson was not yet indicating line breaks, and the uncharacteristically long last line deviates from the meter of the lines that have come before it. It should not be surprising, then, that when Dickinson copied this poem again, this time on formal paper, still torn, but more neatly than before, she copied just the first half of it. In this case, she made the poem shorter by chopping off its final, problematic lines instead of reworking them into their own poem.

In both of these poems, the content of the lines—the way their analogies match up, the sense they try to make out of disparate things—produces a kind of struggle that results in variants that, in turn, result in the excising of the problem- atic part. In "Echo has no Magistrate—" Dickinson ran up against the problem of how to relate the first and second stanzas. In its draft form, the first stanza asserts that while "Echo has no Magistrate," other elements of nature do have some force that governs or frees them, and Dickinson makes the comparison of the Sun's ability to release a "Drop of Dew." When shifting to the second stanza, which is about the distance at which "Orion" exists, the potential comparison, analogy, narrative, or relation between the two is entirely unclear. It is no wonder, then, that Dickinson isolated the second stanza for revision and sending. Taken out of the context of the draft's first lines, the lines sent to Sue are a command to look high and far towards that which is "Dazzling." In "A Drunkard cannot meet a Cork" the poem is set up to be one about temptation and pleasure, as, when confronted with certain items, the "Drunkard" is sent into a "Revery" and the "me" in the poem is sent "reeling in." The second part of the poem shifts to thinking about the "moderate drinker of Delight" (as opposed to the out and out "Drunkard") and the poem stumbles once it has declared that such a person "Does not deserve the Spring—" or, as the variant states, "Has never tasted spring—." The attempt, in the final lines, to bring together the lover of nature and the lover of the "Jug" results in awkward lines that are eventually excised from the poem.

Dickinson's revision process during these years is illuminating because we have the chance to see her producing a variety of options for how her poems will work their way into the forms that ultimately are so dazzling. By seeing the explosions of variants that often come toward the end of her lines on the page and by seeing the cutting away of the problematic parts of the poem that Dickinson often undertakes in subsequent drafts, we can recognize that ending a poem caused a certain crisis for Dickinson, one that the fragmentary nature of the material she was using supported. Without the pressure to set her poems down in formal, finished terms, Dickinson found herself drawn to thinking and rethinking how to finish them.

REVISING FOR A READER

In this section I am going to look at two examples in which variants are not present, but in which the revision and shortening processes that we just saw happening in conjunction with these variants is occurring nonetheless. Throughout this period Dickinson continued to be acutely preoccupied with endings and with the processes by which she could make them, avoid them, and sabotage them. In both of the cases below, a subsequent draft of each poem was sent to one of Dickinson's correspondents, in which case we might assume that the revision process was undertaken with sending in mind. While this is not true of all of Dickinson's revisions, I want to talk about two cases in which this seems to be true, in order to show how, in the midst of having a difficult (albeit fun) time coming to the ends of these poems, Dickinson was often acutely aware of her reader.

In the first example—"The pedigree of Honey" (F 1650)—Dickinson wrote the following lines on a leaf of unlined, slightly heavy paper that had been torn along its left side and was folded once, horizontally, at its center. On this leaf she wrote:

> The pedigree
> of Honey
> Does not con-

> cern the Bee,
> Nor lineage
> of Ecstasy
> Delay the Butterfly
> On spangled
> journeys to the
> peak
> Of some per-
> ceiveless Thing—
> The right of
> way to Tripoli
> A more essential
> thing—

In many ways this seems like a very simple poem. These lines depend on, articulate, and turn on the assertion that the "pedigree"/"lineage" of desired things does not matter to certain creatures. What is, instead, of worth is the journey itself, the getting there, and the power of the "perceiveless Thing" that is the destination but that, by nature of its description, is also an unapprehendible and unarticulatable "Thing." The lines posit valuing one set of things over another, and in doing so the notion of (or the preoccupation with the notion of) pedigree/ lineage is lessened.

When Dickinson shortened this poem and sent it to Mabel Loomis Todd, not only did she do away with this structure, but she also reversed the meaning of this poem. Here, on another leaf of unlined (although slightly yellower) heavy paper, that is torn at the left side and folded once at the center, she wrote:

> The Pedigree
> of Honey
> Does not con-
> cern the Bee—
> A Clover, any
> time, to him
> Is Aristocracy—
>
> E. Dickinson

In this version, the "Pedigree" still does not concern the bee, but not because something else does; instead, it is because the "Clover" is *always* "Aristocracy" to him. In this version, then, the pedigree matters—or, more precisely, the fact of it being pedigreed matters. It is not "concerned" because it is already a fact.

One might say that Dickinson simplified this poem so as to make it palatable to Todd, and indeed Todd must have liked this poem very much, as she pasted it into one of her scrapbooks, the evidence of which remains as faded glue marks on the back of this manuscript. Dickinson, too, must have liked this version, or at least wanted to keep a record of it for some reason, as she made another copy of it, with only slightly different lineation, for herself to keep. Yet this shortened version of the poem seems to me to be a retreat from and simplification of something that the earlier draft is just on the cusp of discovering. In revising and shortening the poem, Dickinson did away with the "perceiveless Thing" that is difficult to let stand in a poem that she was sending in order to communicate something to someone. As we have seen, it is often the end of Dickinson's poems that she fiddled with, as there the "Thing" that is hard to articulate is encountered. In this case, instead of creating lots of variants for it in order to get at the heart of the matter, she cut it out entirely and drastically simplified the situation, the emotion, and the truth that the earlier draft was trying to articulate.

In the second example, the poem becomes much shorter and the fact that it has been shortened for the purposes of sending is embedded into the content of the poem itself. While we do not have the manuscript of the lines that begin "What mystery pervades a well!" (F 1433), Todd's transcription indicates that it was drafted in six stanzas:

> What mystery pervades a well!
> The water lives so far—
> A neighbor from another world
> Residing in a jar
>
> Whose limit none have ever seen,
> But just his + lid of glass—
> Like looking every time you please
> In an abyss's face!
>
> The grass does not appear afraid,
> I often wonder he
> Can stand so close and look so bold
> At what is +awe to me.
>
> Related somehow they may be,
> The sedge stands next the sea
> Where he is floorless
> +And does no timidity betray—
>
> But nature is a stranger yet;
> The ones that cite her most
> Have never passed her haunted house,
> Nor simplified her ghost.

To pity those that know her not
Is helped by the regret
That those who know her, know her less
The nearer her they get.
+ lip + dread + And of fear no evidence gives he

This poem begins by taking the water in a well as its subject and reflecting on how it is unknowable, precisely because, although one can see the top of it, its limits/depths can be neither penetrated nor intuited. In the third stanza Dickinson positioned the grass in relation to this well water, wondering about the fear that it seems not to feel in the face of this, but that the poem assumes one cannot help but feel in proximity to such mystery. While the fourth stanza takes this perception one step further by invoking the parallel situation of "sedge" to "sea," the major shift in the poem occurs in the first stanza. The turn to the explanatory line "But nature is a stranger yet" is both a way of doing away with the fear that was registered in the earlier stanzas and moving away from the particulars of the well water into the more abstract (yet, interestingly, more ubiquitous) "nature." The remaining lines of the poem puzzle over (by calling on the structure of the riddle) the relationship of citing, nearing, and knowing nature, and in Paul Crumbley's estimation, "no Dickinson poem better illustrates her efforts to use nature and art to reveal an incommensurate self."[14]

Todd's inclusion of Dickinson's variants indicate that this six-stanza poem was a working draft of sorts, but her inclination to transcribe it and have it printed in the 1896 *Poems* also indicates that it must have existed in a somewhat finished-feeling (at least to Todd) form. Given that until 1932 all printings of this poem came from Todd's transcript, Todd probably didn't know that around the same time that Dickinson copied this poem in this way, she also revised it in two different ways, both of which indicate that she was rethinking the poem's ending. In one case Dickinson took the final stanza and added four new lines to it, copying all eight lines on a square fragment of graph paper. In the other case she took the last two stanzas of the six-stanza poem, made minor revisions to them, copied them onto a leaf, and sent it to Sue.

As I noted in my reading of the six-stanza version, there is a turn in the final two stanzas, where the specificity of the well water is abandoned in favor of the more abstract concept of "nature." It may be no surprise, then, that Dickinson went on to play with the lines that encompass this idea. In the first of these shortened versions Dickinson took the final stanza and added new lines to the end, working with variants that she ultimately chose between:

To pity those who
know her not ~~that~~
Is helped by the regret
~~soothed~~
That   those who

know her know her less
The nearer her they
get—
How adequate the
Human Heart
To it's emergency—
Intrenchments stimulate
a friend
And stems an enemy
~~balks~~

By starting this version of the poem with the last stanza, Dickinson erases all references to "nature," and who the "her" refers to remains unclear. Instead, the "Human Heart" is introduced as a player here, as potentially the "her" or the thing that helps one cope with the unknowability of the "her." Yet what the "emergency" is or what the "intrenchment" is a reference to is almost completely obscure.

When Dickinson sent a version of this poem to Sue, she dealt with the two final stanzas, making several changes to these lines. Franklin suggests that the version that starts with the final stanza and then adds new lines may have been an attempt at this version sent to Sue.[15] Whether this is true, Dickinson was, once again, drawn to the end of the poem, where the analysis of the well water's mysteriousness becomes a more abstract reflection on nature's (and, with these new revisions, Sue's) unknowability:

But Susan is
a stranger yet—
The ones who
cite her most
Have never scaled
her Haunted House
Nor compromised
her Ghost—

To pity those who
know her not
Is helped by the
regret
That those who
know her know
her less
The nearer her
they get—
                    Emily

Inserting Sue's name where "nature" used to be reveals that the move (within the six-stanza poem) to abstract from well water to "nature" actually produced the possibility that the message/point/emotional truth of the poem could be both transportable and specified. Now "Susan" is the unknowable thing and if we didn't know about the previous draft we would have no idea that this poem started as a reflection about the mysteriousness of water.[16] This third draft ties up the mystery because, whereas in the first version you want to know more, this one doesn't make you want to know "Susan" any more than you already do. The poem passes into an incomprehensible stage but as it emerges from that stage, the mystery is gone and you know exactly where you stand.

Attention to Dickinson's drafting process during these late years shows us that despite the scrap-like materials she was writing on, Dickinson was still acutely attuned to the issue of the identity of poem. She labored over their endings, creating explosions of variants within their final lines, extracting pieces in order to resolve the problem of their endings, and turning and returning both long-finished and newly-finished poems back into drafts that had yet to settle into their endings. In other words, and maybe unexpectedly, in this new material context, Dickinson had the latitude to rethink issues of finality that were largely settled for her when she was working with formal fascicle sheets. She could grapple with issues of variation, unknowability, and indeterminacy in a material context that embodied those very issues. The move to write on small, often torn pieces of paper can be read as her embracing a material that poses, as it obscures, the very problem of formal closure. This is something that Dickinson grappled with throughout her career—there was a resistance to closure in the fascicle poems themselves—and now we see this most fully at work in the late scraps, drafts, and fragments.

Dickinson may have moved to scrap-like paper of many sorts because the formal sheets did not allow for the kind of revisions her poems were embracing, but during this time she also used paper that had previously had other purposes, served other functions, and often had other texts (sometimes handwritten, sometimes printed) on them. These kinds of paper make something different about Dickinson's late process visible. In the next section I will turn to the paper itself—its uses, the other texts and markings on it—in order to discuss the ways in which the parameters of these domestic materials largely governed the ways that Dickinson's poems got made.

READING DOMESTIC MATERIAL CULTURE

In 1875 Dickinson wrote the poem that begins "The Spider as an Artist" (F 1373) onto one of the last sheets of loose formal stationery she would ever use, and here she asserted the unemployable merit and genius of this creature who makes art amongst the items of the household. Not unlike that spider, Dickinson would now turn to what others might see as the scraps, waste, and debris of the house, copying poems on the backs of letters that both she and Lavinia had received, on the insides of turned-out envelopes, and on a variety of other kinds of paper that had once been consumed by, useful to, or of some importance to the everyday life of the Dickinson household.[17] For instance, Dickinson wrote individual poems on, among other things, a guarantee from "The German Student Lamp Co.," an advertisement for *The Children's Crusade*, instructions for laying down carpet from "J. C. Arms & Co." in Northampton, an invitation from twenty-six years earlier, the 1871 schedule for an agricultural college's proceedings, part of a "John Hancock Number One Note," and a "Western Union Telegraph Co." envelope. Whether the other members of the household had discarded these items and each was subsequently preserved by Dickinson, or whether everyone was retaining paper products of all kinds at this moment (and, possibly, long before), we cannot know.[18] What we do know is that Dickinson took these materials and put them to new purposes.

For critics who look closely at these materials, there is the desire not only to explain Dickinson's choice to use such materials, but also to situate this decision in the larger narrative of her life. For instance, Holland reads the turn to domestic materials as related to Dickinson's desire to stay inside, and therefore in terms of (and, as she later makes clear, as a result of) her alleged agoraphobia. In describing the move from fascicles to scraps, Holland plots what she sees as the inevitability of this move, calling it "a logical progression for a poet whose resistance to 'going public' intensified as she grew older."[19] This interpretation depends on both the idea that Dickinson was always resisting the so-called "public" and that she conceived of domestic materials (all of which came into the house from elsewhere and bear the mark of those exterior places) as those that are private. In this section I ask what happens if, instead of reading insularity and containment into these late poems, we read the taking up of domestic materials as an act that makes something new possible for Dickinson at this moment. In order to do this, I will look at three poems and the specific materials onto which they were copied: an early draft of "The Things that never can come back, are several—" (F 1564) that Dickinson first copied on the back of a coconut cake recipe; the lines that begin "To be forgot by thee" (F 1601) that Dickinson copied on the front and back side of a fragment of an advertisement flyer for linens; and the lines that begin "To her derided Home" (F 1617) that Dickinson copied on an opened out wrapper, its original contents having been consumed or discarded.

The problem of how to read Dickinson's domestic material culture is not unlike the problem of how to read the explosions of variants that we saw in the previous sections. When an editor chooses between Dickinson's variants, he or she assumes not only that such a choice can be made, but that there is some entity lurking under the variants that will become visible once all those choices have been made. I would argue that even when Sharon Cameron presents many ways to read variants and goes so far as to suggest that we choose not to choose amomg them, she (in simply trying to figure out how to read such things) must have already assumed that such things, at the most basic level, are readable.[20] Embedded in this assumption of readability is an assumption about the status of the thing one is trying to read. As we move into looking at lines on the backs of recipes, advertisements, and wrappers, I will endeavor to not assume that I know what I am seeing. Suspending such assumptions, even momentarily, can open us up to rediscovering the variety of other relations that might exist between the poems Dickinson was writing and the materials on which she chose to write them.

When Dr. Josiah Gilbert Holland, one of Dickinson's closest friends, died on October 12, 1881, Dickinson wrote a poem and sent it to his wife, a woman with whom she had been a regular correspondent for many years. Between the opening salutation "Dear Sister—" and the closing "Emily, in love," Dickinson wrote the lines that begin "The Things that never can come back, are several—" (F 1564):

> The Things
> that never can
> come back, are
> several—
> Childhood—some
> forms of Hope—the
> Dead—
> Though Joys—like
> Men—may sometimes
> make a Journey—
> And still abide—
> We do not mourn
> for Traveler, or
> Sailor,
> Their Routes are fair—
> But think enlarged
> of all that they
> will tell us
> Returning here—
> "Here"! There are
> typic "Heres"—
> Foretold Locations—
> The Spirit does
> not stand—
> Himself—at whatsoever
> Fathom
> His Native Land—

There are so many strange things about these lines, not the least of which is that in what is seemingly an effort to console, Dickinson opens by reminding her grieving reader that the dead are precisely the ones who never return. There are joys that "may" return to life, and Dickinson compares those joys to "Men," but the men themselves, by nature of the simile into which they are embedded, are not the ones returning. The following lines urge (not by commanding but by invoking the social "we") the reader not to mourn for certain men because "their Routes are fair," a conventional elegiac trope that seems counter to the despair articulated in the earlier, more wistful enumeration of loss. But according to the logic of the lines at this point, the joy that we might feel on certain occasions in the future relies on the very return (and subsequent narration of events) by these men who we have learned will never return. Trapped in its own logic (one that, by its very inscrutable nature, is bound to trap the writer who is attempting to console the inconsolable reader), the poem moves away from the correspondences it has set up and turns to focus on the issue of place. It is hard to know whether Dickinson was defensively backing away from the emotion she had hit on, was simply moving on by shifting focus, or was building on the conundrum she had set up. Regardless, the final lines enact a major shift as they articulate the places (the "typic 'Heres'") to which the dead may return. In doing so, the poem closes the gap between the living and the dead with the repetition and insistence upon "Here" as an actual, physical space that, by repeating it and by employing the languages of place and space ("Locations," "Fathom," and "Land"), the lines themselves witness.[21]

Because this poem was copied in Dickinson's home, sent through the mail, and then received and read in Elizabeth Holland's home, the actual location of "Here" is unclear. But when Dickinson copied an earlier draft of it, that "Here" was most definitely her own home, if not, more specifically, her kitchen. Written on a leaf of stationery, the earlier draft is quite similar to the later one in content and form, but the earlier one was unacceptable for sending presumably because of the material onto which it was written, as the backside of this leaf carries the recipe for Mrs. Carmichael's coconut cake, copied out in Dickinson's hand, and the final lines of the poem are copied on a small fragment of paper that was pinned, face down, to this leaf (fig. 5.3).

There are a number of ways of understanding how both texts ended up here. The most obvious assumption is that Dickinson may have been in the kitchen when she thought of the poem, and wrote it down on the material at hand. As Werner has argued, it is very possible that "the cometary pace of [Dickinson's] thought determines her choice of materials—whatever lies close by."[22] Additionally, Holland's analysis of these materials includes actual accounts of people remembering how Dickinson wrote in the kitchen.[23] Another option is that Dickinson wanted to keep a record of the recipe in the same way that she wanted to keep a record of the poem, and in an effort to do so did not distinguish between them in value. In this case, the poem need not have been written quickly or in the

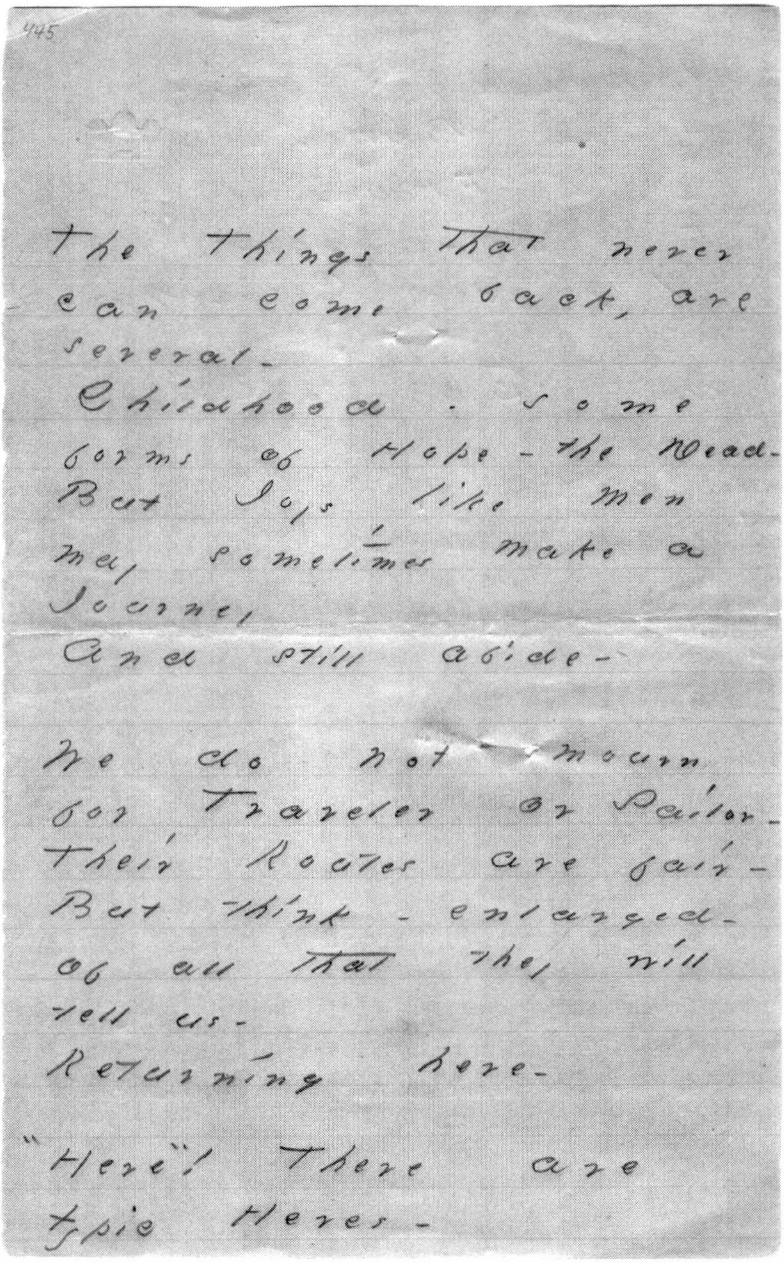

445

the things that never
can come back, are
several.
  Childhood . some
forms of Hope — the Dead.
But Joys like men
may sometimes make a
Journey,
  And still abide —

We do not mourn
for Traveler or Sailor —
their Routes are fair —
But think . enlarged —
of all that they will
tell us —
  Returning here —

"Here"! There are
typic Heres —

Figure 5.3
Draft of "The Things that never can come back, are several—" (F 1564) with pinned slip and cake recipe. Courtesy, Archives & Special Collections, Amherst College.

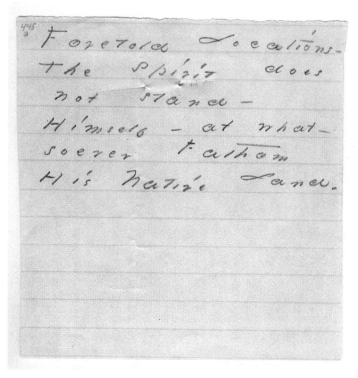

Figure 5.3 (*continued*)

kitchen, and the choice of paper is not nearly as random. A third option is that Dickinson was conserving paper and when faced with a mostly empty leaf (the recipe was most likely copied on the leaf first), regardless of where she was or how she valued either text, she used it to draft the poem. In all of these scenarios, the fact that the cake recipe is there is largely incidental.

A very different way of reading this is to treat the material situation as both intentional and meaningful. In other words, we could say that there might have been something sensory about the cake (its smell, its taste) that Dickinson wanted to call up in relation to the poem; that looking at this cake recipe (and possibly thinking about the cake that is its product) was the occasion for the writing of the poem; or that Dickinson was consciously playing something in the poem off of something in the recipe. In each of these cases, the assumption is that Dickinson was doing something intertextual and that she was creating a situation that, although she would not necessarily have to have imagined this, requires a later interpreter to make the above connections. Werner, for instance, often works along these lines, thinking about the manuscripts as "iconic" and "meta-phorical," as well as "actual containers for thoughts."[24] She writes: "An envelope shaped like a bird carries a text about flight, a seal becomes a space for Dickinson to meditate on the power of secrecy, a torn edge corresponds to a textual verge,

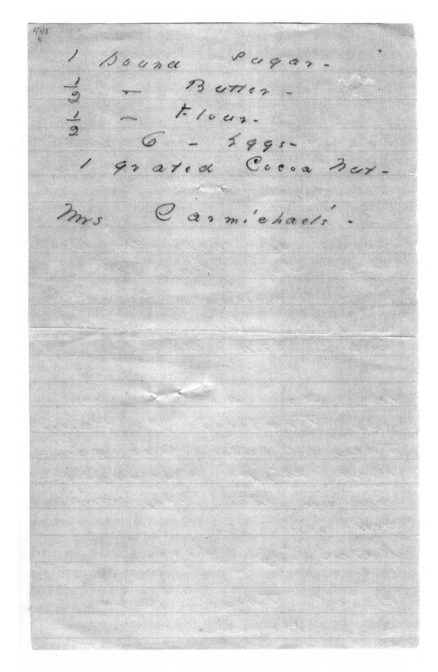

1 Pound Sugar.

½ ~ Butter.

½ ~ Flour.

6 ~ Eggs.

1 grated Cocoa Nut.

Mrs Carmichael's.

Figure 5.3 (*continued*)

the two sides of a manuscript are inscribed with rhyming texts—or texts that cancel each other out. The medium and the message are sometimes one and the same."[25] Jackson shows how enticing these kinds of readings are, as she too spins out ones to which anyone with an investigative eye, an interest in manuscripts, and the impulse to read intertextually will be drawn. But just when we believe that this is what Dickinson must have been after, Jackson tells us that we have fallen into the "double bind" of lyric reading: "while you are imagining these associations, you will realize that you are merely reading a found page lyrically: the maker of the wrapper certainly did not intend for you to interpret those signs in that way.... Yet now that the wrapper has been published as part of a Dickinson poem, associations between literal accident and figurative meaning invite surmise."[26] When looking at lines that Dickinson wrote on the back of a shopping list, then, she states: "All that these two texts have in common is paper."[27]

Faced with the juxtaposition of a poetic text and a non-poetic text and not wanting to over- or under-attribute intention is a tricky endeavor, but looking at Dickinson's actual process for making her poems—a process that we have seen throughout this book is visible in her manuscripts—helps guide us towards what Dickinson was doing in these moments. For instance, it is clear that the recipe was on the leaf before Dickinson started copying the poem on the other side, otherwise she would have copied the rest of the poem on the back of the leaf instead of on the slip that she pinned, face down, to the larger leaf. The break between the leaf and the slip occurs right after the line "'Here'! There are / typic 'Heres'—" and so we might ask what happens in the composition of the poem when Dickinson encountered the recipe and moved to the smaller fragment of paper. While it is clear from the content of the final lines that the interruption of a recipe (of, we *might* say, a representation of or a reminder of both food and labor) does not directly affect where Dickinson took the poem, it is interesting to note that it becomes difficult to understand right at this very moment. We might say, then, that the recipe presents an odd and jarring interruption that the poem registers in the fragmented logic and syntax at its end. As I turn now to lines written on a torn fragment of advertising flyer and those written on an opened-up wrapper, I will continue to read along the lines of Dickinson's process, showing that in these cases even more so, it is not the words, occasion, or meaning of the material itself that we need to focus on, but, instead, the spaces and interruptions that those materials present to Dickinson in the act of writing. By looking closely at the spaces on the paper, we can see the ways in which the movements and strategies of her poems are often made possible, or are even dictated, by the materials themselves. More specifically we will see how the interruptions and constrictions produced by other texts allow the poems to, once again, undo themselves at their ends.

In 1883, Dickinson wrote the lines that begin "To be forgot by thee" (F 1601) on the front and back sides of a torn fragment of an advertising flyer (fig. 5.4). Even less meaning can be drawn from the presence of the advertising flyer than can be from the cake recipe discussed above, as the only words that are visible on the printed side of this fragment make it clear that "Callum's" is the name (or part of the name) of the advertised institution and that "linens" are one of the potentially multiple pieces of merchandise that could be purchased there.[28] The lines that Dickinson drafted on this fragment (ones about the process of forgetting) seem to have nothing to do with the fact of the advertisement itself.

Because Franklin's edition turns these lines into a readable poem, it makes my above judgment possible, but encountering the fragment itself produces a crisis of reading precisely because of the lack of markers for how to read it. Unlike the poem sent to Mrs. Holland, this one was never rendered in complete form as comprehensible to anyone other than Dickinson herself. But because Dickinson left it in a draft state we can see her otherwise invisible compositional methods. If one were to transcribe what is written on this fragment of paper, this is what one would see:

> To be forgot
> by thee
> Surpasses Memory
> Of other minds
> The Heart cannot
> forget
> Unless it Contem-
> Until
> plate
> What it declines
> I was regarded
> then   considered
> Raised from obliv
> ion
> A single time
> royal—signal—
>   hallowed
> To be remembered
> what—Worthy to
> be forgot
> [on other side of leaf]
> My low renown ["renown" and "wan"
> are sectioned off by a curvy line]
> one—meek—wan
> for one must
> recollect
> before
> it
> can
> forget—
> [running vertically between
> lines of the ad: "is my renown"]

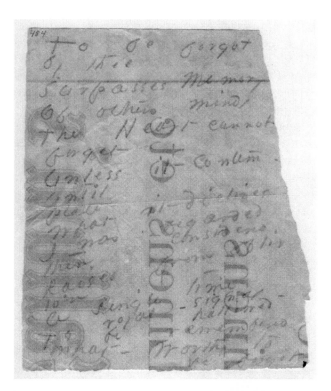

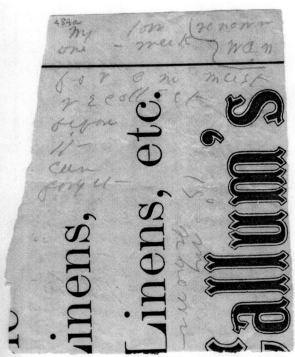

Figure 5.4
"To be forgot by thee" (F 1601). Courtesy, Archives & Special Collections, Amherst College.

The first moment at which these lines become incomprehensible is in line 8 when "Until" interrupts the completion of the word "Contemplate." I would not argue that Dickinson consciously interrupted this word here or that the word "Until" is significant as the thing that comes between "Contem" and "plate." Instead, the manuscript shows that she included the variant "Until" for "Unless" before she wrote the word "Contemplate." In other words, "Unless" and "Until" were generated and recorded at the same time. This observation allows us to see that, while "Unless" appears on top and was therefore written down first, the two words are far more equal in value than we regularly regard Dickinson's variants to be. The second interruption to the flow of these lines occurs when Dickinson wrote "considered" under "regarded," but in this case it is, upon first glance, harder to know when "considered" was recorded because it hugs "regarded" in a way that marks their relation to each other and because there was already the white space after "then" left here. The angle at which both words are written, though, reveals that "considered" was probably recorded either right after "regarded" or right after "then" was set down.

Up until here in the poem, single variants are tucked under the words that were originally set down, and they seem to have been composed within the flow of writing the poem, occurring to Dickinson just as soon as or just after the first word was recorded. But as we get to the bottom of the fragment of flyer, we encounter three variants underneath the line "A single time." Franklin marks "royal," "signal," and "hallowed" as variants for "single," and, as with the variants that came earlier in the poem, these were all written at the same time as the line was recorded, as the next line works around them.[29] As we saw in the previous section, the move into multiple options that can no longer be tightly associated with a singular companion often sets the stage for what will be the poem's unraveling.

This unraveling occurs soon enough: After writing "To be remembered / what—" Dickinson broke with her standard way of indicating a new line and squeezed what seems to be the next line ("Worthy to / be forgot") into the white space at the bottom right of the paper. Then, when Dickinson turned the paper over, she did away with the poem's previous tight sense of relation and coherence that made it possible to read the lines on the first side of the flyer but that is starting to come undone at its bottom. The words at the top of the second side are "My low renown / one—meek—wan," and, as with the three variants under "single," Franklin reads these three adjectives as variants for the noun (in this case, "renown"). But here Dickinson drew a curvy line around "renown" and "wan," as if indicating her favorite of the three variants.

The lines that come beneath this ("for one must recollect before it can forget") seem to have nothing to do with the lines above, and, indeed, Franklin reads them as a variant for the lines "Unless [Until] it contemplate / What it declines" that had appeared on the other side.[30] While this makes sense in terms of the meaning of the poem, for our purposes it is worth noting that this alternative way of phrasing the line did not occur to Dickinson until after she had composed the whole poem. Instead of attempting to squeeze it onto the front side, she placed it, roughly and without any indication of line breaks, on the back side, where the print of the advertisement runs perpendicular to her writing and where the windy line around "renown" and "wan" marks this as a worksheet for no eyes other than her own. As if this side of the flyer had been marked by so many different textual techniques that there is no point in maintaining rules about which lines are meant to be read in relation to which, Dickinson wrote, in a slightly bigger hand, and now perpendicular to her other writing on this side and between the lines of the printed advertisement yet upside down to them, "is my renown." While Franklin reads this as a variant for "My low [one] [meek] [wan] renown," I hope to have shown that such a reading cleans up the textual mess that Dickinson made on the back of this flyer, and yet it is the textual mess that we could say is most important.[31] Seeing the lines in their drafty and largely unreadable form reveals just how the compositional process not only breaks down but how that breaking down incrementally feeds more breaking down—so that the curvy line at the top of the fragment allows for the loss of line breaks in the next section of writing, which then allows for an almost entirely random and untethered "is my renown" written in visual opposition to what has come before it.

Out of these messy final lines Dickinson constructed the two lines that she would send to Helen Hunt Jackson on April 10, 1883. These lines read: "To be remembered what? / Worthy to be forgot, is their renown—." In doing this Dickinson makes sense of her earlier draft for us, showing us that "Worthy to be forgot" is indeed a line in its own right even though it had been squeezed in like a variant, and that "is my renown" (although in the version sent to Jackson the pronoun is changed to "their") is what comes next. Reading backwards from the Jackson version to the version on the fragment of advertising flyer allows us to make sense of how Dickinson eventually made sense of what she had written here. We can see her in the act of creating greater coherence and readability, something that her subsequent drafts often strive for. In other words, while fragmentation was a condition that she could not only live with but that she fostered (by way of her choices of materials) in the process of drafting, coherence and readability were not entirely abandoned. As I read it, this fragment of advertising flyer has nothing to do with the content of these lines (in other words, they are not a response to or a reflection on what the flyer represents or embodies), but instead it is the fragmentary nature of what Dickinson was writing on and the presence of parts of printed words on that fragment that are at least partially responsible for the gradual unraveling of the poem's lines, logic, and order. In other words, the material limits of the paper are related to the production of variants, both of which then affect how the poem navigates its final moves.

The leaf of paper with the recipe written on it and the fragment of advertising flyer both point to, by naming, processes of labor and products of consumption that Dickinson encountered in her daily life. In this third example we see the imprint of such a product not in words, but in a stain and in folds. In the summer of 1883 Dickinson copied the lines that begin "To her derided Home" (F 1617) on a wrapper (fig. 5.5). The stain left on this wrapper, a dark square at the center of its opened-out form, indicates that something (possibly candy) had once been folded within the wrapper that later came to hold Dickinson's words. One of the things that this manuscript makes visible is that Dickinson treated this wrapper not unlike the way she treated a folded sheet of stationery, in that she folded it in half (down the center vertically) and wrote down the front side, ignoring the stain made by the wrapped item. Because the inside of the wrapper may have been less suitable to write on, when Dickinson ran out of room on this panel she turned next to the empty part of this side of the wrapper (in other words, if we see it as a folded sheet, she turned next to its fourth side). The odd thing about this move is that she wrote upside down on this next panel, something that she never did with pieces of folded stationery, an act that marks writing on a wrapper as a less formal endeavor, even as it allows for some of the formal conventions of the sheet.

The tension between formality and informality is evident all over this docu- ment. When looking at the front panel, it is striking how carefully Dickinson cop- ied the words—as if she were copying a fascicle poem or a letter. But at the bottom of this side, she broke in the middle of a line and finished the line upside down on the next side. Once you turn the wrapper over so that the words on this next side are readable, it too looks not like a casual missive jotted on a discarded wrapper, but like a poem rendered in formal lines. Similarly to how she continued the line she left unfinished on the first side, she wrote the final line (for which there was no room) along the margin that had been created by folding the wrapper once down its center. Twice having broken with the formality of the placement of lines, Dick- inson was now free to include a variant (something we have not yet encountered in these lines) above the "him" at the margin. Both the multiplication and inde- terminacy of reference introduced by the "her" that sits over the "him" is a move that does not radically change the meaning of these lines, but instead indicates that Dickinson is unsure about a major aspect of them—namely, if what is being sustained in this situation is male or female. As if this awareness of the poem's instability of reference opens up other instabilities, next Dickinson opened the folded wrapper up and wrote, on its once uninhabitable inside, behind the writing on the second panel but perpendicular to it (in other words, in a totally strange and non-uniform manner), five words that, according to Franklin, are variants for the poem's two final lines.[32] If this is a variant, then here Dickinson chose "him," and so it becomes a variant that presents one choice as its very presence con- structs another.

What my reading of this material artifact and the words that appear on it (if not their meaning, for, you might notice, I have not included a transcription of the lines) are meant to show is that the wrapper itself (its ability to be folded and creased, its various panels and sides) is the very thing that allows the poem to multiply and intensify its inclination to include variants. As in the case of the

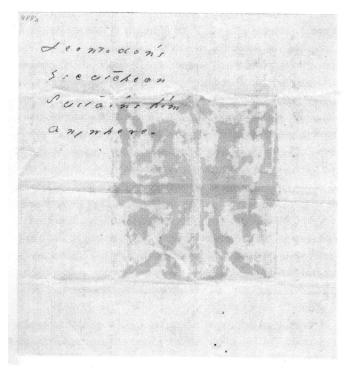

Figure 5.5
"To her derided Home" (F 1617). Courtesy, Archives & Special Collections, Amherst College.

advertising flyer, the constraints presented by the material itself forced Dickinson to renegotiate the relationship of space and text, urging her to press against and play off of its multiple boundaries. We might say, then, that Dickinson's choice of these materials makes possible the sometimes-radical reworkings of lines that gesture at her desire to keep these poems from coming to an end, even if they eventually do.

When Dickinson went on to make another copy of these lines, it is not surprising that she continued to fiddle with the ending. Instead of including the lines that gave her so much trouble on the wrapper (trouble that is made visible by the strange angles at which she wrote them, first in the margin and then on the inside of the wrapper), she copied several lines that she had already copied, as part of another poem, into a letter to Maria Whitney earlier that year. After "As Lady / from her Bower—" Dickinson indicated a stanza break and wrote "The implements / of Bliss are / few—" and then crossed out, with multiple, angular cross strokes, "The implements" and "are," placed a "the" in front of the crossed out "are," and squeezed the words "Codes are" underneath "Of Bliss." She thus created the line "Of Bliss the Codes are few—" and followed it with the remaining lines as sent to Whitney, except for one small revision of the word "says" to "cites." As Dickinson revised the line that she had already sent to Whitney and then attempted to use it (and the ones that follow it) to conclude a poem the ending for which she had not settled on, she further revealed the crisis that exists at this poem's conclusion. Although she signed this folded sheet of letter paper "E. Dickinson," she did not send it, and while she may have copied a new version to send, we can assume that her indecision about the ending on this draft is the reason for this.

In conclusion, I want to return briefly to the presence of the coconut cake recipe on the other side of "The Things that never can come back, are several—," because it made visible all of the different ways we might read how Dickinson came to place the poetic and nonpoetic text on the same material. There I identified that the most radical way of reading intention out of this story is to say that Dickinson is simply writing on whatever materials are on hand. The most radical way of reading intention and purpose into the story is to say that Dickinson is consciously engaging in a kind of coded intertextual play, creating a puzzle of sorts that some later reader will work to decipher. One of the things that I hope to have shown here is that the manuscripts, while not resolving this problem, open up a territory in between, where we can see that Dickinson's turn to these materials is intricately tied to some of the struggles she was having with the movements, choices, and endings of her poems, and that these household materials, in turn, support and intensify those struggles by creating more opportunity for interruption, digression, and rethinking. In other words, it is not so much a story about what Dickinson did or did not intend, but a story about how an evolving compositional process, her developing struggle with her poems' endings, and some very real pieces of domestic material culture come together at this moment.

Poems before this period did not get copied on recipes, advertising flyers, and abandoned wrappers, and once they eventually were, they became more fragmentary, less decisive in their directions and choices, more ready to rethink and reject their own logics and structures. Whether Dickinson had the sense that her poems needed such a context or whether the material contexts allowed for something to develop in the poems that was simply lurking at this moment, we can't know for sure. But we have been able to see that, once here, the poems are pressed by the materials into a more acute state of being. Instead of thinking of this period as one marked by moments of rush and incompletion, I have lingered on the issues of readability, unclear relations, and the tensions between formal and informal gestures that the materials themselves raise.

SCRAPS, PINS, AND THE SMALLEST OF MATERIAL ARTIFACTS

In the final section of this final chapter I will briefly look at the smallest, most jagged, most "scrap-like" materials. Some of these materials will feel visually extreme, even after having seen something like the opened up wrapper or the advertising flyer. I find this most striking when looking at writings on the insides of envelope flaps, or fragments of flaps (figs. 5.6a and 5.6b). On one flap, in which the seal is still visible and where we can see all the places where the paper has been torn in order to produce this writing surface, Dickinson wrote:

> In this short Life
> that only lasts an hour
>   merely
> How much—how
> little—is
> within our
> power
>   (F 1292)

One can't help but associate the shortness of the life, here rendered in temporal terms, with the smallness of the paper. The references to quantity ("how much—how little") is underscored by the smallness of the space, and the gesture at some sort of human community ("our") resonates on a piece of paper that, due to its function, has already engaged in some form of communication between people. And yet, as I have shown in the previous sections, the lines written on all types of stray paper can hardly be said to comment, exactly, on that paper. This becomes clear when we see that the above interpretations are just slightly off, as the torn envelope flap does not actually embody the temporal problem of the lines and does not speak to the problem of quantifying "power."

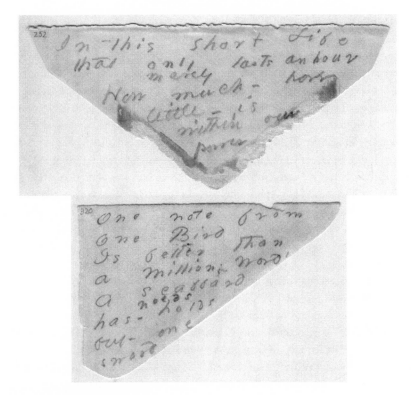

Figures 5.6a and 5.6b
"In this short Life" (F 1292) and "One note from One Bird" (F 1478). Courtesy, Archives & Special Collections, Amherst College.

A similar thing happens on another envelope flap, but this time it is just half of one. There, Dickinson wrote:

> One note from
> One Bird
> Is better than
> a Million Word—
> A scabbard
>   needs
> has—holds
> but one
> sword
>   (F 1478)

This slightest of scraps sets itself in relation to the "One note from / One Bird" that is the very subject of the scrap. It is, possibly, this note itself, except the bird's note is not material but aural, and even if it was, this "note" looks more like a scrap that a bird might pick up and use to make its nest from than like something a bird would actually write. Here the emphasis is on the few words that exist in "one note," as opposed to the "million" that might be found elsewhere. The comparison that emerges, though, is really about singularity. The scabbard "has," "needs," and "holds" only one sword, and by implication not only is one word necessary, but that word is deadly, or protective, or at least prized for both its status and its utility. And in the same way that that sword is contained by the scabbard, and by extension the scabbard's function is to hold it, so the word is being held by something that is unnamed in the lines but that we, seeing it in front of us, know must be paper. In this way these lines are about writing, enclosure, and dissemination. In both of these examples the scrappiness of the literal context is related to the words without the two things being one and the same. In other words, there is always something about the lines that makes it impossible for us to fully collapse the two things (words and torn paper) into one coherent story about Dickinson's manuscripts.

One of the oddest things about Dickinson's smallest scraps is that they are sometimes pinned to each other. Although the pins are no longer present, small holes and thin indentations are evidence of their prior existence. Interestingly, while we can't be certain whether Dickinson was using pins or needles, we can assume that it was one of these items, both of which have another function in the household, most specifically for sewing. Not unlike Dickinson's use of string to sew her sheets together to make fascicles, here she connected poems and pieces of poems (albeit in a stranger and more jagged way) together. In these final pages it feels only right to gesture at this process of pinning that Dickinson took up, not in some attempt to fully understand it or to have it provide closure for this study, but because it raises some of the crucial questions about poetic process and material culture with which this book has been concerned.

While Dickinson sometimes pinned drafts of variant lines together, the most basic thing that this pinning process reveals is that Dickinson was regularly writing on multiple small slips of paper.[33] The breaks we register between slips is often nothing more than a result of the fact that when there was no more room on one slip, she picked up another and continued writing. We can see this in "The Infinite a sudden Guest" (F 1344) and "We never know we go when we are going—" (F 1546), where the lines are started on one slip, finished on another, and the two slips are then pinned together. In "The Infinite a sudden Guest" the break occurs in the middle of the poem:

> The Infinite a
> sudden Guest
> Has been assumed
> to be—
> [next scrap]
> But how can that

stupendous come
Which never went away?

Because these texts were written on two different kinds of paper (one is yellow
with very faint lining and the other is graph paper), one might say that the words
on these two slips could have been written at different times and later pinned together but not as an indication that they make a poem. But it is clear that the
contents of the two scraps are connected, as the sense of the lines on the second
scrap seem to depend for their meaning (otherwise, what would "that stupendous" be referring to?) on the first scrap. The same is true of "We never know we
go when we are going," where only the last line appears on the second scrap:

> We never know we go
> when we are going—
> We jest and shut the
> Door—
> Fate—following—behind us
> bolts it—
> [next scrap]
> And we accost
>   we know
> (no more—)

I assume that these lines were copied in this order because, unlike composing a
first line on its own, one that can roll around for a while until the rest of the lines
follow, it would be strange to generate this last line, which so clearly depends on
the existence of the previous lines, first. In this case not only does the "And" that
begins the second scrap indicate its probable connection to words on the other
scrap, but we know from Frances Norcross' transcripts that Dickinson had sent
the lines that appear on these two scraps together and in this order.

Another example of this mode of relation will drive this point home, as the
break across scraps that occurs within the poem we now call "I noticed People
disappeared" (F 1154) actually disrupts the syntactical unit:

> I noticed People disappeared
> When but a little child—
> Supposed they visited
> remote
> Or settled Regions wild—
> Now know I—^{Or} I know now
> [next scrap]
> They both visited
> And settled Regions

wild—
But | did because |
~~vasted,~~
~~vaster, that~~
| they died |
A Fact withheld
the little child—
a

While this poem is repetitive in interesting ways, it is clear that the lines on the second scrap are not a variant for the lines on the first. The "Now know I" (the choice over "I know now," even though the two mean the same thing) is the hinge in the poem, and the repetition occurs as a result of that subsequent knowing.

The most obvious observation to make about these pins is that they mark Dickinson's desire to keep pieces of her poems in relation to each other. Because the smaller slips are sometimes pinned right side up, upside down, in front of or behind the larger piece of paper, it is clear that Dickinson was simply trying to associate them, but not in some visually uniform way. The pins show us Dickinson's investment in readability and order and in this way we might say they reveal her ambivalence about doing away with the highly organized system that her poetic process had been mostly governed by, for the pins set relationships in motion and kept fragments from scattering into some chaotic form. Dickinson may have rejected sequence, and she may have been troubling the notion of closure, but this does not mean that she did away with all forms of relation and order.

But what is odd about all of the examples above is that in each of these cases, Dickinson could have written the remaining lines on the backs of the original scraps instead of going through the trouble of using a new scrap, pinning it, and then potentially having the two come unattached. The obvious conclusion would be that Dickinson did not want to write on the backs of scraps, but as the following example will show, this is not entirely true. In this chapter's final example we will see that when Dickinson did write on the backs of her scraps, she still used pins, therefore marking the object for preservation not simply the words, but the material artifact itself.

The lines that begin "Power is a familiar growth" (F 1287) were written in 1873 in pencil on a square fragment of paper that had been torn along its bottom and left sides (fig. 5.7). The lines read:

Power is a familiar
growth—
       foreign
Not distant—not to be—
Beside us like a
bland Abyss

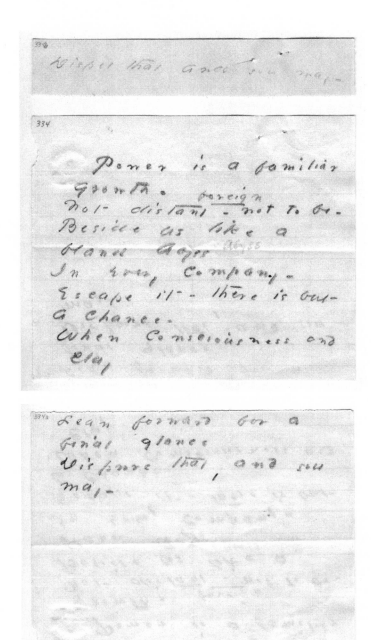

Figure 5.7
"Power is a familiar growth—" (F 1287). Courtesy, Archives & Special Collections, Amherst College.

In every company—
Escape it—there is but
a chance—
When consciousness and
clay
[on other side]
Lean forward for a
final glance
Disprove that, and you
may—

On the slip that Dickinson pinned to this scrap she wrote, "Dispel that and you may—." Although the slip is the same width as the scrap, it is a yellower paper and it does not have lines on it the way the square scrap does. While it may be true that Dickinson came up with this variant at another time and place, it is strange that, once reunited with the square scrap, she didn't simply write "Dispel" as a variant for 'Disprove," either interlined or at the bottom, for there is a good amount of white space left. In other words, why, once Dickinson had already gone onto the other side, did she still pin the variant line instead of copying it onto the scrap itself?

This situation points to the fact that there is something about the material artifact itself that Dickinson wanted to preserve. If all that was at issue was having all of the possible lines for a given poem in the same place, then she would have simply copied the alternate line on the scrap of paper with the poem. Pinning it, though, indicates her desire to associate it while also keeping it separate. In other words, by holding tight to the material remnant, Dickinson retained something of the scene of composition itself. And the trace of that scene is, as it has always been, in the materials. If this pinning process preserved, for Dickinson, all of these small, jagged, strange looking material artifacts, what it raises for us is the status of that artifact. But by holding onto that artifact as material that was important to Dickinson and that is important to us as readers and interpreters of Dickinson's texts, we neither have to turn that material into a piece of a self-referential lyric that it is not nor do we have to abandon the notion that there is something meaningful to read here.

In this chapter we have looked closely at Dickinson's drafts, scraps, and fragments; we have wrestled with the readability and potential meanings of her use of domestic materials; and we have pinned and unpinned the tiniest pieces of paper so as to understand Dickinson's use of paper in her final years. By spending time with these materials I hope to have shown that more so than at any other stage of Dickinson's writing life, it is during this period that she rejected the book as a source of containment, comprehensibility, and authority, navigating new relationships to issues of order, wholeness, finality, and relation in her poetry. As

Dickinson herself would write in 1879 on a small fragment of stationery that was torn along the left-hand side and the bottom, "To see the Summer / Sky / Is Poetry, though / never in a Book / it lie—/ True Poems flee" (F 1491). Yet in that acting of fleeing—in the ways in which these materials scatter and multiply physically—these poems do not drift off beyond our grasp. Dickinson may have imagined that "True Poems flee," but as we have seen, the truest poems are set down, in ink or pencil, on all sizes and sorts of paper, and their meanings, while possibly distant, are still a part of our world.

Afterword

Dickinson is a writer who invites us to look at her paper in part because she explicitly writes about how it shapes what she has to say. To Sue, in February 1852 she wrote, "Susie, what shall I do—there is'nt room enough; not *half* enough, to hold what I was going to say. Wont you tell the man who makes sheets of paper, that I hav'nt the *slightest respect* for him!" (L 77). And later that year, she wrote to Sue again, "[I]f this saucy page did not here bind and fetter me, I might have had no end" (L 93). Aware of the contours of the paper, Dickinson wrote both with and against them. While Dickinson may have been explicit about this, all writers feel the boundaries of the objects on which they write, and they register the kind of texts that might belong there. In other words, Dickinson could not have been the only poet who treated paper as a mode of knowledge production and sociality. She could not have been the only one to imagine that the surfaces of writing make a difference to the lines written there.

Indeed, the history of twentieth-century poetry provides many examples of ways that poets composed their poems. These stories capture our interest and imagination. For instance, scholars have long commented on the fact that William Carlos Williams often wrote poems on his prescription pads.[1] Faced with having to write in between appointments or while a sick child slept, this doctor-poet wrote on the material most readily available to him. And no story is more romantic than the one of Langston Hughes jotting down "The Negro Speaks of Rivers" on the back of an envelope as he crossed the Mississippi River on a train headed for Mexico.[2] Given the methodology of this book, we might ask of these moments, as they become available to us through manuscript and memory, what role the material itself plays in the composition of poems that we have often read as lyrically transcending precisely such material. Might we attribute Williams' short lines not only to the tenets of Imagism, but to the contours of his small prescription pad? Might we wonder about the letter from Hughes' estranged father that lay inside the envelope on which he wrote those tragic and celebratory lines about history? In a recent book on post-World War II poetry, Stephen Fredman asks just such questions, as he not only narrates the moment when Robert Creeley went from composing on the typewriter to writing poems out long-hand, but explains that this is when Creeley "began to see that the size of the notebook page could determine the scope of what he wrote."[3] Faced with the immediacy of the compositional context and set free from the technology that required him to finish his poems, Creeley radically changed the kinds of poems he wrote.

I do not turn to the examples of twentieth-century American poets at the end of this book on Emily Dickinson in order to drag us into the twentieth century, as if to say that this is where Dickinson has been leading us all along. As should be clear by now, I thoroughly resist this trajectory, as it is precisely the move to read Dickinson as proto-everything (modernist, postmodernist, feminist, etc.) that has kept us from returning to her workshop for so long. If Dickinson is simply Gertrude Stein born fifty years too early, then there is little point in understanding her nineteenth-century context. Instead, I raise these examples in order to ask where the comparable stories about nineteenth-century American poetry might be. While it is true that some form of the materials and methods of composition with which we have been immersed in this study are available to every person who sets about composing a poem, in these final pages I would like to suggest that finding the stories about the composition of nineteenth-century poems will be particularly valuable.

No poetry deserves our re-reading more than nineteenth-century American women's poetry. Despite the efforts of scholars to present a more accurate picture of who was writing and publishing in nineteenth-century America, to reinvigorate an interest in what Martha Nell Smith has characterized as the "too-long-neglected or at-best-skimmed American poetry," the poetry that these women wrote is rarely taught in the college classroom.[4] When it is, it is often positioned in opposition to Dickinson's work. Yet as the materials of nineteenth-century American women poets begin to become available—as their archives are processed and opened for use—we might use this study of Dickinson to ask how these other poets too worked in awareness of their own compositional materials and processes. As we do so, it is essential that we resist the impulse to collapse the genres in which they worked, divorce their poems from their material contexts, and dissociate their lines from the historically-specific moments of composition.

One of the ways that we know that nineteenth-century American women poets thought about the paper they used is that they wrote about it in their poems. In "To a Shred of Linen," Lydia Sigourney tells the history of what opens the poem as a piece of household debris, highlighting the labor that went into its creation. After this object emerges as a pillow case that will not tell the secrets of those who lay down on it, the narrator of the poem relegates it to the "paper-mill," from which it will emerge "stainless and smooth" as the "fair page" on which she is writing. Sigourney draws attention to the relationship between paper and linen, foregrounding the domestic and commercial qualities of both. By ending on the paper that makes the poem both writeable and readable, Sigourney calls attention to the material circumstances of writing and the compositional moment.

While Sigourney's poem has made it into anthologies, pieces by Frances Osgood are still rarely read or studied. Yet Osgood seems even more preoccupied than Sigourney with the materials of composition, as can be seen in her poems "Rags! Rags! Any Rags to Sell?" and "To My Pen." As Eliza Richards points out in her study of the women poets who inhabited Edgar Allan Poe's circle, Osgood celebrates even less ambivalently than Sigourney the "world of print" made possible by materials such as rags.[5] Even more to the point, though, Richards draws attention to a story of Osgood's composition that appears in Elizabeth Oakes Smith's autobiography. There, Oakes Smith writes, "I have seen little Fannie Osgood write with a pencil upon slips of paper in her lap surrounded by a room full of company; indeed, she rarely wrote in solitude—she needed the inspiration of human companionship to give form and force to her pen."[6] How might we read such materials ("slips of paper in her lap") and circumstances ("surrounded by a room full of company") as important to, say, Osgood's exhortation to her pen to ignore the words of "critic men" and "publishers"?

As the examples of Sigourney and Osgood make clear, material exists to show that nineteenth-century American women poets were writing explicitly about their materials and modes of composition. In order to find these "slips of paper"—to look at poets who, working before the personal typewriter became available, had no choice but to use paper and who used it in interesting and innovative ways—will send us into the archive and to the manuscripts that live there. Yet what we will find there will not only be the paper itself, but a way out of lyricizing that paper's textual and extra-textual details. By reading the relationship of paper to text (instead of one without the other), we have the opportunity to resist over-reading, or investing with symbolism, either that paper or that text. By returning to the moment of writing to ask what role the paper played in shaping the poem or why the writer may have chosen that particular kind of paper for that poem, we will find ourselves reading through the scene of composition, instead of through the often anachronistic habits of reading that have guided our critical practices up until now.

That being said, it is important not to romanticize the archive, as it does not present the final word on how poems are made and on what they mean. And yet this is precisely why it is so useful to literary critics. The archive, in a nutshell, makes us acutely aware of the often uncomfortable processes behind finished works of literary criticism. We don't usually tell stories about dead ends, unanswered questions, and unreadable texts, as our treatments of literature are meant to produce coherent knowledge where there was no such knowledge before. And yet the archive, for all its promise of information, is filled with faulty paths and sprawling questions. It houses paper that returns us to the moment of composition and that disrupts how we may have read before. By recounting Dickinson's story—one that is full of such paper—I hope to have shown that taking account of the archive is largely about coming to terms with the fact that while the materials and information are not all going to line up, this knowledge is itself a way out of the lyricization of Dickinson and, potentially, her female contemporaries. As we learn this lesson from the archive, and as we allow the story of the archive to wrap back into the work we do, we become readers, writers, and researchers who better understand our own always unfinished, imperfect, and materially-determined business.

NOTES

INTRODUCTION

1. Emily Dickinson, *Poems by Emily Dickinson*, ed. Mabel Loomis Todd and Thomas Wentworth Higginson (Boston: Roberts Brothers, 1890), v–vi.
2. This other way of approaching Dickinson has been most thoroughly undertaken and elaborated in Helen Vendler, *Poets Thinking: Pope, Whitman, Dickinson, Yeats* (Cambridge, MA: Harvard University Press, 2004).
3. Jerome J. McGann, *The Textual Condition* (Princeton, NJ: Princeton University Press, 1991), 4.
4. McGann, *The Textual Condition*, 13.
5. Emily Dickinson, *The Manuscript Books of Emily Dickinson*, ed. R. W. Franklin (Cambridge, MA: Belknap Press of Harvard University Press, 1981).
6. Margaret Dickie, "Dickinson in Context," *American Literary History* 7.2 (1995): 321.
7. See Sharon Cameron, *Choosing Not Choosing: Dickinson's Fascicles* (Chicago: University of Chicago Press, 1992); Martha Nell Smith, *Rowing in Eden: Rereading Emily Dickinson* (Austin: University of Texas Press, 1992); Marta L. Werner, ed., *Emily Dickinson's Open Folios: Scenes of Reading, Surfaces of Writing* (Ann Arbor: University of Michigan Press, 1995); Domhnall Mitchell, *Measures of Possibility: Emily Dickinson's Manuscripts* (Amherst: University of Massachusetts Press, 2005); and Virginia Jackson, *Dickinson's Misery: A Theory of Lyric Reading* (Princeton, NJ: Princeton University Press, 2005).
8. Jackson, *Dickinson's Misery*, 134.
9. Lisa Gitelman and Geoffrey B. Pingree, eds., *New Media, 1740–1915* (Cambridge, MA: MIT Press, 2003), xiv.
10. For two (of the many) studies that mention Emerson's poem as an influence, see Cristanne Miller, *Emily Dickinson: A Poet's Grammar* (Cambridge, MA: Harvard University Press, 1987), 149; and Catherine Tufariello, "'The Remembering Wine': Emerson's Influence on Whitman and Dickinson," *The Cambridge Companion to Ralph Waldo Emerson*, ed. Joel Porte and Saundra Morris (Cambridge, UK: Cambridge University Press, 1999), 185–188. For reference to "The Snow that never drifts—" in relation to "It sifts from Leaden Sieves—," see Martin Bickman, "'The snow that never drifts': Dickinson's Slant of Language," *College Literature* 10.2 (1983): 140–141.
11. Magdalena Zapedowska, "Citizens of Paradise: Dickinson and Emmanuel Levinas's Phenomenology of the Home," *Emily Dickinson Journal* 12.2 (2003): 76–77. For the two readings of the poem by Mitchell, see Domhnall Mitchell, "Emily Dickinson and Class," *The Cambridge Companion to Emily Dickinson*, ed. Wendy Martin (Cambridge, UK: Cambridge University Press, 2002), 203–206 and Domhnall Mitchell, "Revising the Script: Emily Dickinson's Manuscripts," *American Literature* 70.4 (1998): 722.

12. For the ten other poems with four or more contexts from the fascicle period, see F 98, F 112, F 122, F 124, F 325, F 744, F 796, F 804, F 819, and F 846.

13. For the thirty-one poems with four or more contexts from the post-fascicle period, see F 895, F 935, F 1183, F 1194, F 1216, F 1227, F 1234, F 1279, F 1285, F 1286, F 1350, F 1357, F 1372, F 1380, F 1383, F 1384, F 1386, F 1411, F 1416, F 1453, F 1454, F 1484, F 1488, F 1489, F 1570, F 1597, F 1598, F 1616, F 1641, F 1665, and F 1671.

14. Jonathan Culler, *Structuralist Poetics: Structuralism, Linguistics, and the Study of Literature* (Ithaca, NY: Cornell University Press, 1975), 116.

15. Jackson, *Dickinson's Misery*, 55.

16. The first way is the most common and, unless the critic has explicitly addressed his or her resistance to such a methodology, can be found in almost all considerations of Dickinson's poems. For an example of the second way, see Jed Deppman, *Trying to Think with Emily Dickinson* (Amherst: University of Massachusetts Press, 2008), 1, where he argues that Dickinson voices our concerns, asserting that "Emily Dickinson can help us see and think what we are well-nigh thinking and saying," and that "the way she used the language of lyric poetry to respond to her most difficult personal and cultural challenges can help us respond to our own." For examples of the third way, see Gary Lee Stonum, *The Dickinson Sublime* (Madison: University of Wisconsin Press, 1990), 10, where he asserts that "a large number of Dickinson's poems present the self as a romantic quester, searching the secrets of her own mind or of nature and hoping to return triumphantly with what she has found"; see also Vivian R. Pollak, *Dickinson: The Anxiety of Gender* (Ithaca, NY: Cornell University Press, 1984), 9, where she reads the "I" as one who is "erotically bereaved, a self-reliant solitary, or merely weird—a case of permanently arrested development"; and see Paula Bennett, *Emily Dickinson: Woman Poet* (Iowa City: University of Iowa Press, 1990), 12–13, 19, where she reads the speaker as someone who is consciously speaking out of the position of the nineteenth-century poetess.

17. Sharon Cameron, *Lyric Time: Dickinson and the Limits of Genre* (Baltimore: Johns Hopkins University Press, 1979), 23.

18. Jackson, *Dickinson's Misery*, 117.

19. Ibid., 119.

20. Walter Benn Michaels, *The Shape of the Signifier: 1967 to the End of History* (Princeton, NJ: Princeton University Press, 2004), 1–18.

21. Carl Knappett, *Thinking Through Material Culture: An Interdisciplinary Perspective* (Philadelphia: University of Pennsylvania Press, 2005), 1–10. Knappett also points out the shortcomings of this paradigm, explaining how some archeologists have chosen to only move from objects to behavior (claiming the move to thoughts as a faulty one) and how others, like himself, have argued that this system creates a "dualistic conception" of material culture by positing material culture as external and thoughts as internal (4). Knappett also takes issue with the opposition of symbolic and functioning meanings that is embedded in this path from object to thought (7).

22. Cristanne Miller, "Controversy in the Study of Emily Dickinson," *Literary Imagination: The Review of the Association of Literary Scholars and Critics* 6.1 (2004): 45.

23. Ibid., 45–46.

CHAPTER 1

1. Even before Franklin's facsimile copy, people were reading the fascicles as groups of poems. See Ruth Miller, *The Poetry of Emily Dickinson* (Middletown, CT: Wesleyan University Press, 1968), and Martha Lindblom O'Keefe, *This Edifice: Studies in the Structure of the Fascicles of the Poetry of Emily Dickinson* (privately printed, 1986). The following books and articles constitute the most influential readings of the fascicles since Franklin's edition. For a narrative reading of Fascicle 40, see Dorothy Huff Oberhaus, *Emily Dickinson's Fascicles: Method & Meaning* (University Park: Pennsylvania

State University Press, 1995). For a book that treats an overarching, romantic narrative that runs throughout the fascicles, see William H. Shurr, *The Marriage of Emily Dickinson: A Study of the Fascicles* (Lexington: University Press of Kentucky, 1983). For articles that consider specific themes with which certain fascicles work, see William Doreski, "'An Exchange of Territory': Dickinson's Fascicle 27," *ESQ* 32.1 (1986): 55–67, and Daneen Wardrop, "Emily Dickinson and the Gothic in Fascicle 16," *The Cambridge Companion to Emily Dickinson*, ed. Wendy Martin (Cambridge, UK: Cambridge University Press, 2002), 142–166. For a consideration of the fascicles as part of the history of the lyric sequence, see M. L. Rosenthal and Sally M. Gall, *The Modern Poetic Sequence: The Genius of Modern Poetry* (Oxford: Oxford University Press, 1983), and Sharon Cameron, *Choosing Not Choosing: Dickinson's Fascicles* (Chicago: University of Chicago Press, 1992). For an analysis of poems that appear in more than one fascicle (otherwise known as "duplicate" poems), see Eleanor Elson Heginbotham, *Dwelling in Possibilities: Reading the Fascicles of Emily Dickinson* (Columbus: Ohio State University Press, 2003). A repeated argument—especially in Heginbotham, Cameron, and Wardrop—is that context changes the meaning of Dickinson's poems.

2. Emily Dickinson, *The Manuscript Books of Emily Dickinson*, ed. R. W. Franklin (Cambridge, MA: Belknap Press of Harvard University Press, 1981), ix.

3. Barton Levi St. Armand, *Emily Dickinson and Her Culture: The Soul's Society* (Cambridge, UK: Cambridge University Press, 1984), 9.

4. St. Armand, *Emily Dickinson and Her Culture*, 5; Emily Dickinson, *Poems by Emily Dickinson*, ed. Thomas Wentworth Higginson and Mabel Loomis Todd (Boston: Roberts Brothers, 1890), iii.

5. Ralph Waldo Emerson, "New Poetry," *Uncollected Writings: Essays, Addresses, Poems, Reviews and Letters* (New York: Lamb Publishing Co., 1912), 137.

6. Ibid., 139.

7. See Dickinson, *The Manuscript Books of Emily Dickinson*, ix–x, where Franklin argues that the fascicles were Dickinson's way "to reduce disorder" and to make "a systematic and comprehensive record of completed poems."

8. See Heginbotham, *Dwelling in Possibilities*, for a detailed analysis of poems that appear in more than one fascicle.

9. While Franklin argues that this occurs in two instances (Fascicles 2 and 33)—see Dickinson, *The Manuscript Books of Emily Dickinson*, xi—the mutilation of Fascicle 2 that took place after Dickinson's death makes it impossible to deduce this about that fascicle. In the case of Fascicle 33, there may be no explaining Dickinson's change in method here. The way I see it, after having made thirty-two fascicles, Dickinson knew that she could go onto the next sheet if she needed to, even if it wasn't her regular practice to do so.

10. Emily Dickinson, *The Poems of Emily Dickinson: Variorum Edition*, ed. R. W. Franklin (Cambridge, MA: Belknap Press of Harvard University Press, 1998), 9.

11. Dickinson, *The Poems of Emily Dickinson* (1998), 18–19.

12. See F 219, F 325, F 352, F 401, F 420, F 437 (now lost), F 600, and F 846 (fragment).

13. Marta L. Werner, ed., *Emily Dickinson's Open Folios: Scenes of Reading, Surfaces of Writing* (Ann Arbor: University of Michigan Press, 1995), 36, 12.

14. See Paula Bennett, *Poets in the Public Sphere: The Emancipatory Project of American Women's Poetry, 1800–1900* (Princeton, NJ: Princeton University Press, 2003); Mary Loeffelholz, *From School to Salon: Reading Nineteenth-Century American Women's Poetry* (Princeton, NJ: Princeton University Press, 2004); and Eliza Richards, *Gender and the Poetics of Reception in Poe's Circle* (Cambridge, UK: Cambridge University Press, 2004).

15. This observation comes from the wide array of mid-nineteenth-century commonplace books housed at the American Antiquarian Society. Unless otherwise noted, all original documents referred to in this section—aside from the fascicles themselves—are part of its collection.

16. See Earle Havens, *Commonplace Books: A History of Manuscripts and Printed Books from Antiquity to the Twentieth Century* (New Haven, CT: Beinecke Rare Book and Manuscript Library, 2001). Havens highlights the multi-dimensional nature of nineteenth-century commonplace books, at times even referring to them as "hybrid commonplace books/scrapbooks" (90). Havens argues that clippings were widely used in Victorian commonplace books, thereby blurring the boundary between the commonplace book and the scrapbook. According to the holdings at the American Antiquarian Society, however, this practice may have been less widely embraced in America. For a more specific look at the immediate pre-history of the nineteenth-century American commonplace book, see Kenneth A. Lockridge, *On the Sources of Patriarchal Rage: The Commonplace Books of William Byrd and Thomas Jefferson and the Gendering of Power in the Eighteenth Century* (New York: New York University Press, 1992), and Susan M. Stabile, *Memory's Daughters: The Material Culture of Remembrance in Eighteenth-Century America* (Ithaca, NY: Cornell University Press, 2004).

17. Todd S. Gernes, *Checklist of Albums & Commonplace Books at A. A. S.* (Worcester, MA: American Antiquarian Society, 1991), 1.

18. Alice S. Fowler, *Autographs: Verses from New England Autograph Albums, 1825–1925* (Conyngham, PA: Pioneer Books, 1989), iv and Gernes, *Checklist*, 3.

19. Ellen Gruber Garvey, "Scissorizing and Scrapbooks: Nineteenth-Century Reading, Remaking, and Recirculating," *New Media, 1740–1915*, ed. Lisa Gitelman and Geoffrey B. Pingree (Cambridge, MA: MIT Press, 2003), 209.

20. Ibid., 208.

21. Susan Huntington Dickinson's book is currently housed in the Martha Dickinson Bianchi Collection in the John Hay Library at Brown University, where it is labeled a "commonplace book," although it is clearly pushing against this generic classification. A hypertext of the book's cover and pages, with some helpful transcription, is available at http://www.emilydickinson.org/susan/tshdcpb_cov.html.

22. Dickinson, *The Poems of Emily Dickinson* (1998), 1447.

23. Jack L. Capps, *Emily Dickinson's Reading: 1836–1886* (Cambridge, MA: Harvard University Press, 1966), 140. Capps deduces this from the retained documents that indicate a lost clipping, from the fact that Dickinson sometimes referred to things she clipped, and from the fact that she often included a phrase or reference to an article, poem, or cartoon that she would have encountered years before incorporating it in her own writing. See also St. Armand, *Emily Dickinson and Her Culture*, 26, where he argues that Dickinson kept an actual scrapbook and that this affected her poetics: "There is ample evidence from her published letters that Emily Dickinson herself kept a scrapbook of clippings from national magazines, local newspapers, and illustrated books, which she used to ornament some of her own manuscripts, turning them into emblem letters and emblem poems." He also argues that the scrapbook kept by Dickinson's friend, Mary Warner, can act as "a guiding anthology of ideas, models, and patterns that furnishes us with the prototypes, stereotypes, and archetypes of Dickinson's time" (31).

24. On the issue of circulation, see Alfred Habegger, *My Wars Are Laid Away in Books: The Life of Emily Dickinson* (New York: Random House, 2001), 316. Habegger suggests that she may have circulated some of her manuscripts among very close friends. His main example of this, however, occurred during Dickinson's friendship with Henry Vaughan Emmons, which I discussed in the first section of this chapter. See also Martha Nell Smith, *Rowing in Eden: Rereading Emily Dickinson* (Austin: University of Texas Press, 1992), 73, in which Smith argues that Dickinson may have given a fascicle to Helen Hunt Jackson. See Dickinson, *Manuscript Books*, xvi–xvii, for Franklin's assessment of who read, touched, and made markings on the fascicles after Dickinson's death: Susan Huntington Dickinson, Mabel Loomis Todd, Mary Lee Hall, Martha Dickinson Bianchi, Millicent Todd Bingham, and, possibly, Lavinia Dickinson.

25. This pamphlet is undated, but according to the New York City Directories, J. L. Patten & Co. was at 47 Barclay Street (the address that appears on this pamphlet) only from 1878 to 1883.

26. "The Album Writer's Assistant: Being Choice Selections in Poetry and Prose, for Autograph Albums, Valentines, etc." (New York: J. L. Patten & Co., n.d.), 1.

27. Susan Tucker, Katherine Ott, and Patricia P. Buckler, eds., *The Scrapbook in American Life* (Philadelphia: Temple University Press, 2006), 8. Additionally, an advertisement on the last page of "The Album Writer's Assistant" shows that both albums and scrapbooks were being mass-marketed at the time of its printing.

28. Garvey, "Scissorizing and Scrapbooks," 214.

29. See Virginia Jackson, *Dickinson's Misery: A Theory of Lyric Reading* (Princeton, NJ: Princeton University Press, 2005), 58–60, where she makes this argument about Dickinson's Mount Holyoke education.

30. There are a few examples of homemade versions of these books from this period. See Tucker et al., *The Scrapbook in American Life*, 7, where they refer to pre-Civil War scrapbooks that were homemade and then sewn together by the maker, a local bookbinder, or a stationer. Additionally, the collection of Goddard Family Papers at the American Antiquarian Society includes several of Emily Goddard's homemade commonplace books.

31. I am assuming that Cook inserted the sheets inside each other (otherwise known as "nesting") instead of creating signatures. To create a signature one takes a much larger piece of paper, folds it many times, and cuts the pages at their tops. Both processes result in the same product, but I have assumed that Cook nested individually folded sheets because we can see from his first volume that he already had access to paper cut this size. In the case of the Bascom and Gilman examples later in this chapter, it is less clear whether they made signatures or nested individually folded sheets. Because of this I will refer to the products as opposed to the method by which each got there.

32. According to Franklin, spill-over onto single sheets occurred in Fascicles 16, 18, 21 (two instances), 24, 28, and 35, and spill-over onto pinned in slips of paper occurred in Fascicles 7, 16, and 19. See Dickinson, *Manuscript Books*, 1413.

33. Werner, *Emily Dickinson's Open Folios*, 2.

34. Cameron, *Choosing Not Choosing*, 8.

35. Rosenthal and Gall, *The Modern Poetic Sequence*, 47.

36. Cameron, *Choosing Not Choosing*, 96.

37. Sally Bushell, *Text As Process: Creative Composition in Wordsworth, Tennyson, and Dickinson* (Charlottesville: University of Virginia Press, 2009), 173.

38. Ibid., 173.

39. Dickinson, *Manuscript Books*, xii.

40. See Cameron, *Choosing Not Choosing*, 15, where she asserts that for Franklin "the unit of sense is not the individual poem but rather the fascicle book." For a recent move away from this, see Bushell, *Text As Process*, 175–176, where she distinguishes between "poems within a *bifolium*, which have without question been grouped together in this way by the poet" and "poems in a *fascicle*, for which the same level of certainty does not exist."

41. Jackson, *Dickinson's Misery*, 44.

42. See Dickinson, *The Poems of Emily Dickinson* (1998), 462–464 for the history of these drafts. Interestingly, Franklin chooses the second, non-fascicle version for his reading edition, but he situates it in this edition as if it was written in 1862. See R. W. Franklin, ed., *The Poems of Emily Dickinson: Reading Edition* (Cambridge, MA: Belknap Press of Harvard University Press, 1999), 203.

43. Habegger, *My Wars Are Laid Away in Books*, 533.

44. Gary Lee Stonum, *The Dickinson Sublime* (Madison: University of Wisconsin Press, 1990), 142.

45. Eleanor Elson Heginbotham, "Reading Dickinson in Her Context: The Fascicles," *A Companion to Emily Dickinson*, ed. Martha Nell Smith and Mary Loeffelholz (Malden, MA: Blackwell, 2008), 302–303.

46. The notion of "trying" to die struck the first publishers of this poem as wrong. When it first appeared in print, in the *London Mercury*, on February 19, 1929, the word "try" was changed to the more predictable and comfortable "come." As Franklin notes—see Dickinson, *The Poems of Emily Dickinson* (1998), 464–465—this change remained through the next three reprintings of the poem: in *Further Poems of Emily Dickinson* (1929), *The Poems of Emily Dickinson* (1930), and *The Poems of Emily Dickinson* (1937).

47. Fascicles 14, 19, and 20 do not contain sheets with paired poems.

48. Sharon Cameron, *Lyric Time: Dickinson and the Limits of Genre* (Baltimore: Johns Hopkins University Press, 1979), 49.

49. Vivian R. Pollak, *Dickinson: The Anxiety of Gender* (Ithaca, NY: Cornell University Press, 1984), 214.

50. Paula Bennett, *Emily Dickinson: Woman Poet* (Iowa City: University of Iowa Press, 1990), 132.

51. Cynthia Griffin Wolff, *Emily Dickinson* (New York: Knopf, 1988), 383.

52. Cameron, *Choosing Not Choosing*, 168.

53. Cristanne Miller, *Emily Dickinson: A Poet's Grammar* (Cambridge, MA: Harvard University Press, 1987), 137.

54. Dickinson, *Manuscript Books*, ix.

55. See Smith, *Rowing in Eden*, 11–15, on the difference between Dickinson's use of the words "print" and "publish." Informed by Smith's nuanced readings of this distinction, I use the word "print" to describe the medium (and action) with which I am concerned in this section.

56. Emily Dickinson, *Poems by Emily Dickinson*, ed. Mabel Loomis Todd and Thomas Wentworth Higginson (Boston: Roberts Brothers, 1890), iv.

57. Ibid., iv.

58. See Kirsten Silva Gruesz, "Maria Gowen Brooks, In and Out of the Poe Circle," *ESQ: A Journal of the American Renaissance* 54.1–4 (2008): 85, where she describes how this image of the female poet was widespread enough that even Brooks characterized the heroine of her 1838 novel, *Idomen*, this way: "Her words spring (after the clichéd fashion) directly 'from the heart,' with no mediation of craft, revision, or exchange: Idomen herself never attempts to publish her verses."

59. Smith, *Rowing in Eden*, 11; Cameron, *Choosing Not Choosing*, 54; Werner, *Emily Dickinson's Open Folios*, 27; Jerome J. McGann, "Emily Dickinson's Visible Language," *Emily Dickinson Journal* 2.2 (1993): 43.

60. McGann, "Emily Dickinson's Visible Language," 42.

61. Ibid.

62. The list of books that are thought to have resided at the Homestead can be found at http://oasis.lib.harvard.edu/oasis/deliver/deepLink?_collection=oasis&uniqueId =hou00321. According to the Houghton Library, "At the time of the purchase [in 1850], the books were physically located at the Evergreens, many volumes having originally been shelved at the Homestead prior to its sale by Martha Dickinson Bianchi in 1916."

63. See McGann, "Emily Dickinson's Visible Language," 44, where he explains that "in the late nineteenth century 'publication' only came when a poet followed certain textual conventions. These conventions—they are strictly bibliographical rather than more broadly formal—were so dominant that most poets and readers could not imagine poetry without them."

64. Rufus W. Griswold, ed., *Gems from American Female Poets: With Brief Biographical Notices* (Philadelphia: H. Hooker, 1842).

CHAPTER 2

1. See Domhnall Mitchell, *Measures of Possibility: Emily Dickinson's Manuscripts* (Amherst: University of Massachusetts Press, 2005), where he lays out this territory throughout the book, himself coming down on the side of Dickinson as one who upholds generic boundaries.
2. Willis J. Buckingham, ed., *Emily Dickinson's Reception in the 1890s: A Documentary History* (Pittsburgh: University of Pittsburgh Press, 1989), 362.
3. Ibid., 374.
4. See the recent collection of essays on the letters, *Reading Emily Dickinson's Letters: Critical Essays*, ed. Jane Donahue Eberwein and Cindy MacKenzie (Amherst: University of Massachusetts Press, 2009), which offers a wide array of approaches. For a book-length study that situates the letters as Dickinson's primary and authorized writing, see Marietta Messmer, *A Vice for Voices: Reading Emily Dickinson's Correspondence* (Amherst: University of Massachusetts Press, 2001). For a study of the letters sent to Sue, see Martha Nell Smith, *Rowing in Eden: Rereading Emily Dickinson* (Austin: University of Texas Press, 1992), and Ellen Louise Hart and Martha Nell Smith, eds., *Open Me Carefully: Emily Dickinson's Intimate Letters to Susan Huntington Dickinson* (Ashfield, MA: Paris Press, 1998).
5. See Virginia Jackson, *Dickinson's Misery: A Theory of Lyric Reading* (Princeton, NJ: Princeton University Press, 2005), 185–190, for an analysis of this poem in which she argues that the "text stages the act of its own reading in sadomasochistic terms" (187).
6. Messmer, *A Vice for Voices*, 27–28.
7. Ibid., 32.
8. See Messmer, *A Vice for Voices*, which, despite being both the most comprehensive study of Dickinson's letters as well as of those Dickinson sent to Higginson, makes no mention of "As if I asked a common alms—."
9. For other instances of letters that contain embedded poems, see L 290, L 319, L 353, L 381, L 405, L 413, L 458, L 472, L 486, L 498, L 503, L 553, and L 1042.
10. See Martha Nell Smith, "A Hazard of a Letter's Fortunes: Epistolarity and the Technology of Audience in Emily Dickinson's Correspondences," *Reading Emily Dickinson's Letters: Critical Essays*, ed. Jane Donahue Eberwein and Cindy MacKenzie (Amherst: University of Massachusetts Press, 2009), 249, where she suggests that Dickinson may have been urged by Sue to initiate this correspondence.
11. See John Mann, "Dickinson's Letters to Higginson," *Approaches to Teaching Dickinson's Poetry*, ed. Robin Riley Fast and Christine Mack Gordon (New York: Modern Language Association of America, 1989), 41, where he argues for the first option, linking this act with Dickinson's other strategies in this letter: "The mention of her fear of betrayal in the last sentence, the appeal to Higginson's sense of honor, and the shielding of her name in its own envelope can suggest her profound shyness, her state of tension about her work, her peculiar modes of secrecy." See Messmer, *A Vice for Voices*, 120–121, where she points out that this is the only instance in which Dickinson used "Emily" in her signature to Higginson and argues that by placing it on the inserted card she conceals her gendered identity. See Thomas Wentworth Higginson, "Emily Dickinson's Letters," *Atlantic Monthly* 68 (October 1891): 444, where he interprets the inclusion of this card as the "shy writer['s]" desire "to recede as far as possible from view."
12. While Johnson and Ward suggest that Dickinson may have enclosed a poem in her letter of January 11, 1862 to Samuel Bowles, this poem has never been identified; therefore, the enclosures to Higginson have, for a long time, been considered her first. See Emily Dickinson, *The Letters of Emily Dickinson*, ed. Thomas H. Johnson and Theodora Ward (Cambridge, MA: Belknap Press of Harvard University Press, 1958), 390–391.
13. See Emily Dickinson, *The Poems of Emily Dickinson: Variorum Edition*, ed. R. W. Franklin (Cambridge, MA: Belknap Press of Harvard University Press, 1998), 14–17.

14. "Safe in their Alabaster Chambers—" (F 124) had been sent to Sue in three different states of revision, had been published in the *Springfield Daily Republican* on March 1, 1862, and had been copied into both Fascicle 6 and Fascicle 10. For the rich history of the writing, revision, and publication of "Safe in their Alabaster Chambers—," see Dickinson, *The Poems of Emily Dickinson* (1998), 159–164, and Hart and Smith, eds., *Open Me Carefully*, 97–100. "I'll tell you how the Sun rose—" (F 204) and "The nearest Dream recedes—unrealized—" (F 304) had been copied into Fascicles 10 and 14 respectively, the first in early 1861 and the second in early 1862. In both of these cases the fascicle versions contain both variants that Dickinson took up when copying out the versions she sent to Higginson. The earlier version of "I'll tell you how the Sun rose—" appears as four stanzas with a line between the second and third stanzas, indicating that Dickinson may have thought of it as two poems or considered the later stanzas as variants; additionally, the "that" in the second version's line 11 was a "which" in the fascicle version. The earlier version of "The nearest Dream recedes—unrealized—" was copied into the fascicle with variants interlined above three words, all of which were used in the later version: "nearest" for "maddest," "Lifts" for "Spreads," and "bewildered" for "defrauded." "We play at Paste—" (F 282) is the only poem that had not already been copied into a fascicle and may not have been sent to anyone prior to its inclusion in this letter. According to Franklin, three years later Dickinson made a fair copy of this poem on embossed notepaper with the heading "Emily" and signature "Emily," although it was not folded or sent. See Dickinson, *The Poems of Emily Dickinson* (1998), 300.

15. Although Higginson said the enclosures were "Your Riches, taught me, poverty—" (F 418) and "A bird came down the walk" (F 359)—see Dickinson, *The Letters of Emily Dickinson* (1958), 405—Johnson decided otherwise, and Franklin concurs with Johnson's assessment. "There came a Day at Summer's full" had been copied into Fascicle 13, "Of all the Sounds despatched abroad" into Fascicle 12, and "South Winds jostle them—," in addition to having been sent to Louise and Frances Norcross as well as Thomas Gilbert, had been copied into Fascicle 5.

16. Richard B. Sewall, *The Life of Emily Dickinson* (New York: Farrar, Straus and Giroux, 1974), 546.

17. Ibid., 544–545.

18. Cindy MacKenzie, "'This is my letter to the World': Emily Dickinson's Epistolary Poetics," *Reading Emily Dickinson's Letters: Critical Essays*, ed. Jane Donahue Eberwein and Cindy MacKenzie (Amherst: University of Massachusetts Press, 2009), 14.

19. Hart and Smith, *Open Me Carefully*, xxv.

20. Martha Nell Smith, "Suppressing the Books of Susan in Emily Dickinson," *Epistolary Histories: Letters, Fiction, Culture*, ed. Amanda Gilroy and W. M. Verhoeven. (Charlottesville: University Press of Virginia, 2000), 112.

21. Agnieszka Salska, "Dickinson's Letters," *The Emily Dickinson Handbook*, ed. Gudrun Grabher, Roland Hagenbüchle, and Cristanne Miller (Amherst: University of Massachusetts Press, 1998), 175.

22. Sewall, *The Life of Emily Dickinson*, 544.

23. Paul Crumbley, "Dickinson's Correspondence and the Politics of Gift-Based Circulation," *Reading Emily Dickinson's Letters: Critical Essays*, ed. Jane Donahue Eberwein and Cindy MacKenzie (Amherst: University of Massachusetts Press, 2009), 45–46.

24. See Higginson, "Emily Dickinson's Letters," 447, where he states, incorrectly, that there were two poems enclosed with this letter. See Dickinson, *The Letters of Emily Dickinson* (1958), 409, where Johnson corrects this error.

25. For a very different way of reading this, see Robert Graham Lambert, Jr., *A Critical Study of Emily Dickinson's Letters: The Prose of a Poet* (Lewiston, NY: Mellen University Press, 1996), 131, where he argues that Dickinson had been so moved by Higginson's

offer of his hand in the dark that she could no longer write in prose and therefore "shifted into the imagery of poetry": "The poem, then, functions to link her letter to his. Higginson's hand reaches out and Emily's hand receives gifts beyond measure from it."

26. Smith, "Suppressing the Books of Susan in Emily Dickinson," 103, and MacKenzie, "'This is my letter to the World'," 23.

27. It is interesting to note that in Dickinson's fourth letter to Higginson (L 268) she uses similar spacing—spacing that Johnson interprets as paragraph breaks and not the marking off of an embedded poem.

28. Susan Howe, *My Emily Dickinson* (Berkeley, CA: North Atlantic Books, 1985), 132.

29. See Jack L. Capps, *Emily Dickinson's Reading: 1836–1886* (Cambridge, MA: Harvard University Press, 1966), 123.

30. See Messmer, *A Vice for Voices*, 36, for a short treatment of the poetic features of this letter, such as assonance, anaphora, internal rhymes, and alliteration.

31. Dickinson, *The Poems of Emily Dickinson* (1998), 1577.

32. William H. Shurr, ed., with Anna Dunlap and Emily Grey Shurr, *New Poems of Emily Dickinson* (Chapel Hill: University of North Carolina Press, 1993), 2.

33. Dickinson, *The Poems of Emily Dickinson* (1998), 1577.

34. Shurr, *New Poems of Emily Dickinson*, 2–5.

35. Mitchell, *Measures of Possibility*, 237.

36. Ibid., 55.

37. Elizabeth Hewitt, *Correspondence and American Literature, 1770–1865* (Cambridge, UK: Cambridge University Press, 2004), 146.

38. Smith, "A Hazard of a Letter's Fortunes," 252, and Hewitt, *Correspondence and American Literature, 1770–1865*, 165.

39. Jerome J. McGann, "Emily Dickinson's Visible Language," *Emily Dickinson Journal* 2.2 (1993): 44–45.

40. Ibid., 46, 50.

41. Jackson, *Dickinson's Misery*, 21.

42. Ibid., 125.

43. Logan Esdale, "Dickinson's Epistolary 'Naturalness,'" *Emily Dickinson Journal* 14.1 (2005): 2.

44. *The Fashionable American Letter Writer; or Art of Polite Correspondence* (Boston: James Loring, 1826), xvii. Some scholars have argued that Dickinson would neither have owned nor followed the rules of such a manual, which was aimed at those aspiring to middle-class status. See William Merrill Decker, *Epistolary Practices: Letter Writing in America Before Telecommunications* (Chapel Hill: University of North Carolina Press, 1998), 146, who argues, as Karen Lystra had before him, that we cannot assume that Dickinson would have followed the rules found in advice manuals and conduct books, for these were often pitched to women who aspired to a middle-class status that they had already attained.

45. See Capps, *Emily Dickinson's Reading: 1836–1886*, 106–107.

46. See the unpublished manuscripts of L 74a and 74c, L 173, and L 198, available at the Houghton Library.

47. Nan Johnson, *Gender and Rhetorical Space in American Life, 1866–1910* (Carbondale: Southern Illinois University Press, 2002), 79.

48. Ibid., 84.

49. McGann, "Emily Dickinson's Visible Language," 43.

50. See Jackson, *Dickinson's Misery*, 63, where she makes a similar point, arguing that "by sending versions of the same manuscript to several persons, Dickinson herself indicated that the lines were not intended for one reader—as, say, a personal letter might be—but could circulate independently of particular readers or a particular material context."

51. McGann, "Emily Dickinson's Visible Language," 44.
52. Decker, *Epistolary Practices*, 38.
53. Ibid., 38.
54. Ibid., 143–144.
55. Note that the word "flood" in the fascicle version has been changed to "shatter." This was not indicated as a variant in the fascicle and is the only word that has been changed.
56. See Crumbley, "Dickinson's Correspondence and the Politics of Gift-Based Circulation," 48, for a very suggestive reading of just how validating this correspondence was for Dickinson. He writes that it "restored Dickinson's confidence in herself as a writer and gave her the courage to move forward with the daring experiments she was contemplating in her manuscript books."
57. Messmer, *A Vice for Voices*, 42 (italics mine).
58. Ibid., 18.
59. Ibid., 116.
60. Ibid., 184.

CHAPTER 3

1. For a transhistorical study of the elegy, see Peter M. Sacks, *The English Elegy: Studies in the Genre from Spenser to Yeats* (Baltimore: Johns Hopkins University Press, 1985), which treats the American elegy only in the epilogue, admitting that "to undertake a study of the American elegy would be to open yet another book" (312). In the few pages that he then devotes to this subject, Sacks mentions Dickinson only briefly and in relation to his idea about the American elegy's "strong compulsion toward originality and privacy" (313). For a study of British and American elegies of the twentieth century, see Jahan Ramazani, *Poetry of Mourning: The Modern Elegy from Hardy to Heaney* (Chicago: University of Chicago Press, 1994), which considers Dickinson an early practitioner within "the tradition of poetic self-mourning" (30), whose poems of self-elegy are precursors to those by Stevens, Hughes, Auden, and especially Plath. For the most comprehensive study of the genre in the American context, see Max Cavitch, *American Elegy: The Poetry of Mourning from the Puritans to Whitman* (Minneapolis: University of Minnesota Press, 2007). Cavitch sheds new light on Puritan elegies in particular, but because his study concludes with Whitman, he does not treat Dickinson. While there is no book on Dickinson's elegies, a number of scholars have treated specific features of Dickinson's elegies in articles. For an analysis of the ways in which Dickinson's elegies address the issue of immortality, see Ronald A. Sudol, "Elegy and Immortality: Emily Dickinson's 'Lay this Laurel on the One'," *ESQ: A Journal of the American Renaissance* 26 (1980): 10–15; for an analysis of Dickinson relationship to Sigourney and the tradition of the child elegy, see Elizabeth A. Petrino, "'Feet so precious charged': Dickinson, Sigourney, and the Child Elegy," *Tulsa Studies in Women's Literature* 13.2 (1994): 317–338; for a description of Dickinson's "elegiac modes," mostly in relation to her letters, see Patricia Thompson Rizzo, "The Elegiac Modes of Emily Dickinson," *Emily Dickinson Journal* 11.1 (2002): 104–117; and for a consideration of the "elegiac frame" in Dickinson's "Of Death I try to think like this" (F 1588), see Jed Deppman, "Dickinson, Death, and the Sublime," *Emily Dickinson Journal* 9.1 (2000): 1–20. For book-length analyses of Dickinson's poems about death more broadly, see Thomas W. Ford, *Heaven Beguiles the Tired: Death in the Poetry of Emily Dickinson* (University: University of Alabama Press, 1966); Inder Nath Kher, *The Landscape of Absence: Emily Dickinson's Poetry* (New Haven, CT: Yale University Press, 1974); and Katharina Ernst, *"Death" in the Poetry of Emily Dickinson* ([Heidelberg: Winter, 1992).
2. Desirée Henderson, *Grief and Genre in American Literature, 1790–1870* (Burlington: Ashgate, 2011), 4.
3. Cavitch, *American Elegy*, 1.

4. Ibid.

5. Henderson, *Grief and Genre in American Literature*, 4, 16.

6. Cavitch, *American Elegy*, 22.

7. While Franklin does number each sheet and therefore marks them as separate, these numbers are easy to miss if you are not looking for them. Because the facsimiles themselves are bound in a big book, Franklin invites us to read across sheets and through an entire fascicle, until a new title page announces and describes the next fascicle.

8. Dana Luciano, *Arranging Grief: Sacred Time and the Body in Nineteenth-Century America* (New York: New York University Press, 2007), 5.

9. Ibid., 2.

10. Ibid.

11. Herman Salinger, "Time in the Lyric," *Studies in German Literature of the Nineteenth and Twentieth Centuries*, ed. Siegfried Mews (Chapel Hill: University of North Carolina Press, 1970), 157.

12. See Sharon Cameron, *Lyric Time: Dickinson and the Limits of Genre* (Baltimore: Johns Hopkins University Press, 1979). Cameron argues that while it is essential to understand a poem's temporal structures and suppositions, so too must we grasp the speaker's conception of time itself. According to Cameron, Dickinson's speakers try to "stop time dead" (24), attempting "stasis" as the poems "slow temporal advance to the difficult still point of meaning" (25). Some poems, Cameron argues, "seek a way out of time, a reprieve from it" (57); still others are "arrested, framed, and taken out of the flux of history" (71) or constitute a "breathing space, a necessary 'time out'" (90) from action, employing, along the way, Dickinson's desire to "blank out time" (169). See also Dorothy Nielsen, "The Dark Wing of Mourning: Grief, Elegy and Time in the Poetry of Denise Levertov," *Denise Levertov: New Perspectives*, ed. Anne Colclough Little and Susie Paul (West Cornwall, CT: Locust Hill, 2000), 124, which takes this assumption of stopped time one step further by arguing that the text of lyric poems "parallels a monument, so that lyric's characteristic suppression of both its temporal progressions and its relation to historical time allows the text to symbolize permanence."

13. For a discussion of the ways in which a central image in a poem often provides the whole poem with a sense that time and action have been caught in a "timeless moment," see Andrew Welsh, *Roots of Lyric: Primitive Poetry and Modern Poetics* (Princeton, NJ: Princeton University Press, 1978), 67–99. Welsh argues that embedded in this image is the illusion of narration, such that images of the past are brought into the present, but that the effect of this is one of "dynamic stasis," or "peripeteia" (movement caught at the still point of a turn). Along a similar line, he argues that an image often works by reducing and encapsulating into itself *as instantaneous* a wide arc of time.

14. Sacks, *The English Elegy*, 8.

15. Abbie Findlay Potts, *The Elegiac Mode: Poetic Form in Wordsworth and Other Elegists* (Ithaca, NY: Cornell University Press, 1967), 37.

16. Luciano, *Arranging Grief*, 2.

17. Sharon Cameron, *Choosing Not Choosing: Dickinson's Fascicles* (Chicago: University of Chicago Press, 1992), 105.

18. Domhnall Mitchell, *Emily Dickinson: Monarch of Perception* (Amherst: University of Massachusetts Press, 2000), 189.

19. Faith Barrett, "'Drums off the Phantom Battlements': Dickinson's War Poems in Discursive Context," *A Companion to Emily Dickinson*, ed. Martha Nell Smith and Mary Loeffelholz (Malden, MA: Blackwell, 2008), 111.

20. Linda S. Grimes, "Dickinson's 'There's Been a Death in the Opposite House'," *Explicator* 50.4 (1992): 219.

21. Ibid.

22. Ibid.

23. For a treatment of Dickinson's poems written from the perspective of one who has already died, see Diana Fuss, "Corpse Poem," *Critical Inquiry* 30 (2003): 1–30. Fuss distinguishes "the strange literary device of a speaking corpse" (1) from both the epitaph and the elegy, mounting a historical argument about the emergence of corpse poetry in the early nineteenth century and its development into the present. Fuss argues that this form allows Dickinson the latitude to mourn for the living instead of just for the dead, while also granting her the ability to die without actually dying.

24. When this poem was first published, in *Poems by Emily Dickinson* (1890), the editors gave it the title "The Chariot." In doing so, they highlighted the idea of the journey being taken here.

25. See Cameron, *Lyric Time*, 125, where she also writes of the disruption that this stanza causes to the poem's journey.

26. Another instance in which Todd and Higginson removed an entire stanza from a poem was with the 1896 publication of "I measure every Grief I meet" (F 550).

27. See Celeste Schenck, "Feminism and Deconstruction: Re-Constructing the Elegy," *Tulsa Studies in Women's Literature* 5.1 (1986): 13–27, where she argues that women's elegies constitute a countertradition with a revisionist agenda. Schenck reads the "male elegy" as a site of male bonding, power production, and authorial self-identification, and the "female elegy" as a poem about connection (instead of separation) and one that puts aside the issue of careerism that has always been central to the genre. Many critics after Schenck have weighed in on this issue. See, in particular, Ramazani, *The Poetry of Mourning*, 263, 297–299, where he argues for more nuance within these categories, showing that within this countertradition is another one in which modern women's elegies have had to distance themselves from an earlier female sentimentalism. See also Melissa F. Zeiger, *Beyond Consolation: Death, Sexuality, and the Changing Shapes of Elegy* (Ithaca, NY: Cornell University Press, 1997), 63–65, which takes a wholly different approach, denouncing the separate category of the "female elegy" by arguing that women writing elegies were so conditioned by the mainstream elegiac norms and conventions that they retain much of what is at work in them even if they are revising them.

28. See Cheryl Walker, *The Nightingale's Burden: Women Poets and American Culture before 1900* (Bloomington: Indiana University Press, 1982), 87, which makes the case that "among American women poets, [Dickinson] probably knew something of Maria Brooks, Lydia Sigourney, Maria Lowell, Caroline Gilman, and Amelia Welby." Walker bases this on the fact that Samuel Bowles had sent Sue and Austin a copy of *The Household Book of Poetry* (1860), which is likely to have been shared between the households (165).

29. Griswold, Rufus W., ed., *Gems from American Female Poets: With Brief Biographical Notices* (Philadelphia: H. Hooker, 1842).

30. See Paula Bernat Bennett, *Poets in the Public Sphere: The Emancipatory Project of American Women's Poetry, 1800–1900* (Princeton, NJ: Princeton University Press, 2003), 150, where she argues that as part of the burgeoning spiritualism movement, several female poets—including Piatt and Dickinson—attempted to keep the door open between the living and the dead, ending their poems inconclusively in order to leave "the question of the afterlife open, forcing readers to confront the epistemological conundrum that death is."

31. Paula Bernat Bennett, ed., *Palace-Burner: The Selected Poetry of Sarah Piatt* (Urbana: University of Illinois Press, 2001), xxviii. All poems by Piatt in this section come from this text.

CHAPTER 4

1. See Gary Lee Stonum, *The Dickinson Sublime* (Madison: University of Wisconsin Press, 1990), 173, where he refers to it as one of Dickinson's "traumatic poems" in which "some previous belief or reliable form of understanding is suddenly shattered

and the speaker thus left in anguish." See Sharon Cameron, *Lyric Time: Dickinson and the Limits of Genre* (Baltimore: Johns Hopkins University Press, 1979), 205, where she specifies the terms of this shattering, taking the poem as an example of Dickinson's productive distrust of the poem's temporal scheme, as "the very sequence the speaker claims she is at a loss to reconstruct is that structure which elements the poem." See Betsy Erkkila, "Dickinson and the Art of Politics," *A Historical Guide to Emily Dickinson*, ed. Vivian Pollak (Oxford: Oxford Univerity Press, 2004), 155, where she argues, along very different lines, that "the self-divided, terrorized, and incoherent speaker" in this poem "suggest[s] a problem in liberal and democratic theory with putting individuals—even elite ones—in charge."

2. See Emily Dickinson, *The Manuscript Books of Emily Dickinson*, ed. R. W. Franklin (Cambridge, MA: Belknap Press of Harvard University Press, 1981), 1408, for Franklin's initial decision that Dickinson copied poems onto loose sheets from 1862–1866 and then again from 1870–1877. See his later reevaluation of this dating as it pertains to individual poems in Emily Dickinson, *The Poems of Emily Dickinson: Variorum Edition*, ed. R. W. Franklin (Cambridge, MA: Belknap Press of Harvard University Press, 1998).

3. "Dont put up my Thread & Needle—" (F 681), copied on the second and third sides of the first sheet of folded stationery that was sewn into Fascicle 32, is Dickinson's most extended musing on sewing, stitches, thread, and seams. In other instances, Dickinson refers to stitches and stitching in "'Twas like a Maelstrom, with a notch" (F 425), "I saw no Way—The Heavens were stitched—" (F 633), "Death sets a Thing significant" (F 640), and "This Chasm, Sweet, opon my life" (F 1061). She refers to sewing, surprisingly, in only two poems, "A fuzzy fellow, without feet—" (F 171) and "A Spider sewed at Night" (F 1163). References to threads and threading are far more present, as we can see in "On such a night, or such a night" (F 84), "A feather from the Whippowil" (F 208), "My first well Day—since many ill—" (F 288), "A Shady friend—for Torrid days—" (F 306), "She sweeps with many-colored Brooms—" (F 318), "I'm ceded—I've stopped being Their's" (F 353), "The Grass so little has to do" (F 379), "From Blank to Blank—" (F 484), and "To mend each tattered Faith" (F 1468). She mentions strings in "Bring me the sunset in a cup—" (F 140), "Tie the strings to my Life, My Lord" (F 338), "I'll clutch—and clutch—" (F 385), "The first Day's Night had come—" (F 423), "Sang from the Heart, Sire" (F 1083), and "In Winter in my Room" (F 1742). She refers to seams and seamlessness in "It sifts from Leaden Sieves—" (F 291), "Of all the Sounds despatched abroad—" (F 334), "A Bird came down the Walk—" (F 359), "I tend my flowers for thee—" (F 367), "Without this—there is nought—" (F 464), "They dropped like Flakes—" (F 545), "You'll know Her—by Her Foot—" (F 604), "The Crickets sang" (F 1104), "Step lightly on this narrow spot—" (F 1227), "A Word dropped careless on a Page" (F 1268), "How fits his Umber Coat" (F 1414), "This Me—that walks and works—must die" (F 1616), and "Of Yellow was the outer Sky" (F 1733).

4. Although Franklin refers to the existence of 15 sets, he uses an a-b designation (as in the case of 4a and 4b and 8a and 8b) and the a-b-c designation (as in the case of 6a, 6b, and 6c), bringing the actual number of sets to 19. See Dickinson, *The Manuscript Books of Emily Dickinson*, 1410.

5. Dickinson, *Manuscript Books*, xi.

6. This is not to imply that the distinction is lost on all Dickinson scholars, for, indeed, see Sharon Cameron, *Choosing Not Choosing: Dickinson's Fascicles* (Chicago: University of Chicago Press, 1992), 15, where she points out their difference by stating, about the sets, that "no internal order could be established for the sets since they were never bound."

7. Domhnall Mitchell, *Measures of Possibility: Emily Dickinson's Manuscripts* (Amherst: University of Massachusetts Press, 2005), 307.

8. Ibid., 185. Additionally, when discussing a particular set—in this case, Set 6C—Mitchell calls them Dickinson's "unbound manuscript miscellanies" in the same sentence in which he lumps them in with the fascicles and describes *both* fascicles and sets as "the only collections or anthologies (outside the correspondence) that she supervised and collated (and presumably approved) herself" (36). I do not mean to imply that Mitchell is intentionally trying to make us think that the sets and the fascicles are the same thing, for he has worked extensively with the manuscripts and knows very well the difference between sewn and not-sewn sheets. I mean to call attention to the fact that because he always ties the sets to the fascicles, he makes the interpretive situation murky.

9. Cameron, *Choosing Not Choosing*, 13.

10. Ibid., 7.

11. See Alexandra Socarides, "Rethinking the Fascicles: Dickinson's Writing, Copying, and Binding Practices," *Emily Dickinson Journal* 15.2 (2006): 88–89, where I articulate the argument about Dickinson's mother's stroke, one that I have rethought in light of the work with the loose sheets that I have subsequently done.

12. Dickinson, *Manuscript Books*, xii. Also, see R. W. Franklin, "The Emily Dickinson Fascicles," *Studies in Bibliography* (1983): 1–20, where he explains that once there were too many poems, Dickinson would have found it easier to locate poems if they weren't bound. Later, in 1981—see Dickinson, *Manuscript Books*, xii—Franklin argues, "That she continued to copy fascicle sheets without binding them suggests that she found the bound books difficult to use." In an interesting moment of combining the something-happened argument with the use argument, Franklin goes on to write, "By 1864 unbound sheets may have been easier for her to use—connected perhaps to the eye trouble of 1864 and 1865 that forced her to spend several months in Cambridge under the care of a physician" (xii–xiii).

13. Alfred Habegger, *My Wars Are Laid Away in Books: The Life of Emily Dickinson* (New York: Random House, 2001), 525.

14. Cameron, *Lyric Time*, 43.

15. This happened with the first three sheets of Fascicle 1, which Dickinson copied in summer 1858 but did not sew into a fascicle until late that summer when she finished copying the fourth sheet. This happened with the first two sheets of Fascicle 3, which she copied in autumn of 1858 but did not sew into a fascicle until spring 1859. This happened with the first two sheets of Fascicle 10, which she copied in early 1861 but did not sew into a fascicle until the second half of 1861. This happened with one sheet of Fascicle 12, which she copied in early 1861 but did not sew into a fascicle until early 1862. And this happened in the case of Fascicle 14, which is the only fascicle that was written over three time periods: a single leaf was copied in late summer 1858; the next two sheets were copied in early 1862; and the last three sheets were copied in autumn 1862, before all of them were sewn together. Fascicle 11 is the one other case in which Dickinson copied a single leaf before copying the other sheets that she would sew to it, but because leaves and sheets are different materials, I do not consider Fascicle 11 here.

16. Dickinson, *Manuscript Books*, xii. According to Franklin's later dating of the manuscripts—see Dickinson, *The Poems of Emily Dickinson* (1998), 651–655, 790–794, 811–814—the two sheets that become Set 1 were copied in the second half of 1863, before the last nine fascicles were made (Fascicles 32–40, although not in that order); the two sheets that would become Set 4 (Franklin designates one sheet Set 4a and the other Set 4b, for no apparent reason) were both copied in early 1864, after which only 2 more fascicles would still be made (Fascicles 38 and 39); and the one sheet that makes up Set 2 was copied between the making of the final two fascicles.

17. Jed Deppman, *Trying to Think with Emily Dickinson* (Amherst: University of Massachusetts Press, 2008), 99.

18. Cameron, *Choosing Not Choosing*, 41.

19. While I am arguing that the loose sheets resist the sequences that the fascicles approximate, it is interesting to note that other critics unproblematically call the fascicles sequences and ask us to read them as such. Indeed, whether we are reading Dickinson's fascicles or sets, our only access to them (besides visiting the archive, which, as I have shown in the case of the sets, is already a complicated enterprise) is through Franklin's *The Manuscript Books of Emily Dickinson*, which, Cameron tells us in *Choosing Not Choosing*, presents "poems that have the appearance of a sequence" (6). Cameron does not challenge this presentation, as she reads the fascicles as sequences and suggests that they be read in relation to other sequences. See Cameron, *Choosing Not Choosing*, 39, where she writes that "The fascicles invite us to read Dickinson's poems in the context of other sequences—Herbert's *The Temple*, Barrett Browning's sonnets, Tennyson's *In Memoriam*, Shakespeare's sonnets—which we can presume Dickinson had read." Franklin and Cameron's attention to sequence makes visible the very structure that Dickinson was attempting to sidestep but that ultimately could not be avoided. For more on Dickinson and sequence, see M. L. Rosenthal and Sally M. Gall, *The Modern Poetic Sequence: The Genius of Modern Poetry* (Oxford: Oxford University Press, 1983).

20. See Dickinson, *The Poems of Emily Dickinson* (1998), 812, where Franklin dates both as written in "early 1864." See Ellen Louise Hart and Martha Nell Smith, eds., *Open Me Carefully: Emily Dickinson's Intimate Letters to Susan Huntington Dickinson* (Ashfield, MA: Paris Press, 1998), 141, which dates this vaguely as "mid-1860s." Given that one had to occur before the other in time and, as I will discuss in this section, my research points to the fact that Dickinson was inclined to send pieces of her poems to Sue first, I read the order of copying in this way.

21. The following poems, or pieces of what later became poems, were sent to Sue before being copied on loose sheets: F 192, F 501, F 738, F 797, F 798, F 799, F 804, F 811, F 816, F 817, F 818, F 819, F 867, F 940, F 951, F 956, F 962, F 964, F 966, F 972, F 995, F 1016, F 1081, F 1090, F 1096, F 1098, F 1102, F 1103, F 1113, F 1120, F 1216, F 1227, F 1234, F 1239, F 1275, and F 1372. Although Franklin says that F 974, F 1022, and F 1104 were sent to Sue after Dickinson copied these poems onto loose sheets, this dating is debatable. The following poems were sent to Sue after having been copied on loose sheets: F 933, F 1096 (this poem went to Sue both before and after the loose sheet version was copied), F 1110, and F 1208.

22. Dickinson, *The Poems of Emily Dickinson* (1998), 225.

23. The editors of the Dickinson Electronic Archives—see www.emilydickinson.org— suggest that "perhaps this was another poem Dickinson was developing via Sue's commentary," but I would argue that while this interpretation of its circumstances acknowledges the ways in which Sue and Dickinson worked on her poems together, it does not take into account the details of the manuscript itself, which indicate it might be more note than poem.

24. David Porter, *Dickinson: The Modern Idiom* (Cambridge, MA: Harvard University Press, 1981), 94.

25. During the years in which she was sewing fascicles, Dickinson sent at least one hundred poems to Sue before she copied them into the fascicles, yet only four of them were sent as pieces of what would later become longer poems. These four poems are F 28, F 724, F 862, and F 888. Additionally, the compositional history of F 773 is unclear, as the final ten lines of what will become a twenty-line poem that is copied into Fascicle 37 were sent to Sue, but, according to Franklin the first leaf of the version to Sue is simply missing (Dickinson, *The Poems of Emily Dickinson* [1998], 729–730). Even in the case of the four pieces of poems that were sent to Sue first and then copied onto sheets as longer poems and were sewn into fascicles, each of these instances took place late in her fascicle-making stage (these poems appear in Fascicles 33, 35, 38, and 39), indicating that it was a process that Dickinson developed over time and that was connected to her

decision to stop sewing sheets. This can be seen in contrast to the at least thirty-six poems that Dickinson sent to Sue that would later be copied onto loose sheets, twelve of which first came to her as pieces of what would become longer poems. Also, it is worth noting that the three I have discussed at length are not the exception, as there are at least nine other instances in which Dickinson employs a similar method. These poems are F 798, F 811, F 818, F 951, F 1102, F 1120, F 1227, F 1239, and F 1275. There is also the chance that F 1104 was sent to Sue first, although (see Dickinson, *The Poems of Emily Dickinson* [1998], 962–964) Franklin dates the version sent to Sue as later than the one copied onto the sheet.

26. Dickinson, *Manuscript Books*, 1010.

27. Dickinson, *The Poems of Emily Dickinson* (1998), 811–814.

28. Although Franklin does not explain why he has changed his mind about these dates, it is clear from the manuscripts that Dickinson's handwriting and her convention for including variants is the same across these sheets, indicating that they were, indeed, probably copied around the same time.

29. See Dickinson, *The Poems of Emily Dickinson* (1998), 1538–1541 for Franklin's timeline of Dickinson's copying.

30. Another factor that reveals the deliberateness of this process is that there is a break of many years between copying Sets 6a, 6b, and 6c and Set 8. There are two stages in the process of copying loose sheets and, as I will discuss in Chapter 5, during the second most of her final poems were copied onto scraps. The fact that she still copied multiple poems on individual folded sheets of stationery marks this act as deliberate.

31. See S. P. Rosenbaum, *A Concordance to the Poems of Emily Dickinson* (Ithaca, NY: Cornell University Press, 1964), which lists it twenty-four times; because I am counting the draft of the second stanza of "Cleaving" to Sue, I count twenty-five. Also, it is worth noting that another of these usages of "Dust" occurs in "We can but follow to the Sun—" (F 845), which was copied, around the same time, onto the loose sheet that is now referred to as "Set 4b."

32. See "Her final Summer was it—" (F 847) on sheet 1; "'I want'—it pleaded—All it's life—" (F 851) on sheet 2; "She staked Her Feathers—Gained an Arc—" (F 853) on sheet 3 (here, much like in "All overgrown by cunning moss" (F 146) in Fascicle 7, we can read the bird as a symbol for the dead woman); "She rose to His Requirement—dropt" (F 857) on Sheet 4; "No Notice gave She, but a Change—" (F 860) on Sheet 5; and "A Plated Life—diversified" (F 864) on Sheet 6.

33. These lines were first sent to Sue as "The Definition of Beauty, is / That Definition is none—" and later copied onto the loose sheet that would become Set 6a (F 797).

CHAPTER 5

1. Emily Dickinson, *The Poems of Emily Dickinson: Variorum Edition*, ed. R. W. Franklin (Cambridge, MA: Belknap Press of Harvard University Press, 1998), 26 and Alfred Habegger, *My Wars Are Laid Away in Books: The Life of Emily Dickinson* (New York: Random House, 2001), 526.

2. For the first time that Mabel Loomis Todd called them "scraps" in print, see Emily Dickinson, *Letters of Emily Dickinson* (Boston: Roberts Brothers, 1894), 268.

3. See Jeanne Holland, "Scraps, Stamps, and Cutouts: Emily Dickinson's Domestic Technologies of Publication," *Cultural Artifacts and the Production of Meaning: The Page, the Image, and the Body*, ed. Margaret J. M. Ezell and Katherine O'Brien O'Keeffe (Ann Arbor: University of Michigan Press, 1994), 140–141, where she writes, "I do not perceive resignation or carelessness in this activity," and goes on to argue that "much of Dickinson's late work interrogates the relation of sexuality and textuality." See Melanie Hubbard, "Dickinson's Advertising Flyers: Theorizing Materiality and the Work of Reading," *Emily Dickinson Journal* 7.1 (1998): 27, where she proposes "that Dickinson's

practice, after abandoning the fascicles, was to make her compositions literally 'of their milieu,' both by appropriating the print environment of her time and by theorizing thought's specific and material appearing. Dickinson's eschewal of print for her poems was both theoretical and practical: it was not a problem with print per se, but it came increasingly to be a problem with the resistance inherent in a project intent on investigating the materiality of representation." Howe deals with these issues throughout her writing, especially in Susan Howe, *The Birth-mark: Unsettling the Wilderness in American Literary History* (Hanover: Wesleyan University Press, 1993), 131–154.

4. Marta L. Werner, ed., *Emily Dickinson's Open Folios: Scenes of Reading, Surfaces of Writing* (Ann Arbor: University of Michigan Press, 1995), 4.

5. Ibid., 3.

6. Ibid.

7. Jackson, *Dickinson's Misery*, 50. Jackson also argues that Werner's analysis follows on the heels of Howe's "deeply lyrical interpretation of the difference between Dickinson-in-manuscript and Dickinson-in-print" (37). Although Jackson does not discuss Hubbard's work on the late fragments, Hubbard's position that "Dickinson's fugitive productions in the scraps take the lyric's logic, its refusal of totality and metaphysic, to its extreme by drawing attention to a thought's materiality in time" (Hubbard, "Dickinson's Advertising Flyers," 27) positions her approach squarely within Jackson's critique. Instead of reading the manuscripts as lyrics, Jackson theorizes the various ways in which Dickinson's manuscripts don't do what lyrics are supposed to do: "Rather than turning privacy public, her work tended to take all kinds of public and private, artificial and natural materials into the everyday life of a private person. Rather than give us immediate access to the private perceptions of that person, the literate traces of that everyday life tend to emphasize our distance from the time and place of her practice—of her culture. Rather than address themselves to an horizon of literary interpretation in the future (to future literary critics), Dickinson's manuscripts were addressed to particular individuals or to herself" (53).

8. See Dickinson, *The Poems of Emily Dickinson* (1998), 1185, where Franklin calls this a "working draft in which different moments of writing and revision can be discerned." He argues that Dickinson "worked all the way through the poem, then went back over the whole, suggesting additional possibilities and underscoring a few readings."

9. In some cases these variants completely dominate the page on which a poem has been drafted. "A Sparrow took a slice of Twig" (F 1257), for example, is a seven-line poem for which Dickinson generated twenty-three variant lines, all of which are for the final three: five variants for line 5, eight variants for line 8, and ten variants for line 7. "To see her is a Picture—" (F 1597) is another example of a poem whose final lines were heavily reworked. Dickinson had sent a previous draft to Sue, but in the draft that Dickinson retained she did the work of rethinking the whole second half of the poem. What's striking about this manuscript is that over half of this leaf is filled with variants for the final line; they take up all of the space below the fold at the center of the page. In other words, there is as much space on this leaf is devoted to variants for one line as there is for the whole poem.

10. There is a word along this margin, before "Were exquisite extents," which I cannot decipher and which Franklin does not include in his transcription of this poem.

11. Marta L. Werner, "'A *Woe* of Ecstasy': On the Electronic Editing of Emily Dickinson's Late Fragments," *Emily Dickinson Journal* 16.2 (2007): 31. Werner also argues that this type of text "seem[s] capable of illuminating with particular clarity the principles at the core of an artist's production" and that "in Dickinson's case, the fragments, the limit texts, are the latest and furthest affirmation of a centrifugal impulse, a gravitation away from the center, that is expressed at every level and at every phase of her work, and is revealed in the starkest possible manner in the leading formal problem of Dickinson's work: the problem of variant readings."

12. For an example of a poem that Dickinson revised on the fascicle paper, see "I meant to find Her when I Came—" (F 881), which was copied into Fascicle 39 in 1864, after which Dickinson heavily revised it in the mid-1870s. For an example of an earlier poem that Dickinson copied out on a new leaf or sheet in order to revise it, see "Two Butter-flies went out at Noon" (F 571), which was copied on a sheet that Dickinson sewed into Fascicle 25 in 1863, but fifteen years later she copied out a different version and revised it so heavily that, in this particular case, there ended up being more variants than there were lines of the poem. For an example of simple extraction, see "The Soul selects her own Society—" (F 409), which Dickinson copied onto a sheet that she sewed into Fascicle 20, but two years later she copied just one stanza onto a leaf that had (or would soon have) the lines beginning "Love reckons by itself—alone—" (F 812) copied on the other side. Another example is the lines that begin "These are the days when Birds come back—" (F 122), which was a long poem that Dickinson had sent to Sue in 1859, had been published in *Drum Beat*, and had been copied onto a sheet of stationery that was sewn into Fascicle 6; despite all of these gestures at finality, in 1883 Dickinson went back to this poem and made a pencil copy of just the first two stanzas, which she retained for herself. A third example is the lines beginning "A Drop fell on the Apple Tree—" (F 846), which Dickinson had copied onto a sheet that she had sewn into Fascicle 38, and yet nine years later she sent just the second half of the poem to Sue. (When she made the fascicle copy, she also made a copy of the poem's first two lines. At the same time that she shortened the poem, she made another copy of the poem's opening lines.) See also "Just to be Rich" (F 635), which Dickinson had copied into Fascicle 31 after which she sent a variation of the first stanza to Samuel Bowles, and this shorter version was then copied onto a sheet in what we now call "Set 7." In other cases the version that was in the set got shortened later: "As imperceptibly as Grief" (F 935) had been an eight-stanza poem when it was copied onto a sheet in "Set 5" in 1865, but then in 1866 Dickinson copied out just four stanzas of it and retained it, at which point she also sent a similar version of this shorter version to Higginson. In an act of double revision through shortening, Dickinson would return to this poem seventeen years later to copy out one of its stanzas and retain it.

13. Dickinson, *The Poems of Emily Dickinson* (1998), 1371–1372.

14. Paul Crumbley, "Dickinson's Uses of Spiritualism: The 'Nature' of Democratic Belief," *A Companion to Emily Dickinson*, ed. Martha Nell Smith and Mary Loeffelholz (Malden, MA: Blackwell, 2008), 247.

15. Dickinson, *The Poems of Emily Dickinson* (1998), 1253–1255.

16. See Habegger, *My Wars Are Laid Away in Books*, 544, where it doesn't seem to matter how the poem was drafted, since for him it is about the well and Susan at once: "The definitive treatment of Sue as unknowable alien is found in a version of a poem on the mystery of wells in which her first name is substituted for the original word, 'nature'."

17. See Holland, "Scraps, Stamps, and Cutouts," 162, where she points out that the spider is often Dickinson's shorthand for poet. Alternatively, see Aife Murray, "Architecture of the Unseen," *A Companion to Emily Dickinson*, ed. Martha Nell Smith and Mary Loeffelholz (Malden, MA: Blackwell, 2008), 28–29, where she reads this poem as articulated by an "Irish maid-of-all-work" who does not have "the sensibility to recognize a spider's artistry" and so "whisks away ephemera that is a thing of beauty and mastery." In both of these readings, as well as my own, Dickinson values the work of the spider; that being said, by representing the spider as male, she does not collapse their two positions. For examples of other poems in which Dickinson used the spider as the figure of an artist, see "The Spider holds a Silver Ball" (F 513) and "A Spider sewed at Night" (F 1163). For examples of poems written on the back of letters and envelopes, see F 1366, F 1367, F 1404, F 1405, F1409, and F 1443.

18. There is no evidence that points to the availability or price of paper changing drastically during this time, or that the finances of the Dickinson household changed in such a way that made them more attuned to conserving paper.

19. Holland, "Scraps, Stamps, and Cutouts," 141. While at first Holland writes that "It is significant that her writing on household refuse coincides with her agoraphobic withdrawal from public life," later in the article she argues that "her domestic technologies of publication result from her 'agoraphobia'" (151). One of the things that seems odd about Holland's assumptions here is that she goes on to read these materials not as if they are so private that they can't be read. In fact, she argues that Dickinson's "late works meld literary creativity and domesticity" (152), theorizing that "rather than themes of domesticity dominating her writing, Dickinson's poetry reflects her engagement with domesticity's ideology of intimacy, privacy, and self-protection" (155).

20. Sharon Cameron, *Choosing Not Choosing: Dickinson's Fascicles* (Chicago: University of Chicago Press, 1992), 41–42.

21. See Mary Loeffelholz, "Really Indigenous Productions: Emily Dickinson, Josiah Holland, and Nineteenth-Century Popular Verse," *A Companion to Emily Dickinson*, ed. Martha Nell Smith and Mary Loeffelholz (Malden, MA: Blackwell, 2008), 199–201, where she reads this poem as, at least partially, a response to *The Century*'s reproduction of Josiah Holland's manuscript of "Two Homes" as well as to Helen Hunt Jackson's "The Last Words."

22. Werner, *Emily Dickinson's Open Folios*, 21. In quoting Werner here, I do not mean to imply that she believes that the choice of material is totally random, for, when she argues that Dickinson is writing on whatever materials are at hand, she also implies, at some level, that the shift in how Dickinson was writing (now more speedily, now more impulsively and less formally) demands these new material contexts. For Werner, then, there is a relationship between poetics and materials.

23. Holland, "Scraps, Stamps, and Cutouts," 155.

24. Werner, "'A *Woe* of Ecstasy'," 42.

25. Ibid.

26. Jackson, *Dickinson's Misery*, 67. Jackson mostly thinks about pastings and enclosures, which is different from thinking about the paper she wrote on, in that there is more room to talk about Dickinson's intentional play with pastings. But even in these cases, Jackson resists reading connections. In regards to "the three-cent stamp with a picture of a steam engine on it stuck to clippings from *Harper's Weekly* that read 'GEORGE SAND' and 'Mauprat,'" Jackson writes that they seem "to have little to do with the lines Dickinson wrote around it" (166) and that "whatever these lines may be about, they are not (except in the most literal sense) about the stamp and clippings" (167). Jackson also points out that enclosures (and, more specifically, now-missing enclosures) became a problem for later interpreters: "If Vanderbilt understood the wit of the lines in relation to an enclosed bouquet from Dickinson's garden or conservatory, then how do we understand the lines without the enclosure?" (71). In the end she argues that "the point of Dickinson's familiar circulation of these enclosures was not their survival but their ephemeral recognition" (197–198).

27. Jackson, *Dickinson's Misery*, 171.

28. See Dickinson, *The Poems of Emily Dickinson* (1998), 1405, where Franklin tells us that Alexander McCallum's was a dry goods store in Northampton.

29. Dickinson, *The Poems of Emily Dickinson* (1998), 1405–1406.

30. Ibid.

31. Ibid.

32. Ibid., 1418–1419.

33. For an example of the pinning of variants, see "The Clover's simple Fame" (F 1256). Dickinson wrote all eight lines of the poem on a square scrap of paper and then

reworked the final four lines on a separate slip that she pinned to the original square. The two types of paper are different (one has lines while the other doesn't; the square piece is wider than the slip), and so it is conceivable that Dickinson simply continued to work on the final four lines after having produced the eight-line version. The major thing that gets tinkered with in the variant lines is a single word: Dickinson had written "degrades" on the square scrap and then indicated "profanes" as a variant below, and so on the slip Dickinson uses "profanes" but then interlines "pollutes" and "defiles," before underlining "defiles" three times. By pinning the variant stanza to the original, Dickinson keeps these different possibilities for that line in play. It is worth noting that there is another manuscript of just the first four lines.

AFTERWORD

1. See Paul Mariani, *William Carlos Williams: A New World Naked* (New York: Norton, 1990), 187, 288, 297, 396, 695.
2. To hear Langston Hughes's recollection of the writing of this poem, visit http://www. poets.org/viewmedia.php/prmMID/15722.
3. Stephen Fredman, *Contextual Practice: Assemblage and the Erotic in Postwar Poetry and Art* (Stanford, CA: Stanford University Press, 2010), 50.
4. Martha Nell Smith, "Afterword: The Literary World Has Always Been Read/Write," *ESQ: A Journal of the American Renaissance* 54:1–4 (2008): 269.
5. Eliza Richards, *Gender and the Poetics of Reception in Poe's Circle* (Cambridge, UK: Cambridge University Press, 2004), 70.
6. See Richards, *Gender and the Poetics of Reception in Poe's Circle*, 73, where she references this story as it appears in *A Human Life: Being the Autobiography of Elizabeth Oakes Smith.*

BIBLIOGRAPHY

"The Album Writer's Assistant: Being Choice Selections in Poetry and Prose, for Autograph Albums, Valentines, etc." New York: J. L. Patten & Co., n.d.

Barrett, Faith. "'Drums off the Phantom Battlements': Dickinson's War Poems in Discursive Context." *A Companion to Emily Dickinson*. Ed. Martha Nell Smith and Mary Loeffelholz, 107–132. Malden, MA: Blackwell, 2008.

Bennett, Paula. *Emily Dickinson: Woman Poet*. Iowa City: University of Iowa Press, 1990.

———. *Poets in the Public Sphere: The Emancipatory Project of American Women's Poetry, 1800-1900*. Princeton, NJ: Princeton University Press, 2003.

———, ed. *Palace-Burner: The Selected Poetry of Sarah Piatt*. Urbana: University of Illinois Press, 2001.

Bickman, Martin. "'The Snow that never drifts': Dickinson's Slant of Language." *College Literature* 10.2 (1983): 139–146.

Buckingham, Willis J., ed. *Emily Dickinson's Reception in the 1890s: A Documentary History*. Pittsburgh: University of Pittsburgh Press, 1989.

Bushell, Sally. *Text As Process: Creative Composition in Wordsworth, Tennyson, and Dickinson*. Charlottesville: University of Virginia Press, 2009.

Cameron, Sharon. *Lyric Time: Dickinson and the Limits of Genre*. Baltimore: Johns Hopkins University Press, 1979.

———. *Choosing Not Choosing: Dickinson's Fascicles*. Chicago: University of Chicago Press, 1992.

Capps, Jack L. *Emily Dickinson's Reading: 1836-1886*. Cambridge, MA: Harvard University Press, 1966.

Cavitch, Max. *American Elegy: The Poetry of Mourning from the Puritans to Whitman*. Minneapolis: University of Minnesota Press, 2007.

Crumbley, Paul. "Dickinson's Uses of Spiritualism: The 'Nature' of Democratic Belief." *A Companion to Emily Dickinson*. Ed. Martha Nell Smith and Mary Loeffelholz, 235–257. Malden, MA: Blackwell, 2008.

———. "Dickinson's Correspondence and the Politics of Gift-Based Circulation." *Reading Emily Dickinson's Letters: Critical Essays*. Ed. Jane Donahue Eberwein and Cindy MacKenzie, 28–55. Amherst: University of Massachusetts Press, 2009.

Culler, Jonathan. *Structuralist Poetics: Structuralism, Linguistics, and the Study of Literature*. Ithaca, NY: Cornell University Press, 1975.

Decker, William Merrill. *Epistolary Practices: Letter Writing in America Before Telecommunications*. Chapel Hill: University of North Carolina Press, 1998.

Deppman, Jed. "Dickinson, Death, and the Sublime." *Emily Dickinson Journal* 9.1 (2000): 1–20.

———. *Trying to Think with Emily Dickinson*. Amherst: University of Massachusetts Press, 2008.

Dickie, Margaret. "Dickinson in Context." *American Literary History* 7.2 (1995): 320–333.

Dickinson, Emily. *Poems by Emily Dickinson*. Ed. Mabel Loomis Todd and Thomas Wentworth Higginson. Boston: Roberts Brothers, 1890.

——. *Letters of Emily Dickinson*. Ed. Mabel Loomis Todd. 2 vols. Boston: Roberts Brothers, 1894.

——. *Poems by Emily Dickinson*. Ed. Mabel Loomis Todd. Boston: Roberts Brothers, 1896.

——. *The Complete Poems of Emily Dickinson*. Ed. Martha Dickinson Bianchi. Boston: Little, Brown, 1924.

——. *The Poems of Emily Dickinson*. Ed. Martha Dickinson Bianchi with Alfred Leete Hampson. Boston: Little, Brown, 1930.

——. *Letters of Emily Dickinson*. Ed. Mabel Loomis Todd. New York: Harper, 1931.

——. *The Poems by Emily Dickinson*. Ed. Martha Dickinson Bianchi with Alfred Leete Hampson. Boston: Little, Brown, 1937.

——. *The Letters of Emily Dickinson*. Ed. Thomas H. Johnson and Theodora Ward. Cambridge, MA: Belknap Press of Harvard University Press, 1958.

——. *The Manuscript Books of Emily Dickinson*. Ed. R. W. Franklin. 2 vols. Cambridge, MA: Belknap Press of Harvard University Press, 1981.

——. *The Poems of Emily Dickinson: Variorum Edition*. Ed. R. W. Franklin. 3 vols. Cambridge, MA: Belknap Press of Harvard University Press, 1998.

——. *The Poems of Emily Dickinson: Reading Edition*. Ed. R. W. Franklin. Cambridge, MA: Belknap Press of Harvard University Press, 1999.

Doreski, William. "'An Exchange of Territory': Dickinson's Fascicle 27." *ESQ: A Journal of the American Renaissance* 32.1 (1986): 55–67.

Eberwein, Jane Donahue, and Cindy MacKenzie, eds. *Reading Emily Dickinson's Letters: Critical Essays*. Amherst: University of Massachusetts Press, 2009.

Emerson, Ralph Waldo. "New Poetry." *Uncollected Writings: Essays, Addresses, Poems, Reviews and Letters*, 137–152. New York: Lamb Publishing Co., 1912.

Erkkila, Betsy. "Dickinson and the Art of Politics." *A Historical Guide to Emily Dickinson*. Ed. Vivian Pollak, 133–174. Oxford: Oxford University Press, 2004.

Ernst, Katharina. *"Death" in the Poetry of Emily Dickinson*. Heidelberg: Winter, 1992.

Esdale, Logan. "Dickinson's Epistolary 'Naturalness.'" *Emily Dickinson Journal* 14:1 (2005): 1–23.

The Fashionable American Letter Writer; or Art of Polite Correspondence. Boston: James Loring, 1826.

Ford, Thomas W. *Heaven Beguiles the Tired: Death in the Poetry of Emily Dickinson*. University: University of Alabama Press, 1966.

Fowler, Alice S. *Autographs: Verses from New England Autograph Albums, 1825-1925*. Conyngham, PA: Pioneer Books, 1990.

Franklin, R. W. "The Emily Dickinson Fascicles." *Studies in Bibliography* 36 (1983): 1–20.

Fredman, Stephen. *Contextual Practice: Assemblage and the Erotic in Postwar Poetry and Art*. Stanford, CA: Stanford University Press, 2010.

Fuss, Diana. "Corpse Poem." *Critical Inquiry* 30 (2003): 1–30.

Garvey, Ellen Gruber. "Scissorizing and Scrapbooks: Nineteenth-Century Reading, Remaking, and Recirculating." *New Media, 1740-1915*. Ed. Lisa Gitelman and Geoffrey B. Pingree, 207–227. Cambridge, MA: MIT Press, 2003.

Gernes, Todd S. *Checklist of Albums & Commonplace Books at A.A.S.* Worcester, MA: American Antiquarian Society, 1991.

Gitelman, Lisa, and Geoffrey B. Pingree, eds. *New Media, 1740-1915*. Cambridge, MA: MIT Press, 2003.

Grimes, Linda S. "Dickinson's 'There's Been a Death in the Opposite House.'" *Explicator* 50.4 (1992): 219.

Griswold, Rufus W., ed. *Gems from American Female Poets: With Brief Biographical Notices*. Philadelphia: H. Hooker, 1842.

Gruesz, Kirsten Silva. "Maria Gowen Brooks, In and Out of the Poe Circle." *ESQ: A Journal of the American Renaissance* 54.1–4 (2008): 75–110.

Habegger, Alfred. *My Wars Are Laid Away in Books: The Life of Emily Dickinson*. New York: Random House, 2001.

Hart, Ellen Louise, and Martha Nell Smith, eds. *Open Me Carefully: Emily Dickinson's Intimate Letters to Susan Huntington Dickinson*. Ashfield, MA: Paris Press, 1998.

Havens, Earle. *Commonplace Books: A History of Manuscripts and Printed Books from Antiquity to the Twentieth Century*. New Haven, CT: Beinecke Rare Book and Manuscript Library, 2001.

Heginbotham, Eleanor Elson. *Dwelling in Possibilities: Reading the Fascicles of Emily Dickinson*. Columbus: Ohio State University Press, 2003.

———. "Reading Dickinson in Her Context: The Fascicles." *A Companion to Emily Dickinson*. Ed. Martha Nell Smith and Mary Loeffelholz, 288–308. Malden, MA: Blackwell, 2008.

Henderson, Desirée. *Grief and Genre in American Literature, 1790-1870*. Burlington, VT: Ashgate, 2011.

Hewitt, Elizabeth. *Correspondence and American Literature, 1770-1865*. Cambridge, UK: Cambridge University Press, 2004.

Higginson, Thomas Wentworth. "Emily Dickinson's Letters." *Atlantic Monthly* 68 (October 1891): 444–456.

Holland, Jeanne. "Scraps, Stamps, and Cutouts: Emily Dickinson's Domestic Technologies of Publication." *Cultural Artifacts and the Production of Meaning: The Page, the Image, and the Body*. Ed. Margaret J.M. Ezell and Katherine O'Brien O'Keeffe, 139–181. Ann Arbor: University of Michigan Press, 1994.

Howe, Susan. *My Emily Dickinson*. Berkeley, CA: North Atlantic Books, 1985.

———. *The Birth-mark: Unsettling the Wilderness in American Literary History*. Hanover: Wesleyan University Press, 1993.

Hubbard, Melanie. "Dickinson's Advertising Flyers: Theorizing Materiality and the Work of Reading." *Emily Dickinson Journal* 7.1 (1998): 27–54.

Jackson, Virginia. *Dickinson's Misery: A Theory of Lyric Reading*. Princeton, NJ: Princeton University Press, 2005.

Johnson, Nan. *Gender and Rhetorical Space in American Life, 1866-1910*. Carbondale: Southern Illinois University Press, 2002.

Kher, Inder Nath. *The Landscape of Absence: Emily Dickinson's Poetry*. New Haven: Yale University Press, 1974.

Knappett, Carl. *Thinking Through Material Culture: An Interdisciplinary Perspective*. Philadelphia: University of Pennsylvania Press, 2005.

Lambert, Robert Graham, Jr. *A Critical Study of Emily Dickinson's Letters: The Prose of a Poet*. Lewiston, NY: Mellen University Press, 1996.

Lockridge, Kenneth A. *On the Sources of Patriarchal Rage: The Commonplace Books of William Byrd and Thomas Jefferson and the Gendering of Power in the Eighteenth Century*. New York: New York University Press, 1992.

Loeffelholz, Mary. *From School to Salon: Reading Nineteenth-Century American Women's Poetry*. Princeton, NJ: Princeton University Press, 2004.

———. "Really Indigenous Productions: Emily Dickinson, Josiah Holland, and Nineteenth-Century Popular Verse." *A Companion to Emily Dickinson*. Ed. Martha Nell Smith and Mary Loeffelholz, 183–204. Malden, MA: Blackwell, 2008.

Luciano, Dana. *Arranging Grief: Sacred Time and the Body in Nineteenth-Century America*. New York: New York University Press, 2007.

MacKenzie, Cindy. "'This is my letter to the World': Emily Dickinson's Epistolary Poetics." *Reading Emily Dickinson's Letters: Critical Essays*. Ed. Jane Donahue Eberwein and Cindy MacKenzie, 11–27. Amherst: University of Massachusetts Press, 2009.

Mann, John. "Dickinson's Letters to Higginson." *Approaches to Teaching Dickinson's Poetry.* Ed. Robin Riley Fast and Christine Mack Gordon, 39–46. New York: Modern Language Association of America, 1989.

Mariani, Paul. *William Carlos Williams: A New World Naked.* New York: Norton, 1990.

Martin, Wendy, ed. *The Cambridge Companion to Emily Dickinson.* Cambridge, UK: Cambridge University Press, 2002.

McGann, Jerome J. *The Textual Condition.* Princeton, NJ: Princeton University Press, 1991.

———. "Emily Dickinson's Visible Language." *Emily Dickinson Journal* 2.2 (1993): 40–57.

Messmer, Marietta. *A Vice for Voices: Reading Emily Dickinson's Correspondence.* Amherst: University of Massachusetts Press, 2001.

Michaels, Walter Benn. *The Shape of the Signifier: 1967 to the End of History.* Princeton, NJ: Princeton University Press, 2004.

Miller, Cristanne. *Emily Dickinson: A Poet's Grammar.* Cambridge, MA: Harvard University Press, 1987.

———. "Controversy in the Study of Emily Dickinson." *Literary Imagination: The Review of the Association of Literary Scholars and Critics* 6.1 (2004): 39–50.

Miller, Ruth. *The Poetry of Emily Dickinson.* Middletown, CT: Wesleyan University Press, 1968.

Mitchell, Domhnall. "Revising the Script: Emily Dickinson's Manuscripts." *American Literature* 70.4 (1998): 705–737.

———. *Emily Dickinson: Monarch of Perception.* Amherst: University of Massachusetts Press, 2000.

———. "Emily Dickinson and Class." *The Cambridge Companion to Emily Dickinson.* Ed. Wendy Martin, 191–214. Cambridge, UK: Cambridge University Press, 2002.

———. *Measures of Possibility: Emily Dickinson's Manuscripts.* Amherst: University of Massachusetts Press, 2005.

Murray, Aife. "Architecture of the Unseen." *A Companion to Emily Dickinson.* Ed. Martha Nell Smith and Mary Loeffelholz, 11–36. Malden, MA: Blackwell, 2008.

Nielsen, Dorothy. "The Dark Wing of Mourning: Grief, Elegy and Time in the Poetry of Denise Levertov." *Denise Levertov: New Perspectives.* Ed. Anne Colclough Little and Susie Paul, 119–137. West Cornwall, CT: Locust Hill, 2000.

Oberhaus, Dorothy Huff. *Emily Dickinson's Fascicles: Method & Meaning.* University Park: Pennsylvania State University Press, 1995.

O'Keefe, Martha Lindblom. *This Edifice: Studies in the Structure of the Fascicles of the Poetry of Emily Dickinson.* Privately printed, 1986.

Petrino, Elizabeth A. "'Feet so precious charged': Dickinson, Sigourney, and the Child Elegy." *Tulsa Studies in Women's Literature* 13.2 (1994): 317–338.

Pollak, Vivian R. *Dickinson: The Anxiety of Gender.* Ithaca, NY: Cornell University Press, 1984.

Porter, David. *Dickinson: The Modern Idiom.* Cambridge, MA: Harvard University Press, 1981.

Potts, Abbie Findlay. *The Elegiac Mode: Poetic Form in Wordsworth and Other Elegists.* Ithaca, NY: Cornell University Press, 1967.

Ramazani, Jahan. *Poetry of Mourning: The Modern Elegy from Hardy to Heaney.* Chicago: University of Chicago Press, 1994.

Richards, Eliza. *Gender and the Poetics of Reception in Poe's Circle.* Cambridge, UK: Cambridge University Press, 2004.

Rizzo, Patricia Thompson. "The Elegiac Modes of Emily Dickinson." *Emily Dickinson Journal* 11.1 (2002): 104–117.

Rosenbaum, S. P. *A Concordance to the Poems of Emily Dickinson.* Ithaca, NY: Cornell University Press, 1964.

Rosenthal, M. L., and Sally M. Gall. *The Modern Poetic Sequence: The Genius of Modern Poetry.* Oxford: Oxford University Press, 1983.

Sacks, Peter M. *The English Elegy: Studies in the Genre from Spenser to Yeats.* Baltimore: Johns Hopkins University Press, 1985.

Salinger, Herman. "Time in the Lyric." *Studies in German Literature of the Nineteenth and Twentieth Centuries.* Ed. Siegfried Mews, 157–173. Chapel Hill: University of North Carolina Press, 1970.

Salska, Agnieszka. "Dickinson's Letters." *The Emily Dickinson Handbook.* Ed. Gudrun Grabher, Roland Hagenbüchle, and Cristanne Miller, 163–182. Amherst: University of Massachusetts Press, 1998.

Schenck, Celeste. "Feminism and Deconstruction: Re-Constructing the Elegy." *Tulsa Studies in Women's Literature* 5.1 (1986): 13–27.

Sewall, Richard B. *The Life of Emily Dickinson.* New York: Farrar, Straus and Giroux, 1974.

Shurr, William H. *The Marriage of Emily Dickinson: A Study of the Fascicles.* Lexington: University Press of Kentucky, 1983.

Shurr, William H., ed., with Anna Dunlap and Emily Grey Shurr. *New Poems of Emily Dickinson.* Chapel Hill: University of North Carolina Press, 1993.

Smith, Martha Nell. *Rowing in Eden: Rereading Emily Dickinson.* Austin: University of Texas Press, 1992.

———. "Suppressing the Books of Susan in Emily Dickinson." *Epistolary Histories: Letters, Fiction, Culture.* Ed. Amanda Gilroy and W. M. Verhoeven, 101–125. Charlottesville: University Press of Virginia, 2000.

———. "Afterword: The Literary World Has Always Been Read/Write." *ESQ: A Journal of the American Renaissance* 54.1–4 (2008): 269–281.

———. "A Hazard of a Letter's Fortunes: Epistolarity and the Technology of Audience in Emily Dickinson's Correspondences." *Reading Emily Dickinson's Letters: Critical Essays.* Ed. Jane Donahue Eberwein and Cindy MacKenzie, 239–256. Amherst: University of Massachusetts Press, 2009.

Smith, Martha Nell, and Mary Loeffelholz, eds. *A Companion to Emily Dickinson.* Malden, MA: Blackwell, 2008.

Socarides, Alexandra. "Rethinking the Fascicles: Dickinson's Writing, Copying, and Binding Practices." *Emily Dickinson Journal* 15.2 (2006): 69–94.

Stabile, Susan M. *Memory's Daughters: The Material Culture of Remembrance in Eighteenth-Century America.* Ithaca, NY: Cornell University Press, 2004.

St. Armand, Barton Levi. *Emily Dickinson and Her Culture: The Soul's Society.* Cambridge, UK: Cambridge University Press, 1984.

Stonum, Gary Lee. *The Dickinson Sublime.* Madison: University of Wisconsin Press, 1990.

Sudol, Ronald A. "Elegy and Immortality: Emily Dickinson's 'Lay this Laurel on the One'." *ESQ: A Journal of the American Renaissance* 26 (1980): 10–15.

Tucker, Susan, Katherine Ott, and Patricia P. Buckler, eds. *The Scrapbook in American Life.* Philadelphia: Temple University Press, 2006.

Tufariello, Catherine. "'The Remembering Wine': Emerson's Influence on Whitman and Dickinson." *The Cambridge Companion to Ralph Waldo Emerson.* Ed. Joel Porte and Saundra Morris, 162–191. Cambridge, UK: Cambridge University Press, 1999.

Vendler, Helen. *Poets Thinking: Pope, Whitman, Dickinson, Yeats.* Cambridge, MA: Harvard University Press, 2004.

Walker, Cheryl. *The Nightingale's Burden: Women Poets and American Culture before 1900.* Bloomington: Indiana University Press, 1982.

Wardrop, Daneen. "Emily Dickinson and the Gothic in Fascicle 16." *The Cambridge Companion to Emily Dickinson.* Ed. Wendy Martin, 142–164. Cambridge, UK: Cambridge University Press, 2002.

Welsh, Andrew. *Roots of Lyric: Primitive Poetry and Modern Poetics.* Princeton, NJ: Princeton University Press, 1978.

Werner, Marta L. "'A *Woe* of Ecstasy': On the Electronic Editing of Emily Dickinson's Late Fragments." *Emily Dickinson Journal* 16.2 (2007): 25–52.

———, ed. *Emily Dickinson's Open Folios: Scenes of Reading, Surfaces of Writing.* Ann Arbor: University of Michigan Press, 1995.

Wolff, Cynthia Griffin. *Emily Dickinson.* New York: Knopf, 1988.

Zapedowska, Magdalena. "Citizens of Paradise: Dickinson and Emmanuel Levinas's Phenomenology of the Home." *Emily Dickinson Journal* 12.2 (2003): 69–92.

Zeiger, Melissa F. *Beyond Consolation: Death, Sexuality, and the Changing Shapes of Elegy.* Ithaca, NY: Cornell University Press, 1997.

POEMS REFERENCED

"Awake ye muses nine, sing me a strain divine" (F 1), 65

"On this wondrous sea" (F 3), 24

"I had a guinea golden—" (F 12), 49

"There is a morn by men unseen—" (F 13), 49–51

"As if I asked a common alms—" (F 14), 14, 49–77

"She slept beneath a tree—" (F 15), 49–51

"If those I loved were lost" (F 20), 25–26

"On such a night, or such a night" (F 84), 185n3

"South Winds jostle them—" (F 98), 55–57, 180n15

"These are the days when Birds come back—" (F 122), 190n12

"Safe in their Alabaster Chambers—" (F 124), 54–56, 114, 180n14

"Bring me the sunset in a cup—" (F 140), 185n3

"All overgrown by cunning moss" (F 146), 81–89, 91, 94–96, 101, 104, 188n32

"She died—this was the way she died" (F 154), 86–89

"She went as quiet as the Dew" (F 159), 86–89

"A fuzzy fellow, without feet—" (F 171), 185n3

"A Wife—at Daybreak—I shall be—" (F 185), 25–26

"Through the strait pass of suffering—" (F 187), 56

"'Tis Anguish grander than Delight" (F 192), 116–118

"I'll tell you how the Sun rose—" (F 204), 54–56, 180n14

"A feather from the Whippowil" (F 208), 185n3

"Would you like Summer? Taste of our's—" (F 272), 56

"Going to Him! Happy letter!" (F 277), 53

"We play at Paste—" (F 282), 54–56, 180n14

"My first well Day—since many ill—" (F 288), 185n3

"It sifts from Leaden Sieves—" (F 291), 6–13, 18, 185n3

"The nearest Dream recedes—unrealized—" (F 304), 54–56, 180n14

"A Shady friend—for Torrid days—" (F 306), 185n3

"She sweeps with many-colored Brooms—" (F 318), 185n3

"There came a Day at Summer's full" (F 325), 55–56, 100, 180n15

"Of all the Sounds despatched abroad" (F 334), 55–56, 180n15, 185n3

"Before I got my eye put out" (F 336), 58

"Tie the strings to my Life, My Lord" (F 338), 185n3

"I'm ceded—I've stopped being Their's—" (F 353), 185n3

"It was not Death, for I stood up" (F 355), 40–44

"If you were coming in the Fall" (F 356), 41–44

"A Bird came down the Walk—" (F 359), 180n15, 185n3

"I tend my flowers for thee—" (F 367), 185n3

"After great pain, a formal feeling comes—" (F 372), 97

"The Grass so little has to do" (F 379), 185n3

"It dont sound so terrible—quite—as it did—" (F 384), 87

"I'll clutch—and clutch—" (F 385), 185n3

"Over and over, like a Tune—" (F 406), 87

"The Soul selects her own Society—" (F 409), 190n12

"Your Riches, taught me, poverty—" (F 418), 180n15

"The first Day's Night had come—" (F 423), 105–106, 185n3

"'Twas like a Maelstrom, with a notch" (F 425), 185n3

"I—Years—had been—from Home—" (F 440), 37–40, 105–106

"You'll find—it when you try to die—" (F 441), 39–40

"They shut me up in Prose—" (F 445), 52–53

"This was a Poet—" (F 446), 53

"Without this—there is nought—" (F 464), 185n3

"I dwell in Possibility—" (F 466), 53

"Because I could not stop for Death—" (F 479), 94–96, 98, 102, 104, 131

"He fought like those Who've nought to lose—" (F 480), 97

"Wolfe demanded during Dying" (F 482), 97

"Most she touched me by her muteness—" (F 483), 97

"From Blank to Blank—" (F 484), 97–98, 102, 185n3

"The Whole of it came not at once—" (F 485), 97

"Presentiment—is that long shadow—on the Lawn—" (F 487), 97

"You constituted Time—" (F 488), 97

"The World—feels Dusty" (F 491), 97

"The Day undressed—Herself—" (F 495), 97

"The Beggar Lad—dies early—" (F 496), 97

"The Spider holds a Silver Ball" (F 513), 190n17

"This is my letter to the World" (F 519), 53

"They dropped like Flakes—" (F 545), 185n3

"There's been a Death, in the Opposite House" (F 547), 89-94, 104

"I measure every Grief I meet" (F 550), 92–93, 184n26

"There is a Langour of the Life" (F 552), 93

"It's Coming—the postponeless Creature—" (F 556), 93

"Did Our Best Moment last—" (F 560), 93

"She hideth Her the last—" (F 564), 93

"Two Butterflies went out at Noon" (F 571), 190n12

"You'll know Her—by Her Foot—" (F 604), 185n3

"I saw no Way—The Heavens were stitched—" (F 633), 185n3

"Just to be Rich" (F 635), 190n12

"Death sets a Thing significant" (F 640), 185n3

"I started Early—Took my Dog—" (F 656), 131

"I could not prove the Years had feet—" (F 674), 129

"Dont put up my Thread & Needle—" (F 681), 185n3

"My Life had stood—a Loaded Gun—" (F 764), 131

"The Definition of Beauty, is" (F 797), 188n33

"Love reckons by itself—alone—" (F 812), 190n12

"This Consciousness that is aware" (F 817), 114-116

"We can but follow to the Sun—" (F 845), 188n31

"A Drop fell on the Apple Tree—" (F 846), 124, 190n12

"Her final Summer was it—" (F 847), 124, 188n32

"By my Window have I for Scenery" (F 849), 124–128

"'I want'—it pleaded—All it's life—" (F 851), 188n32

"It was a Grave—yet bore no Stone—" (F 852), 124

"She staked Her Feathers—Gained an Arc—" (F 853), 188n32

"She rose to His Requirement—dropt" (F 857), 188n32

"Time feels so vast that were it not" (F 858), 124–125

"No Notice gave She, but a Change—" (F 860), 188n32

"They say that 'Time assuages'—" (F 861), 125

"On the Bleakness of my Lot" (F 862), 125

"A Plated Life—diversified" (F 864), 188n32

"This Dust, and it's Feature—" (F 866), 119–120, 128–129

"I felt a Cleaving in my Mind—" (F 867), 15, 105–129, 184–185n1, 188n3

"Fairer through Fading—as the Day" (F 868), 120–121, 124

"What I see not, I better see—" (F 869), 121–122

"I meant to find Her when I Came—" (F 881), 190n12

"Further in Summer than the Birds" (F 895), 12

"She sped as Petals from a Rose—" (F 897), 100

"Split the Lark—and you'll find the Music—" (F 905), 53, 129, 179n5

"As imperceptibly as Grief" (F 935), 190n12

"Crumbling is not an instant's Act" (F 1010), 111

"This Chasm, Sweet, opon my life" (F 1061), 185n3

"Sang from the Heart, Sire" (F 1083), 185n3

"A narrow Fellow in the Grass" (F 1096), 45

"The Crickets sang" (F 1104), 185n3

"I noticed People disappeared" (F 1154), 163–164

"The Snow that never drifts—" (F 1155), 6

"A Spider sewed at Night" (F 1163), 185n3, 190n17

"Contained in this short Life" (F 1175), 134–138

"Step lightly on this narrow spot—" (F 1227), 185n3

"Fortitude incarnate" (F 1255), 133–134

"The Clover's simple Fame" (F 1256), 191–192n33

"A Sparrow took a slice of Twig" (F 1257), 189n9

"A Word dropped careless on a Page" (F 1268), 185n3

"Power is a familiar growth—" (F 1287), 164–166

"In this short Life that only lasts an hour" (F 1292), 160–162

"The Infinite a sudden Guest" (F 1344), 162–163

"Crisis is sweet and yet the Heart" (F 1365), 133–134

"The Spider as an Artist" (F 1373), 145–146, 190n17

"How fits his Umber Coat" (F 1414), 185n3

"What mystery pervades a well!" (F 1433), 142–145

"To mend each tattered Faith" (F 1468), 185n3

"One note from One Bird" (F 1478), 161–162

"To see the Summer Sky" (F 1491), 166–167

"We never know we go when we are going—" (F 1546), 162–163

"The Things that never can come back, are several—" (F 1564), 146–152, 159

"Echo has no Magistrate—" (F 1569), 138–140

"Of Death I try to think like this" (F 1588), 182n1

"To see her is a Picture—" (F 1597), 189n9

"To be forgot by thee" (F 1601), 146, 152–156

"This Me—that walks and works—must die" (F 1616), 185n3

"To her derided Home" (F 1617), 146, 157–159

"A Drunkard cannot meet a Cork" (F 1630), 139–140

"The pedigree of Honey" (F 1650), 140–142

"A Letter is a joy of Earth—" (F 1672), 53

"Of Yellow was the outer Sky" (F 1733), 185n3

"In Winter in my Room" (F 1742), 185n3

INDEX

"The Album Writer's Assistant," 30, 177n27
American Antiquarian Society, 175n15, 176n16, 177n30
Amherst College Archive, 108
anaphora, 96, 181n30
archive, 34–35, 107–108, 169–171, 187n19
Atlantic Monthly, 54, 58, 103, 179n11
Auden, W. H., 182n1
autograph albums, 14, 27–30, 34

Barrett, Faith, 87
Bascom, Ruth Henshaw, 32, 177n31
Bennett, Paula, 26, 43, 174n16, 184n30
Bianchi, Martha Dickinson, 116, 176n24, 178n62
Bickman, Martin, 173n10
Bingham, Millicent Todd, 176n24
book making, conventions of, 14, 22, 31–35
Boston Herald, 52
Bowdoin, Elbridge G., 63–66, 70
Bowles, Samuel
    books sent from and to, 82, 184n28
    death of, 131
    Dickinson's relationship with, 53
    poems and letters sent to, 51, 56, 57, 179n12, 190n12
Bradlee, Miss, 27, 28, 30
Brontë, Charlotte, 80–82
    "Mementos," 82
Brontë sisters, *Poems by Currer, Ellis, and Acton Bell*, 46, 82
Brooks, Maria Gowen, 178n58, 184n28
    Idomen, 178n58
Browning, Elizabeth Barrett, 46, 187n19
Bryant, William Cullen, 46
Buckler, Patricia P., 30, 177n30
Bushell, Sally, 35–36, 177n40

Callum's. *See* McCallum's
Cameron, Sharon
    on Dickinson's decision not to publish, 45
    on the fascicles, 5, 35, 36, 43, 87, 174–175n1, 177n40, 187n19
    on the loose sheets, 110, 185n6
    readings of poems by, 43, 111
    on time and the lyric, 16, 43, 85, 183n12, 184n25, 184–185n1
    on the variants, 112, 146–147
Capps, Jack, 30, 176n23, 181n29, 181n45
Carmichael, Mrs., 148, 151
Cavitch, Max, 79, 182n1
The Century, 191n21
Chandler, Elizabeth Margaret, 100
Charlestown Seminary, 27
The Children's Crusade, 146
circulation and recirculation, 29, 31, 67, 69, 70, 77, 176n24, 191n26
Civil War, 110
commonplace books, 14, 27–30, 34, 175n15, 176n16, 176n21, 177n30
Cook, Ichabod, 31–32, 34, 177n31
Cooper, Abby, 68
correspondence. *See* letters
Creeley, Robert, 169
Crowell, Mary Warner. *See* Warner, Mary
Crumbley, Paul, 58, 143, 182n56
Culler, Jonathan, 13

death
    of Dickinson's family and friends, 131
    poems about, 14, 39–42, 43, 53, 78–104, 115–116, 120–121, 124–125, 182n1, 184n23
Decker, William, 71–72, 181n44
Deppman, Jedd, 112, 174n16, 182n1
diaries, nineteenth-century, 14, 31–32, 34
Dickie, Margaret, 5

Dickinson, Austin, 24, 47, 64, 184n28
Dickinson, Edward, 64, 131
Dickinson Electronic Archive, 187n23
Dickinson, Emily. *See also* drafts; fascicles;
     letters; "letter-poems;" loose sheets;
     poems; variants
  and agoraphobia, 146, 191n19
  at Amherst Academy, 24
  Bible of, 30
  books of, 46–47, 55, 65, 178n62
  dog of, 55, 59
  eye trouble of, 186n12
  handwriting of, 188n28
  at Mt. Holyoke, 31, 68
  myths about, 45
  print, relationship to, 14, 22, 30, 32, 36,
     44–48, 178n55
  scrapbook of, 176n23
  signature of, 54, 56, 179n11, 180n14
  tutor of, 55, 57, 58
Dickinson, Emily Norcross, 110, 131,
    186n11
Dickinson, Gilbert, 131
Dickinson, Lavinia, 65, 131, 146, 176n24
Dickinson, Susan Huntington
  criticism on, 179n4, 190n16
  Dickinson, relationship to, 7, 53, 56,
    179n10, 184n28, 187n23
  drafts, letters, "letter-poems," and poems
    sent to, 7–12, 24, 51, 55, 56, 57,
    68, 100, 107, 113–118, 125, 129,
    139–140, 143–145, 168, 179n4,
    180n14, 187n20, 187n21, 187n23,
    187–188n25, 188n31, 188n33,
    189n9, 190n12
  fascicles, relationship to, 176n24
  letters of, 68
  loose sheets, relationship to, 114–118,
    187n21, 187–188n25
  scrapbook of, 29–30, 176n21
Doreski, William, 174–175n1
drafts
  destroying, 23, 75, 133
  first, 25, 26
  individual instances of, 6–7, 9–13, 18,
    25–26, 55, 74, 107, 113, 114,
    133–167, 177n42, 180n14, 188n31,
    189n8, 189n9, 190n12, 190n16
  intermediate, 25, 26
  making, 3, 15, 17, 24, 26, 45, 60, 110–111,
    117, 130
  paper, relationship to, 6, 133–134, 145
  post-fascicle, 15, 76, 114, 130–133, 145

  pre-fascicle, 22
  sending, 56, 180n14
  of sermons, 33–34
dramatic monologue, 16
"The Dream," 27–28
Drum Beat, 190n12
Dwight, Edward S., 100

elegy, 78–104
  American, 182n1
  by Charlotte Brontë, 82
  for Charlotte Brontë, 80–84
  child, 182n1
  and closure, 14, 80, 84, 86, 87, 89, 98, 99,
    100, 101, 102, 103, 104
  and consolation, 14, 80, 86, 89, 97, 98, 99,
    100–101, 102, 103, 104
  conventions of, 13, 14, 78–79, 81–82, 86,
    90, 99–100, 103, 104, 148
  criticism on, 78–79, 99, 182n1, 184n23,
    184n27
  and epitaph, 184n23
  "male" and "female," 99–100, 184n27
  nineteenth-century, 78, 79, 86, 89, 99–103
  pastoral, 86
  Puritan, 86, 103, 182n1
  Romantic, 86
  self, 182n1
  sentimental, 89
  twentieth-century, 182n1, 184n27
  by Amelia Welby, 100–101, 103
Embury, Emma, 100
Emerson, Ralph Waldo, 6–7, 21, 46
  "New Poetry," 21
Emmons, Henry Vaughn, 24–25, 176n24
epistolary conventions, nineteenth-century,
    22, 53, 57, 62, 67, 68, 69, 70, 74
epistolary manuals, 53, 68, 69, 181n44
  The Fashionable American Letter Writer, 68
epitaph, 79, 184n23
Erkkila, Betsey, 184–185n1
Ernst, Katharina, 182n1
Esdale, Logan, 68
Evergreens, 178n62

Fascicle 1, 25, 49–51, 71, 74–75, 76, 186n15
Fascicle 2, 175n9
Fascicle 3, 94, 186n15
Fascicle 5, 180n15
Fascicle 6, 180n14, 190n12
Fascicle 7, 81–89, 94, 104, 177n32, 188n32
Fascicle 9, 94
Fascicle 10, 180n14, 186n15

Fascicle 11, 40, 186n15
Fascicle 12, 180n15, 186n15
Fascicle 13, 94, 180n15
Fascicle 14, 178n47, 180n14, 186n15
Fascicle 15, 111
Fascicle 16, 94, 177n32
Fascicle 17, 37, 40–44
Fascicle 18, 177n32
Fascicle 19, 177n32, 178n47
Fascicle 20, 94, 178n47, 190n12
Fascicle 21, 37–40, 44, 177n32
Fascicle 23, 94–98, 104
Fascicle 24, 9, 177n32
Fascicle 25, 190n12
Fascicle 27, 40, 89–94, 104
Fascicle 28, 177n32
Fascicle 31, 190n12
Fascicle 32, 25, 185n3
Fascicle 33, 175n9, 187–188n25
Fascicle 35, 177n32, 187–188n25
Fascicle 37, 187–188n25
Fascicle 38, 107, 123–128, 186n16,
    187–188n25, 190n12
Fascicle 39, 123, 186n16, 187–188n25,
    190n12
fascicles
  bound books, relation to, 14, 22, 27–31,
    34, 35, 36, 37, 39, 40, 46, 48, 78,
    112–113, 186n12
  circulation of, 12, 30, 176n24
  construction of, 14, 20, 22–23, 25–26, 30,
    31, 32, 34, 36, 48, 78, 80, 104, 106,
    108, 111
  copying poems into, 4, 13, 14, 21, 22–26,
    31, 34–35, 46, 47, 48, 51, 54–55,
    104, 106, 111, 118, 123, 130, 157
  end of, 13, 15, 106–107, 110–111, 118,
    125, 128–129, 187–188n25
  dismantling of, 20, 32, 34, 48
  finding the, 130–131
  homemade objects, relation to, 14,
    31–35
  letters, relation to, 56–57
  loose sheets, relation to, 110–112,
    117–118, 122–129, 186n8
  mutilation of, 175n9
  paired poems within, 40, 178n47
  poems in multiple, 23, 174–175n1
  poems written prior to, 24–26
  possible early, 24
  readings of
    narrative, 14, 20, 21–22, 35, 37, 44,
      174–175n1

sequential, 14, 21–22, 35, 44, 106,
    174–175n1, 187n19
  thematic, 20, 21–22, 35, 37, 174–175n1
  reconstruction of, 20, 21–22
  returning to, 75–76
  sewing of, 13, 14, 15, 20, 22–24, 31, 32, 34,
    48, 56–57, 78, 80, 89, 97, 104, 106–
    107, 110, 111, 118, 123, 128, 129, 130,
    162, 186n8, 186n15, 187–188n25
  sheets of
    poems across, relation of, 48, 80,
      92–94, 97–98, 99, 104, 123–128
    poems on single, relation between,
      21–22, 37–44, 49–51, 86–89
    print and, relation between 45–46
    relation between, 21–48, 79–80, 87,
      183n7
    spill-over from, 24, 34, 36, 177n32
    size of, 22, 32
    studies of, 5, 14, 20–23, 26, 35–36, 39, 43,
      87, 174–175n1, 177n40, 187n19
    unique and not unique features of, 21,
      26–27, 34–35
Fern, Fanny, 21
Fields, James T., 58
"Flowers of Genius," 27, 29
Ford, Thomas W., 182n1
"Forest Leaves," 24
form
  of Ichabod Cook's diary entires, 31
  Dickinson's experiments with, 22, 44, 47,
    72–73
  of individual poems, 40, 44, 84–86, 88,
    94, 98, 104, 120, 121–122, 127–128,
    129, 148
  poetic, 4, 14, 18, 35, 38, 51, 53, 85, 86, 89,
    101, 102, 140
  materials and, 106
Fowler, Alice S., 27–29
fragmentation, 36, 156
Franklin, Ralph
  on Dickinson's decision not to publish, 44
  on Dickinson's method, 25, 186n12,
    188n29
  editorial decisions of, 25, 55, 65–66, 76,
    80, 83, 84, 108, 116, 123, 139, 144,
    154–157, 177n42, 180n14, 180n15,
    180n16, 186n16, 187n20, 187n21,
    187–188n25, 188n28, 189n8,
    189n10
  on the fascicles, 5, 20–22, 24, 108, 110,
    123, 175n7, 175n9, 176n24, 177n32,
    177n40, 183n7, 186n12

Franklin, Ralph (*continued*)
  on the folded fascicle sheet, 36
  on the loose sheets, 107–108, 110, 111,
    123, 185n4, 186n12
  on the "scraps," 130
Fredman, Stephen, 169
Fuss, Diana, 184n23

Gall, Sally M., 35, 174–175n1, 187n19
Garvey, Ellen Gruber, 29, 30–31
Gems from American Female Poets, 47,
  100
genre. *See also* elegy; lyric
  blending of, 67
  boundaries between, 62, 66, 67, 69, 70,
    73, 179n1
  critical approaches to, 13, 16, 66–67, 79,
    99–100, 182n1, 184n27
  Dickinson's relationship to issues of, 13,
    15–16, 36, 51, 53, 68
  diversity of nineteenth-century, 5, 13, 68,
    69, 79, 169
  editorial approaches to, 54, 63–70
  instability of, 13, 52–53, 63, 70
  and media, 106
"The German Student Lamp Co.," 146
Gernes, Todd, 27, 29
Gilbert, Thomas, 180n15
Gilman, Caroline, 34, 177n31, 184n28
Gitelman, Lisa, 6
Goddard, Emily, 34
Goddard Family Papers, 177n30
Grimes, Linda, 91–92
Griswold, Rufus, 47
Gruesz, Kristen Silva, 178n58

Habegger, Alfred, 38–39, 110, 130, 176n24,
  190n16
Hall, Mary Lee, 176n24
The Hampshire and Franklin Express, 30
handwriting, 6, 20, 36, 188n28
Harper's Weekly, 191n26
Hart, Ellen Louise, 56, 67, 179n4, 180n14,
  187n20
Havens, Earle, 176n16
Heginbotham, Eleanor Elson, 39,
  174–175n1, 175n8
Henderson, Desirée, 79
Herbert, George, *The Temple*, 187n19
Hewitt, Elizabeth, 67
Higginson, Thomas Wentworth
  criticism of Dickinson by, 55, 58

Dickinson, relationship to, 53, 55, 56, 57,
  60, 72
  on Dickinson's decision not to publish ,
    45–48
  on Dickinson's poetry, 3, 21
  editorial decisions of, 96, 184n26
  "Emily Dickinson's Letters," 180n24
  essays of, 55
  "Letter to a Young Contributor," 54, 55, 58
  letters and poems sent to, 11, 12, 16, 51,
    53, 54–62, 63, 66–67, 69, 70, 71–74,
    76, 179n8, 179n11, 179n12, 180n14,
    180n15, 180–181n25, 181n27,
    190n12
Holland, Elizabeth, 147, 148, 153
Holland, Jeanne, 131, 146, 148, 188–189n3,
  190n17, 191n17
Holland, Josiah Gilbert, 147, 191n21
Holmes, Oliver Wendell, 46
Holt, Dr. Jacob, 30
homemade books, 14, 31–35
  of poetry, 34
Houghton Library, 178n62, 181n46
Household Book of Poetry, 184n28
Howe, Susan, 17, 62, 131, 188–189n3,
  189n7
Hubbard, Melanie, 131, 188–189n3, 189n7
Hughes, Langston, 168–169, 182n1
  "The Negro Speaks of Rivers," 168,
    192n2

intention, 17–18, 52, 84, 137, 150–151, 152,
  159, 174n21, 191n26
Irving, Washington, 21

Jackson, Helen Hunt, 45, 46, 156, 176n24,
  191n21
Jackson, Virginia
  on Sharon Cameron, 36
  central argument of, 5
  on circulation, 67, 181n50
  on Dickinson's copying process, 177n29
  on Dickinson's manuscripts, 5, 132,
    189n7, 191n26
  on individual poems, 179n5
  on lyric and genre, 13, 16, 67
  on "lyric reading," 5, 67, 152
  on Marta Werner, 132, 189n7
J. C. Arms & Co., 146
John Hancock Number One Note, 146
John Hay Library, 176n21
Johnson, Nan, 69

Johnson, Thomas
  editorial decisions of, 54–55, 60, 62, 65,
    76, 179n12, 180n15, 180n24, 181n27
  transcriptions by, 58–59, 76, 82–83, 96

Kher, Inder Nath, 182n1
Knappett, Carl, 17–18, 174n21

Lambert, Robert Graham, 180–181n25
Lee, Mary E., 100
"letter-poems," 51, 56, 57
letters, 49–77
  abandoned, 25, 74, 159
  announcements for Dickinson's, 52
  in autograph albums, 27
  critical treatments of, 52–53, 54, 55–56,
    58, 60, 65, 66–67, 69–71, 73–74,
    78, 179n4, 179n8, 180–181n25,
    181n30, 181n50, 182n1
  of Dickinson's contemporaries, 68
  early, 24
  editions of, Dickinson's
    The Letters of Emily Dickinson (1894),
      52, 58, 188n2
    The Life and Letters of Emily Dickinson
      (1924), 58
    The Letters of Emily Dickinson (1931),
      58, 65
    The Letters of Emily Dickinson (1958),
      58–63, 65–66, 76, 179n12, 180n15,
      180n24, 181n27
  editorial practices concerning, 54, 58–77,
    179n12, 180n24, 181n27
  fascicles, relation to, 56–57, 157
  of Langston Hughes, 169
  "I" in, 71–74
  L 23, 68
  L 41, 63–66
  L 77, 168
  L 93, 168
  L 105, 24
  L 110, 24
  L 121, 24
  L 150, 24
  L 183, 68
  L 229, 56
  L 251, 56
  L 260, 54–56
  L 261, 55–56
  L 265, 51, 56, 57–63, 66–67, 69–77
  L 268, 16, 71, 181n27
  L 299, 82

L 470, 74
L 813, 12
L 813a, 82
L 813b, 82
L 964, 74–76
  loose sheets, relation to, 118
  method of writing, 14, 56, 68, 110
  paper of, 3, 6, 18–19, 56, 71, 190n17
  poems about, 52–53
  poems embedded in, 4, 13, 14, 51, 54,
    58–62, 70–76, 179n9, 181n27
  poems enclosed in, 14, 51, 53, 54–57, 59,
    72, 73, 179n12, 180n14, 180n15,
    180n24
  poems inserted in, 13, 14, 51, 57, 58, 60,
    68, 72
  poems, relation to, 48, 51–77, 78, 116,
    145–146, 159
  women's, 68, 69
  writing of, 51, 56
Lockridge, Kenneth A., 176n16
Loeffelholz, Mary, 26, 191n21
London Mercury, 178n46
Longfellow, Henry Wadsworth, 46
loose sheets, 105–129
  characteristics of poems on, 111, 112, 118,
    128–129
  critical studies of, 110–111, 186n11,
    187n19
  and Susan Dickinson, 114–118, 187n21,
    187–188n25
  editorial approaches to, 108–110, 185n2,
    185n4
  of Emily Goddard, 34
  fascicles, relationship to, 110–112,
    117–118, 122–129, 186n8
  method of making, 106, 107, 111, 114,
    118, 188n30
  readings of, 107, 119–123, 124–128
  scattering of, 13, 14–15
  "Set 1," 111, 123, 129, 186n16
  "Set 2," 106, 107, 108, 109, 111, 118–124,
    128, 186n16
  "Set 3," 111
  "Set 4a," 111, 123, 185n4, 186n16
  "Set 4b," 111, 123, 185n4, 186n16,
    186n31
  "Set 5," 108, 129, 190n12
  "Set 6a," 108, 115–116, 185n4, 188n30,
    188n33
  "Set 6b," 108, 185n4, 188n30
  "Set 6c," 186n8, 185n4, 188n30

loose sheets (*continued*)
  "Set 7," 108, 117, 124, 190n12
  "Set 8a," 185n4, 188n30
  "Set 8b," 185n4, 188n30
  "sets" as another name for, 107–110
Lord, Otis, 131
Lowell, Maria, 184n28
Luciano, Dana, 84–85, 86
lyric, 13, 16, 36, 40, 45, 48, 51, 67, 87, 104,
  129, 132, 166, 183n12
lyricization, 171
"lyric reading," 5, 36, 38–39, 67, 132, 152
lyric voice, 16, 74
Lystra, Karen, 181n44

MacKenzie, Cindy, 55–56, 60, 179n4
manuscripts
  in the archive, 170
  circulation of, 176n24
  critical studies of, 5–6, 35, 36, 66–67, 73,
    110, 130–132, 150–152, 186n8,
    189n7
  and Ralph Franklin, 5, 44, 186n16,
    188n28
  issues raised by, 16–18, 67–68, 69, 70, 71,
    74, 132, 133, 152, 159, 162
  and Thomas Johnson, 96
  print, relation to, 18
  represented in this book, 8–10, 12, 28, 29,
    33, 50, 61–63, 64, 75, 83, 92, 109,
    135, 138, 149–151, 154, 158, 161,
    165
  as a source of interpretation, 15–16
Marvel, Ik, *Reveries of a Bachelor*, 65
McCallum's, 153–154, 191n28
McGann, Jerome
  on correspondence, 69
  on Dickinson's decision not to print,
    45–46, 178n63
  on the fascicles, 46
  on the letters and poems, relation between
    67, 70
  on scenes of reading v. scenes of
    writing, 4
  on textual materials, 4
media, 6, 35, 46, 52, 71–72, 77, 104, 106,
  152, 178n55
  studies, 6
Messmer, Marietta, 53, 73–74, 179n4,
  179n8, 179n11, 181n30
meter, 18, 32, 62, 65, 66, 67, 70, 73, 100, 116,
  117, 120, 139

Michaels, Walter Benn, 17
Miller, Cristanne, 18, 44, 173n10
Miller, Ruth, 174–175n1
Milton, John, "Lycidas," 86
Mitchell, Dohmnall 5, 6, 66–67, 75, 87, 110,
  179n1, 186n8
Murray, Aife, 190n16

narrative, 13, 14, 20, 21–22, 35, 36, 44, 48,
  98, 118, 139, 174–175n1
Newman, Samuel Phillips, *A Practical
  System of Rhetoric*, 68
Nielsen, Dorothy, 183n12
Niles, Thomas, 11, 12, 82
Norcross, Fanny and Louise, 51, 53, 56, 163,
  180n15

Oberhaus, Dorothy Huff, 174–175n1
O'Keefe, Martha Lindblom, 174–175n1
"or," 80, 81–89, 91, 95–98, 101
Osgood, Frances, 170
  "Rags! Rags! Any Rags to Sell?," 170
  "To My Pen," 170
Ott, Katherine, 30, 177n30

paper
  clippings of, 29–30, 176n16, 176n23,
    191n26
  conservation of, 33, 150, 191n18
  critical treatments of, 4–5, 148, 150–152,
    191n26
  editorial work with, 108
  folded and creased, 11, 12, 16, 17, 26, 63,
    113, 136, 139, 140, 141, 157, 159,
    189n9
  fragments of, 13, 15, 29, 114, 118, 130,
    132, 133, 137, 143, 145, 146, 148,
    152–153, 155–156, 164, 166–167,
    175n12, 189n11
  inserted, 31–34, 112–113, 177n31
  leaves of, 3, 22, 25, 51, 56, 57, 63, 89,
    108, 113, 133, 134, 135, 139,
    140–141, 143, 148, 150, 152, 156,
    186n15, 187–188n25, 189n9,
    190n12
  marked by pins, 16, 17, 18, 20, 21, 34,
    131–133, 148, 149, 152, 162–166,
    177n32, 191–192n33
  as media, 6
  poetics, relation to, 3–4, 11, 13, 15, 19,
    36, 39, 106, 130, 132, 137, 145, 156,
    166–167, 168–171

scraps of, 3, 4, 6, 15, 18, 130–133, 145–146, 160–167, 188n30, 188n2, 188–189n3, 189n7, 191n19, 191–192n33

slips of, 16, 22, 34, 36, 89, 149–150, 152, 162, 164, 166, 170, 177n32, 191–192n33

stacked, 22, 31, 32, 34, 36, 56, 80, 112–113

torn, 3, 13, 25, 113, 131, 132, 139, 140, 141, 145, 150–151, 152, 160, 162, 164, 166–167

types of
  advertisements, 15, 130, 131, 133, 146–147, 152–156, 158–159, 160
  bills, 15
  candy wrappers, 6, 133, 146–147, 152, 157–159, 160
  envelopes, 3, 6, 15, 131, 146, 160–162, 168
  graph paper, 133, 143, 163
  household paper, 3, 4, 6, 13, 130, 131, 132, 133, 145, 146, 159, 166, 169–170, 191n19
  invitations, 146
  labels, 130
  memoranda, 130
  note paper, 38, 180n14
  recipes, 15, 131, 133, 146–147, 148, 150, 152, 156, 159, 160
  shopping lists, 15, 16, 131, 152
  signatures, 177n31
  stationery. *See* fascicle, sheets of

pedagogy, 13

periodicals, nineteenth-century, 46–47, 102

Petrino, Elizabeth, 182n1

Piatt, Sarah, 100, 102–103, 184n30
  Palace-Burner: The Selected Poetry of Sarah Piatt, 102

Pierpont, 68

Pingree, Geoffrey B., 6

Plath, Sylvia, 182n1

poems. *See* "Poems Referenced," 199–201
  editions of, Dickinson's
    Poems by Emily Dickinson (1890), 3, 21, 45–47, 62, 96, 184n24
    Poems by Emily Dickinson (1891), 62
    Poems by Emily Dickinson (1896), 82, 83, 91, 112, 143, 184n26
    The Single Hound (1914), 116
    The Complete Poems of Emily Dickinson (1924), 82, 96

    Further Poems of Emily Dickinson (1929), 178n46
    The Poems of Emily Dickinson (1930), 82, 96, 178n46
    The Poems of Emily Dickinson (1937), 82, 96, 178n46
    The Poems of Emily Dickinson (1955), 55, 62, 65, 76, 82–83, 96
    The Complete Poems of Emily Dickinson (1960), 83
    The Manuscript Books of Emily Dickinson (1981), 5, 21, 50, 80, 83, 92, 108, 109, 123, 175n7, 175n9, 176n24, 177n32, 183n7, 185n2, 185n4, 186n12, 187n19
    The Poems of Emily Dickinson: Variorum Edition (1998), 55, 65, 76, 83, 123, 130, 177n42, 178n46, 180n14, 185n2, 186n16, 187n20, 187–188n25, 188n29, 189n8, 191n28
    The Poems of Emily Dickinson: Reading Edition (1999), 83, 177n42

poetics, definition of, 3–4

poetry anthologies, 6, 46–47, 100

Pollak, Vivian, 43, 174n16

Porter, David, 118

Potts, Abbie Findlay, 86

print culture, 46–48, 70, 170

public, relation to private, 46, 47, 53, 69–70, 77, 99

Putnam, Lucy, 68

Ramazani, Jahan, 182n1, 184n27

recovery, of women's writing, 102, 169–170

revision. *See* drafts

rhyme, 21, 32, 66, 73, 120, 181n30

Richards, Eliza, 26, 170, 192n6

riddle, 143

Rizzo, Patricia Thompson, 182n1

Roberts Brothers, 11

Root, Abiah, 68

Rosenthal, M. L., 35, 174–175n1, 187n19

Sacks, Peter, 86, 182n1

Salinger, Herman, 85

Salska, Agnieszka, 57

Sand, George, 191n26

Sawyer, Caroline M., 100

Schenck, Celeste, 184n27

Scott, Julia H., 100

The Scrapbook, 30–31

scrapbooks, 14, 29–31, 142, 176n16,
  176n23, 177n27, 177n30
seams, 10, 106, 111, 112, 127, 185n3
self, split, 38, 40, 105–106
sequence, 105–129
  coordinates of
    spatial, 15, 107, 111–113, 118–122,
      123–124, 128, 129
    temporal, 15, 107, 111–113, 118, 120,
      123, 129, 184–185n1
  as a genre, 13, 45, 174–175n1, 187n19
  problems of, 36, 129, 164
  reading and not reading the fascicles as,
    14, 21, 35, 44, 106, 174–175n1,
    187n19
  as a structuring devise, 44, 112, 120, 123,
    128
sermons, 14, 32–34
"Sets." *See* loose sheets
Sewall, Richard B., 55, 180n22
Shakespeare, William, 187n19
Shelley, Percy Bysshe, "Adonais," 81
Shurr, William H., 65–66, 174–175n1
  New Poems of Emily Dickinson, 65–66
Sigourney, Lydia, 169–170, 182n1, 184n28
  "To a Shred of Linen," 169–170
Smith, Elizabeth Oakes, 170, 192n6
Smith, Martha Nell
  on Dickinson's decision not to publish, 45,
    178n55
  on Dickinson's relationship to Susan, 56
  on the fascicles, 176n24
  on the letters, "letter-poems," and poems,
    60, 67, 179n4, 179n10, 180n14,
    187n20
  on the manuscripts, 5, 60
  on nineteenth-century American poetry, 169
Socarides, Alexandra, 186n11
speaker, in poems, 16–17, 174n16, 183n12,
  184–185n1
Springfield Daily Republican, 45, 180n14
St. Armand, Barton Levi, 21, 176n23
Stabile, Susan M., 176n16
stationery. *See* paper
Stein, Gertrude, 169
Stevens, Wallace, 182n1
Stonum, Gary Lee, 39, 174n16, 184–185n1
string
  cutting the, 20–21, 32, 48
  language of, 106, 185n3
  as material, 16, 128
  sewing with, 17, 22, 80, 106, 128, 162

Sudol, Ronald, 182n1
suicide, 103
syntax, 44, 88, 89, 102, 115, 116, 121, 152

Tennyson, Alfred Lord, 35–36
  In Memoriam, 187n19
time. *See also* sequence, coordinates of,
    temporal
  and death, 84–85, 96, 98
  Dickinson's approach to, 71–72, 98
  expansion of, 80
  looped or circular, 89, 94, 96, 98
  poetic, 16, 47, 84–85, 86, 95, 98, 101, 102,
    103, 104, 107, 124–125, 183n12,
    184n25, 184–185n1
  of reading, 96
  stopped, 42, 85, 98, 183n12
  and timelessness, 85, 183n12, 183n13
Todd, Mabel Loomis
  as editor of Dickinson's letters, 52, 65
  as editor of Dickinson's poems, 45, 62
  editorial decisions of, 65, 83, 84, 91,
    141–142, 143, 184n26
  and the fascicles, 20, 32, 48, 176n24
  on the loose sheets, 108
  scrapbook of, 30, 141–142
  on the "scraps," 131, 188n2
  transcriptions by, 62, 142–143
transcriptions, 18, 56, 58–60, 62–67,
    142–143, 157, 163, 176n21, 188n29,
    189n10
Tucker, Susan, 30, 177n30
Tufariello, Catherine, 173n10
typewriter, 169

valentines, 63–65, 70
variants
  Sharon Cameron on the, 112,
    146–147
  editorial treatments of, 18, 83, 96, 112,
    146–147, 157
  individual instances of, 10, 25, 84, 88,
    89, 97, 112, 120–122, 127–128,
    133–137, 138–140, 143, 155–157,
    164, 166, 180n14, 182n55, 189n9,
    190n12, 191–192n33
  marking of, 10
  method of recording, 22–23, 122, 127,
    132–133, 138, 145, 162, 188n28,
    189n9
  Marta Wener on the, 137, 189n11
Vendler, Helen, 173n2

verse copying, nineteenth-century
  conventions for, 14, 22, 26–31, 35

Wadsworth, Charles, 131
Walker, Cheryl, 184n28
Ward, Theodora, 58–59, 60, 65, 76,
  179n12
Wardrop, Daneen, 174–175n1
Warner, Mary, 68, 176n23
Welby, Amelia, 100–102, 103, 184n28
Welsh, Andrew, 183n13
Werner, Marta 175n13
  on Dickinson's decision not to publish, 45
  on Dickinson's late stage of writing,
    131–132, 148
  on the fascicles, 26

on the manuscripts, 5, 150–152, 189n7,
  189n11, 191n22
on the variants, 137
Western Union Telegraph Co., 146
Whitman, Walt, 55, 182n1
  Drum-Taps, 124
Whitney, Maria, 159
Williams, William Carlos, 168
Wolff, Cynthia Griffin, 43
women poets, nineteenth-century, 5, 14,
  46, 80, 89, 99–104, 169–170,
  184n28
Worcester Spy, 52

Zapedowska, Magdalena, 6
Zeiger, Melissa F., 184n27